Conference Participants—Other Than Those Whose Contributions are Found in This Volume

Stuart Ahn, Chair, Koreatown Redevelopment Committee
Yong-Shik Ahn, The Oriental Mission Church
Larry Aubry, Human Relations Commission, L. A. County
Robert Biller, Vice President for Undergraduate Affairs, USC
Gordon Berger, Professor of History, USC
Lawrence Bobo, Professor of Sociology, UCLA
March Fong Eu, Secretary of State of California
Annie Cho, Rebuild LA
John Cho, Koryo Health Foundation
Mehyun Cho, YWCA Asian Pacific Center
Yohngsohk Choe, Adviser, Korean Chamber of Commerce, L.A.
James Choi, Reporter, The Korea Central Daily
Young Choi, Reporter, Korean Television Enterprise (KTE)
John Ferraro, President, City Council of Los Angeles
Ho Chung, Coluncilman, Garden Grove, California
Leon E. Faniel, Pastor, Saint Paul's Presbyterian Church
David Heer, Assoc. Director, Population Research Laboratory, USC
Joe R. Hicks, Exec. Dir., Southern Christian Leadership Conference
Chull Huh, Korean Chamber of Commerce, Los Angeles
Ik-Soo Hwang, Exec. Dir., Koreatown YMCA
Laura Jeon, Korean Health, Ed., Info., and Referral Center (KHEIR)
Al Kim, Vice President, Korean Student Association, USC
Brian Kim, President, Korean American Coalition
Chan-Hee Kim Professor of Theology, Claremont Theological Seminary
Christina Kim, Department of Sociology, UCLA
Dong-Suk Kim, President So. Cal. Korean College Students Assn.
Sung Yong Kang, Esq., son of former Prime Minister Kang Young Hoon
Wayne Kim, Co-Chair, Friends of the USC Korean Heritage Library
Hang-Kyung Kim, Korean Consul General, Los Angeles
David D. Kim, Vice President, Korean Chamber of Commerce
Jay C. Kim, U.S. Congressman from 41 Dist., California
Yun-Hee Kim, Special Assistant of L.A. Mayor Tom Bradley
Charles Kwack, Past Chair, Korean American Relief Fund
Jin Hyang Kwag, Composer, Music School, USC
Robert Levine, Senior Economist, RAND

Chae-Jin Lee, Dir., Keck Center, Claremeont McKenna College
Han-Kook Lee, Reporter, The Korea Times, Los Angeles
Jin Lee, Assn. of Korean American Victims of the L.A. Riots
John Lee, Professor of Accounting CSULA
Kwon-Suk Lee, Reporter, KCB Radio
Lilia Huiying Li, President, China Seminar (L.A.)
Moon-Song Oh, School of Business and Economics, CSULA
Melvin L. Oliver, Professor of Sociology, UCLA
Min Paek, Exec. Dir., Korean American Relief Fund
Julie Paik, Asian Pacific American Legal Center
Gary Park, Law Student, Loyola Marymount University
Hee-Min Park, Senior Pastor, Young-Nak Presbyterian Church
Jong-Mae Park, Fed. of Korean Buddhist Temples in So. Calif.
Kyeyoung Park, Department of Anthropology, UCLA
Derrick Pedranti, President, Student Senate, USC
Tony Salazar, Co-Chair, Rebuild LA
Soo-Bong Seung, Reporter Korean American Television (KATV)
John D. Song, President, Association for Korean Studies
Ryan Song, Exec. Dir., Korean American Grocers Association (KAGRO)
Duncan Suh, Reporter, Radio Korea, U.S.A.
Chase Chonggwang Rhee, Past President, Korean Chamber of Commerce
Michael Robinson, Professor of History, USC
Chong-Sook Suh, Asian Pacific Counseling & Treatment Center
John G. Tomlinson, Associate Dean for Library Advancement
Karin Wada, Assistant Managing Editor, The Los Angeles Times
Ron Wakabayashi, Exec. Director, Japanese American Citizens League
Sung-Soo Whang, Past Pres., Council of Korean Churches in So. Cal.
Lorain Wong, Director of Communications, AT&T
John Won, Father, St. Christopher Korean Community Catholic Church
Michael Woo, Councilman, City of Los Angeles
Hyun-Seung Yang, President, Korean American Food & Shelter Services
Dae-Shik Yoo, Reporter, Korean Moonhwa Broadcasting Co. (KMBC)
Jongpyo Grace Yoon, Principal, Wilton Place Elementary School
Jerry C. Yu, Exec. Dir., Korean American Coalition

Note: Titles, abbreviated or partial, are for identification purposes only, refer to time of Conference, and refer to Los Angeles or California unless otherwise indicated.

Community in Crisis

The Korean American Community After the Los Angeles Civil Unrest of April 1992

Edited by

George O. Totten III
and
H. Eric Schockman

Center for Multiethnic and Transnational Studies
University of Southern California
Los Angeles, California

Thanks to the Following Persons for the Photographs in This Volume and for the Many Others Which Were Displayed at the Conference:
Jae-Min Chang, President, *The Korea Times, Los Angeles*
Se Hoon Park, Chief Photographer, *The Korea Times, Los Angeles*
Young-Sup Lee, President, *The Korea Central Daily*
Young Whan Pyo, Photo Editor, *The Korea Central Daily*

Note: All the photographs are copyrighted and used with permission here.

Thanks to the Following Person for Videotaping the Whole Conference:
Dianne Lee, Graduate Student, Department of Anthropology, USC

ISBN 1-885229-00-3
ISBN 1-885229-01-1 paper

Center for Multiethnic and Transnational Studies
University of Southern California
Los Angeles, California

Manufactured in the United States of America.

CONTENTS

INTRODUCTION

George O. Totten III
H. Eric Schockman

The Los Angeles riot of 1992 had a devastating effect on the city as a whole, but especially on the Korean American community. In the three-day period of conflagrations, looting, and other violence, which incidentally did not seem to be targeted at individuals, some 58 persons lost their lives and some 2,382 were reported injured. The main targets were businesses, stores, shops, swapmeet markets, and banks; some 5,200 structures were damaged or burned to the ground with an estimated loss of some $360 million. About 30 percent of these were owned or leased by Korean Americans. According to Juna Byun, et al., whose paper appears in this volume, this riot was the worst in contemporary U.S. history. And as an ethnic minority, Korean Americans were the most victimized.

Korean Americans were shocked to discover that they had been especially singled out and that such a whole-sale destruction could occur in what is considered an advanced Western country; indeed, the land of their dreams. They had come not as economic or political refugees, but as industrious immigrants who simply sought new opportunities where they could work hard and succeed. They had not, by and large, seen a need for developing special relationships with non-Korean communities. For them, the everyday responsibility of making a living was the main reason, perhaps the only reason, for engaging in "interethnic" relationships. They said, in effect, "If we earn our living through honest, productive work, everything will be all right." This, they believed, was the promise of America. They have suddenly come to realize that it is more complicated than that.

The riot had a galvanizing effect on the entire Korean American community. In the midst of the disaster, previously antagonistic factions became allies, and Korean Americans mobilized, at least for a moment, on a scale hitherto considered unimaginable. This suggested the possibility of major structural change within the community, such as creating a more effective infrastructure to deal with the "other" reality, of which they had so far taken scant notice.

In the field of politics, this possibility has, in part, already materialized: new Korean American political organizations have sprung up, while some of the old ones formed new alliances in order to more powerfully represent Koreans in local, state, and federal politics. Previously only a few Korean Americans had been elected to political office on various levels of government. After the riot, Korean Americans, for the first time, began to take legal action against local government in cases where they thought their political rights had been violated. In short, political action on behalf of Korean Americans rested on the belief that they had not been properly participating in the American democratic political process. Greater participation, the proponents of political action claimed, would solve the problem. This would lead to greater political equality with other groups.

On the non-political front, major change for Korean Americans has not been all that apparent. This has to do with the difficulty of defining the "other" reality, which so surprised Koreans during the riot. Attempts at this definition take several forms. Some people maintain that, prior to the riot, Koreans were unwilling to admit the existence of a "racial conflict" between themselves and other ethnic minorities. Most proponents of this argument believe that racial conflicts have their underlying cause in economic "inequality" with various racial groups. This inequality is their definition of the reality they did not take notice of before the riot, but which certainly came to the surface during those turbulent days. This view led some to believe that the looting mobs were merely attempting to abolish economic inequality by wiping out the property of business owners. Since many Korean Americans were shop owners in economically disadvantaged neighborhoods, they were part of the social inequity by virtue of operating those stores. Thus, in this view, the "real" victims were not the shop owners, but the economically disadvantaged residents of these neighborhoods. Moreover, some felt the looters' behavior sprang from the simple fact that, for a very long time, they had been on the low end of the socio-economic equation and could bear it no more.

While this rationale is wrong in a sense, so is the destruction of property. The stores were located mainly in the poorer areas and the people affected by the disappearance of the shops were mainly residents of the poorer neighborhoods. Two wrongs do not make a right. Attacking the "better off" to balance the inequality only creates a greater equality of poverty. The reformers, therefore, want it the other way, and speak of large-scale urban renewal and redevelopment.

Others separate the ideas of political and economic inequality. The economic inequality of certain groups cannot, in their opinion, be abolished. Since throughout history inequality between various segments of society was the norm, it is likely that it will continue to remain so. Therefore, in this view, there should be a floor on poverty. The whole of Los Angeles' inner city should be improved. The "better off" who work there have fled to the suburbs to live, thus depriving the inner city of its economic local tax base. This is seen as an economic injustice. Cynical about the possibilities for change in the political and legal areas, some of the looters felt they were righting injustice by their own hands. For example, during the riot a looter carrying a television set out of a store, when confronted by a TV camera, justified his action by shouting, "It belongs to me anyway!". Thus, there are those who call for legislative action to improve the economic environment of the inner city through better schools, more jobs, and easier access to financial assistance for local enterprises.

Then there are those who believe that Korean Americans were especially heavily victimized during the riot because of cultural misunderstandings, and resultant insensitivity, between this ethnic group and others. To state it positively: if there were more understanding of Korean culture by non-Koreans and, conversely, if Korean Americans had had more knowledge of non-Korean culture, they would not have found such an outpouring of rage against them. In this opinion, the behavior of the looters was determined by their cultural disposition, they acted out a frustration resulting from cultural differences. Thus, to solve the problem, one would have to educate each side about the other.

These were just some of the arguments and explanations about the Korean community's plight during the riot. To be sure, most people hold a mixture of these opinions, in which the intensity of each component reflects the person's predilection for certain approaches. However, to judge the merits of complex opinions, one needs to isolate its components by a process of reduction, determine the validity of each, and then, if the components prove to be true, to re-assemble the complex view by the method of integration. If the components do not withstand the trial of truth, the complex view which they comprise would loose its full or partial validity as well. Since invalid ideas are invalid because they clash with reality, no one can act upon them with success. It is therefore worth examining in detail the various views pertaining to the Korean American community's plight during the riot, because only by acting upon valid hypotheses can we better our chances of not having to suffer such destruction again. This is not to say that only Korean Americans would have to check their premises; the riot elaborately demonstrated that human beings are not immune to the actions of their fellows. But identifying the ideas that manifested themselves during and after the riot can provide a form of self-protection from, or at least preparedness against, malignant actions from others.

It was the need for a re-examination of these and other ideas that led us to organize this Conference on New Directions For the Korean American Community After the Civil Unrest of April 1992. The conference was held on April 19-20, 1993, about one month before the first anniversary of the riot. This would help, we thought, enable the community to be prepared for whatever might occur on the symbolically significant exact anniversary of that frightening event. In addition, several trials related to the original Rodney King trial, which in part had set off the riot in the first place, were coming to a conclusion with uncertain repercussions. The civil unrest had been started by still unidentified persons who took advantage of the almost universal dissatisfaction with the light sentences meted out to the police officers who had kicked and beaten Rodney King, unaware that their actions were being videotaped by an amateur cameraman. Our hope was that this Conference would bring a measure of mutual understanding into this charged atmosphere. In addition to trying to understand the Korean community's situation during the riot, we also wanted to look ahead to the future. That is why the conference called for "new directions." We hoped the conference would provide a benchmark on the road to creating cogent public policy proposals as well as action on the part of Korean Americans.

As mentioned, during the riot the factional and other differences within the Korean American community momentarily faded away, uniting the community as never before. For example, on May 11, 1992, over 30,000 Korean Americans participated in a "peace march" which turned out to be the largest gathering Korean Americans had ever held in Los Angeles. They were united in bewailing the injustice that all felt had been inflicted on them. They were joined by a sprinkling of almost all other ethnic minorities as well as members of the dominant Anglo community. But, while united in protest, some called for revenge, some expressed hatred, some sought other scapegoats, some expressed forgiveness, some proposed specific economic and/or political measures, while still others called for solidarity with other groups to realize such measures.

That unity, therefore, masked and temporarily overcame a number of fissures that had existed in the Korean American community long before the riot—fissures which had undermined attempts to create a strong and respected leadership within the community. Such intra-community tensions still have not entirely dissipated.

These fissures had grown up along with the maturation of the so-called "one-point-five" (1.5) generation—namely those who were brought over from Korea when they were between one and ten years of age. These children readily took on the culture of their new homeland, but the first generation held to traditional views and values. Nonetheless, upon arrival in America the first generation set to and worked long, hard hours to save enough money to send their children to college for professional degrees.

Many in the first generation had learned very little English and knew a minimal amount about American culture in general and the American political system in particular. They were interested only in starting up small businesses, shops or garages, often being unable to utilize the professional capabilities they had acquired in Korea. As referenced in some of the following papers, certain scholars have called this phenomenon "status disfunctionalism:" Koreans who had earned advanced professional degrees in their homeland had to work in America in inferior-level jobs or enterprises.

Scholars have pinpointed the irony that, in the mania of pursuing economic attainment and projecting ahead their children's college and professional goals, many parents in the Korean American community have eventually lost touch with their children's daily educational achievements, even on the elementary level. The result was a breakdown in communication between these two generations before the end result was achieved. In Los Angeles, many immigrants had never really become comfortable with American ways and their own children's reactions to their surroundings.

Some conference participants noted that after the riot the older generation seemed to engage in self-introspection. A good number of them came to the realization, rightly or wrongly, that the riot may have been part of the fate of a community that defines its upward mobility purely in economic terms, without also considering the importance of becoming politically engaged and thus cognizant of where power truly resides.

It might be hypothesized that the wider society was partly to blame for the community's lack of engagement because it built up a special image of Korean Americans as constituting a "model community," i.e., one that did not engage in crime, that did not depend on social welfare, and that did not make waves on the political waters. This labeling, however, served to inhibit the growth of practical, realistic, and popularly supported leadership in the community. What leadership there was consisted, in part, of self-appointed, locally successful business people who had gained access to the established political order, both in Los Angeles and Seoul. It relied on vertical patterns of respect without also reaching out for horizontal ties of solidarity.

Upon reflection, the community by and large has come to realize the need for local organizations, organized from the bottom up, that include persons of similar interests, willing to "fight for their rights." The need has always been for umbrella organizations that have trans-ethnic "stakeholders" who, when united, would present a controlling political force on the urban scene.

Illustrative of the community's lack of political empowerment was Korean Americans' reluctance to resist the reapportionment—some would say gerrymandering—of Koreatown. That action divided the community into different political districts, leaving Korean Americans separated and thus politically impotent. Another example was witnessed when the Federal Emergency Management Agency (FEMA) responded to the results of the civil unrest with a clear lack of understanding of Korean culture. FEMA did not even employ any Korean-speaking agents. This gave rise to a "victim pathology mentality" in which riot victims found themselves *further* victimized because of their lack of political strength.

Perhaps as important, Korean Americans felt isolated from other ethnic communities. To correct this, they organized discussion groups and prayer meetings, especially with African Americans. Here the clergies from both communities were very responsive. They arranged inter-racial exchanges of clergy and congregations. Certain Korean American groups sent selected African Americans to Korea for the first time in their lives. Those who visited Korea could and did come back with much information on how people in South Korea were caring, polite, highly advanced technologically, and had, over the years, absorbed a surprising number of cultural elements from other societies. In both the African American and Korean American communities a high percentage of the population attend church, many on a regular basis. The ecumenical spirit is strong in both communities.

As demonstrated in this collection of conference papers, there are multiple grounds for political cooperation. We discovered wide-spread, inter-ethnic support for an Asian American candidate for Mayor of Los Angeles. While Michael Woo did not win the election, the coalition he was able to forge could, if it becomes broad enough, become successful in the future. In the mayoral election of 1993, the African American and Asian American votes overwhelmingly supported Michael Woo, whereas the Hispanic and Anglo votes were split, contributing in part to the election of Richard Riordan. Mayor Riordan shows a deep interest in the Korean American community, especially as entrepreneurs and key players in building a new "neo-conservative rainbow coalition." This would be an attempt to split the earlier "rainbow coalition" along more economic class lines.

Now the question is: How should the Korean American community structure its political realignments with other groups in Los Angeles and beyond? While the Korean American community is not very large in terms of numbers and raw votes, it does have economic strength and is gaining maturity. Will it be able to convince other groups that what is good for Korean Americans is also good for them? Or will it remain isolated and unaligned? The papers in this collection shed light on this, and give us food for reflection.

When viewed from the long-term perspective, the question is will the situation remain, both in Los Angeles and beyond, wherein unrest could again erupt? Some people see the Los Angeles riots as a repeat (albeit on a larger scale) of the so-called Watts riot of 1965—a civil disturbance largely confined to one geographic area of the city. At present, it appears that we will not have a recurrence in the near future; but unless the structural conditions fostering civil disturbance—racial, economic and political—are not ameliorated, who knows how long this tranquillity will last.

On the national level, the Clinton administration's urban policy has yet to be fully articulated. When it is, it will be easier to evaluate its impact on Los Angeles. Natural disasters still appear to get faster and more thorough relief, as exemplified in the fall of 1993 fires in Los Angeles and Orange counties. Human-made disasters are still looked upon as though they do not warrant as much relief; the rationale being "because some people were 'bad,' the communities involved deserve to suffer."

The aftermath goes on, even in local politics. For instance, members of the Los Angeles City Council have drawn up an ordinance that affects a section of the Korean American community, and in turn, that community's relations with other communities. The ordinance in question mandates that the re-establishment of any store in South Central L.A. that sold liquor, either partially or predominantly, would be subject to new city requirements. For example, under the proposed ordinance store owners would be required to: hire a security guard, be open for business only until 11:00 p.m., and meet other conditions that the average Korean "mom and pop" store owner simply could not afford. Does such a request conflict with their Constitutional rights? Are they being doubly victimized? What is the social impact of these establishments in the South Central community, especially given the over-concentration of liquor stores? This is just one example of the continuing problems that cry for solutions. Many more can be found in these pages.

The following papers present a variety of viewpoints and have been authored by people of diverse backgrounds, experiences, and interests. Some papers are by scholars, some by community activists, and some by persons who represent a combination of the two. Some papers have been meticulously researched, others are impressionistic. Thus, throughout the text, the reader will be treated to different styles as well as to different viewpoints, philosophies, recommendations, and conclusions. Far from being an oversight, we believe this approach is a strength, and thereby gives greater liveliness to the volume as a whole.

The last section is a list of the recommendations that came out of the conference. They were elicited by H. Eric Schockman and edited by the two of us. They are the expression of a specific time and place and of the people present at the very end of the conference—that collective authorship, however, had been soaked in the barrage of presentations, and as a result, reflects that enlightenment along with its own insights. We commend these recommendations, both to policy makers and to the community as a whole, as sign posts and guidelines; we do not, however, intend that they are definitive, complete, or even "correct." We hope you enjoy the book as much as we enjoyed preparing it for you, and if some insight can come from this compendium, if even one injustice can be corrected, then our efforts will have been richly rewarded.

*   *   *   *   *   *

There are many people we have to thank who have made this conference, whatever its worth, a reality and a success. First of all we must mention Dr. Yong Mok Kim and Mr. Yongsohk Choe, President and Executive Director, respectively, of the Korean American Forum. They got in touch with us shortly after the riot. We met with them and others, discussing at first the idea of a small seminar to mull over the events; but as time passed, our ideas became bigger and bolder until finally we set our sights on a conference, and then sought ways to fund it. We all worked diligently to make the conference a reality and we were helped along the way by graduate students Su Hwan Im and Frank Sommers, and by Mr. Eric Chang from the community.

What eventuated was far beyond our original intentions or expectations. It was natural to decide that USC would be the best venue—it was neutral ground, where different types of people with very different viewpoints could gather in a calm, academic environment. Also, the sponsorship and support from the University, specifically the Department of Political Science and the Center for Multiethnic and Transnational Studies, enabled us to raise the necessary funding. The support we received from Rebuild LA and from the Korea Foundation was vital to our success. We also wish to acknowledge the support we generously received from the following: Pacific Bell, AT&T, the Oriental Mission Church, the Young-Nak Presbyterian Church of L.A., the Korean Philadelphia Presbyterian Church, the L.A. Christian Reformed Church, the L.A. Choong-Hyun Presbyterian Church, the *Korea Times*, *Los Angeles*, Inc., the *Korean Central Daily News*, the Korean Senior Citizens Association, Inc., the Association of Korean American Victims of the L.A. Riot, the California Center Bank, the Pacific Century Institute, and Park & Foster Advertising, Inc. To these we and all the participants, and, hopefully, the readers, are thankful.

We are also grateful to all those at the University interested in, or connected with, Korean studies who encouraged us, including but not limited to: President Steven B. Sample, Dr. C. Sylvester Whitaker, Dr. Peter Lyman, Dr. Marshall Cohen, Dr. Carol Nagy Jacklin, Dr. Stephen Toulmin, Dr. Alvin Rudisill, Dr. Michael B. Preston, Dr. Robert Friedheim, Dr. John E. Wills, Jr., Dr. Gordon M. Berger, Dr. Michael B. Robinson, Dr. Nam Gil Kim, Dr. Eun Mee Kim, Dr. Kay Song, and Dr. Kenneth D. Klein. We also appreciate the administrative assistance of Clare Walker and Veronica Pete of USC, and the technical assistance of Dr. Richard D. Burns and Joey Parker. To these we and all the participants, and, hopefully, the readers, are thankful. And finally, thanks must go to the authors whose contributions made this volume possible.

I

KOREAN AMERICANS
IN
SOUTHERN CALIFORNIA

April 29th, 1992   L.A. City Hall

THE KOREAN AMERICAN COMMUNITY IN SOUTHERN CALIFORNIA

Yong Mok Kim
President, Korean American Forum

An overview of the Korean peoples' development in southern California should include their emigration and settlement patterns, demographic characteristics, occupational patterns, social and community life and institutions, economic activities, and their views on family, children and education, as well as the racial prejudice and discrimination these immigrants had to suffer.

The migration of Koreans to the Los Angeles area dates back to the early years of the twentieth century. At that time, the Korean influx into Los Angeles was mainly in the form of transmigration from Hawaii, where Koreans had sought employment on sugar plantations.[1] However, the majority of the Korean American immigrants into southern California in the 1960s and early 1970s arrived directly from Korea, largely as a result of the liberalized immigration law of 1965.[2]

Los Angeles has had a special appeal to Korean immigrants throughout the century. Because of its geographic location, Los

---

[1] Lee Houchins and Chang-su Houchins, "The Korean Experience in America," in Morris Hundley, Jr., ed., *The Asian American: The Historical Experience* (Santa Barbara, CA: ABC-Clio, 1976), pp. 129-136. Also, Yong Mok Kim, "Formation and Tasks in the History of Korean Emigration to the United States of America," in Korean American Historical Society, ed. *Immigrant Life in America* (Los Angeles: Korean American Historical Society, 1979), pp. 7-10.

[2] Ivan Light and Edna Bonacich, *Immigrant Entrepreneurs: Koreans in Los Angeles, 1965-1982* (Berkelely: University of California Press, 1988), pp. 106-126.

Angeles—and to a lesser degree San Francisco—served as the chief gateway to America from the Far East. The mild climate of southern California, its growing and booming economy, its multiethnic setting and life style were additional benefits to Korean immigrants. Los Angeles was also the site of the Korean independence movement in America.[3]

Before 1945, the Korean population in southern California was not more than 2,000 at most. The total Korean population in the continental United States was approximately 3,000, besides 7,000 or so Koreans who settled in Hawaii. Between 1945 and 1965 Korean immigrants to the United States consisted mainly of "war brides," adopted orphans, and students, numbering not more than 15,000. Southern California attracted a large percentage of these postwar immigrants, possibly as many as 2,000-3,000 (about 20%). With its small number, the Korean American community in southern California remained largely unnoticed. In 1965, liberal immigration legislation led to a large influx of Korean immigrants to America. The main result of that influx was the fast-growing Korean American community of southern California.[4]

In explaining the movement of immigrants from one country to another, historians often use the "push and pull" theory. According to this theory, emigrants leave their home country for various reasons, including political turmoil, economic uncertainty, or religious or ideological persecution (the "push" side). They then immigrate to a country that has a special appeal for them (the "pull" side).[5]

South Korea's postwar history supplies plenty of reasons why immigrants would leave the country. Following the thirty-year Japanese colonization of Korea, the end of World War II left the country in utter poverty. Five years later, in 1950, the Korean War broke out, bringing unspeakable devastation to

---

[3] Ibid., pp. 147-155.

[4] Yi Kwang-gyu, *Chaemi Hangugin* (Koreans in America), (Seoul: Ilchogak, 1989), pp. 98-102.

[5] Light and Bonacich, pp. 152-153.

Korea and privations to its people. In 1961, a military junta took over the government of South Korea, suppressing political dissent in the most brutal ways. Meanwhile, the regime introduced aggressive programs of urbanization and industrialization to the hitherto agricultural country, bringing about rapid and often painful social change. Despite the fast-growing industrial sector, massive unemployment was a burning problem in Korea during the1960s and 1970s. These factors were major forces driving people to the conclusion that it would be better for them to seek success and fulfilment in some other country. Severe entrance competition in Korea made sending their children to college so frustrating that many Koreans sought better opportunities for their children's education in the United States.

On the "pull' side, the United States was a country where immigrants could have a fresh start and, by dint of hard work, could achieve success. The United States was the richest and strongest nation in the world. Many Koreans who considered emigrating to America already had family connections here. The idea of joining one's relatives was enticing. American culture, as they perceived it, was attractive enough for many Koreans to make the decision to emigrate.

Currently, the Korean American community in southern California has an estimated population of 500,000, or approximately one third of the total number of Korean immigrants and their offspring in the United States. The Korean immigrants formed several communities in southern California, including the large Korean American community in Los Angeles, and in several urban centers such as the San Fernando Valley, Monterey Park, Cerritos, Anaheim, San Diego, and Riverside. [6]

Of the many "Koreatowns," as these Korean population centers are often called, the one in Los Angeles is the largest and attracts the most attention and interest, both from Koreans and from others. Los Angeles' Koreatown reflects a typical

---

[6] Ibid., pp. 152-153.

settlement pattern of newly arrived immigrants, particularly ethnic minorities, similar to Little Tokyo and Chinatown. The area that has become Koreatown—which is bounded roughly by Beverly Boulevard on the north, Crenshaw on the west, Pico on the south, and Hoover on the east—witnessed many turbulent times throughout the 1960s. Its northern border was adjacent to South Central Los Angeles, an area that, following the 1965 riots, was quickly abandoned by major business establishments, thus sowing the seeds of future economic depression and resulting social conflict. The Korean immigrants who settled in this area during the 1960s, assumed ownership of many businesses formerly owned by Jews and other ethnic minorities—the same minorities who had been the chief targets of the 1965 riots.[7]

Koreatown is often the first stopping place for newly arriving Korean immigrants. To satisfy their needs, Koreans established many churches, social and personal service organizations, retail businesses, restaurants, gas stations, real estate offices, laundry shops, grocery markets, and so forth. The colorful Korean-language signs and billboards virtually turned Koreatown into a Little Seoul. As Korean immigrants achieve a degree of economic security through the hard work invested in running their businesses, they tend to move out of Koreatown into the suburban areas. Today, although the majority of business establishments in Koreatown are owned and operated by Koreans, the residents of the area are predominantly Latino. This notwithstanding, Los Angeles' Koreatown continues to be the social, economic, and cultural center of the Korean population in southern California.

The Korean American community developed some unique characteristics in its demographic patterns. For instance, the median age of the Korean population in southern California was 23.7 years for males and 27.1 years for females, vis-a-vis 28.8 years for males and 31.2 years for the average American population. While only 8 percent of Korean Americans were 50

---

7 Ibid., pp. 145-148; Yi, pp. 99-100.

years or older, 26 percent of the general American population has passed that age. The typical Korean family had three to four members, averaging 3.8 persons per household; 74.5 percent of Korean families can be described as a "nuclear family." The male-female ratio was 72 to 100. Of Korean households, 72 percent had male heads, 11 percent had female. This compares with 63 percent male and 10 percent female heads of household in the general American population. The same survey listed 93.5 percent of Korean males and 90.4 percent females in the 25-29 age bracket as having graduated from high school; the numbers are 87 percent and 87.2 percent for white males and females, respectively. A 1987 survey found that, prior to their immigration to America, 73 percent of Korean men and 63 percent of Korean women had received a college education.[8]

A 1985 survey about Koreans' employment patterns revealed some interesting results. Roughly 40 percent of the adult Korean population is self-employed, and is predominantly in the retail and service industries. Only about 6.5 percent of Koreans were in manufacturing and 1.4 percent in construction, while 38.6 percent were engaged in some form of wholesale and retail trade, such as general trade (7%), food (8%), electrical appliances (2.1%), jewelry (2.2%), automotive (3.9%). In addition, 8.1 percent was in the restaurant business, 4.7 percent in real estate, 3.5 percent in the hotel and transportation businesses, 6.1 percent in various social services, 8.9 percent in such personal services as legal and accounting, 7.9 percent in laundry and hairdressing businesses, and 5.7 percent were engaged in some form of religious occupation. Another survey estimated that there were about 800 hamburger stores, 200 gas stations, and 356 garment factories owned by Koreans in southern California.

To be sure, these patterns of occupation are not commensurate with the Korean immigrants' level of education.[9] Before many Koreans enter self-employment, they find

---

[8] Yi, pp. 217-219.

[9] Ibid., pp. 100-112.

employment in menial labor or jobs requiring semi-skilled workers. When we consider that about 70 percent of Korean immigrants had received college education in Korea and 30 to 40 percent of them were professionals in Korea, many Koreans find that their employment as mechanics, welders, gas station attendants, or garment workers does not make use of their professional skills. But, in spite of their higher education in Korea, many of these immigrants cannot communicate in English well enough to find employment in their learned professions. Also, many Koreans are not familiar with the American working style, which can cause friction between them and their employers. It is also true that some Korean immigrants have to face racial prejudice and discrimination in American society. Thus, Koreans often have no choice but to accept low-paying jobs. In this light, perhaps it is not surprising that 32 percent of male and 42 percent of female Korean garment workers had a college education. [10]

Much perseverance and hard work are required from Koreans to achieve relative independence in the form of self-employment. It takes usually between three and six years before most Korean small-business owners can establish themselves. According to a study on self-employment patterns in the Los Angeles area, 28.3 percent of Korean small-business owners worked in menial jobs for three years before they could establish their businesses; for women, the figure is 18.9 percent. But the majority did not enjoy such rapid prosperity. It took six years of low-paying menial labor for 47.6 percent of Korean males and 45.7 percent of females to establish their own businesses. Even as independent business owners, these Koreans are not free of worry. The rate of failure of small businesses is alarmingly high among Korean American owners. One study estimates that in the Los Angeles area 50 percent of such business ventures fail within the first year of operation, and as many as 70 percent fail within three years. There is,

---

[10] Ronald Takaki, *Strangers from a Different Shore: A History of Asian Americans* (Boston: Little, Brown, 1989), pp. 432-445.

therefore, a high percentage of evident risk in a newly established Korean American business. But this level of risk must be put into perspective. In the United States, it is estimated that 80 percent of new business ventures fail within the first five years of operation. This reflects not only the large number of business start-ups in America, but also indicates that Korean American entrepreneurs are about as successful as the average American business owner. [11]

These days more and more people start some form of small business, often as a part-time occupation to complement their regular income. The spectacular success of some well-known, and many lesser-known, franchises and other types of business opportunities indicate the sharply increasing trend in Americans' desire to own their own businesses. The unique aspect of Korean business owners, therefore, is not their desire for financial independence, or even self-employment. Rather it is the fact that, due to the language handicap, most Korean Americans simply had no other opportunity to earn a living than by owning their own businesses.[12]

According to a survey of Korean immigrants' ability to speak English, 5.7 percent responded as "fluent," 35 percent as "fairly good," 39.6 percent as "not so good," 17.7 percent as "poor," and 2 percent identified themselves as "not being able to speak English at all." In reading English, 15.2 percent thought that they were "excellent," 41.7 percent "fair," 33.9 percent "not so good," while 7.4 percent responded as "bad," and 1.8 percent said they were "not able to read at all." In writing English, 8.8 percent felt that they were "excellent," 35.5 percent "fair," 41.3 percent "not so good," 12.1 percent "bad," and 2.1 percent "could not write English at all." Observe that the majority of respondents belong to the "not so good" or "so-so" category, and that the categories established by the survey were rather subjective. Being able to get along in English on the everyday conversational level is one thing; being able to rapidly absorb

---

[11] Yi, pp. 200-204.

[12] Ibid., pp. 200-205.

sophisticated business information and develop highly elaborate communication skills, both being essential to business success, is another. Not being able to speak fluent English is a handicap, not only in the job market, but in small-business ownership as well.[13]

Most new Korean business owners lack the necessary knowledge to successfully develop their enterprises, especially if that enterprise is in a field in which they had no previous training or experience. In addition to the lack of specific knowledge about a product or service, there is the lack of general knowledge about American business culture. The latter factor limits Koreans' ability to successfully network among non-Koreans in seeking advice with regard to management, financial or legal matters, marketing, and other crucial aspects of a business enterprise.[14]

Koreans heavily depend on other Koreans in financing their ventures. Although an organized form of raising capital has been developed and transplanted from Korea, the rotating credit association (*kye*) has many limiting factors. The most important among them is the difficulty of properly assessing the risk involved in the ventures in which their money is invested. It follows that many Korean small businesses are tremendously undercapitalized. One survey found that 20.3 percent of Korean-owned small businesses had less than $10,000 in capital assets, 20.9 percent had between $10,000 and $20,000, 28.1 percent between $20,000 and $50,000, 18.1 percent between $50,000 and $100,000, and only 12.4 percent of businesses had more than $100,000. Actually, these numbers are not bad vis-a-vis the capitalization of small businesses in America in general. What makes these numbers alarming is that they reflect not the owners' risk capital, not even their savings above daily expenditures, but their families' only assets. Also, because of the nature of their financing through the *kye*, most Korean businesses lack the recourse to secondary and tertiary financing.

---

[13] Ibid., pp. 222-224.
[14] Ibid., pp. 183-208.

Because of their lack of established credit, these owners can hardly obtain loans; and given the small size of their operations, they have little opportunity to receive venture capital either. Literally, those wanting to start a new business are limited to whatever resources they have available at that time. Under such conditions, few native-born Americans would be willing to start a business. But the Korean immigrants, if they are to survive, often have no other option.[15]

Particularly in retail businesses, which form the majority of Korean-owned ventures, the lack of ability to speak American English and the lack of understanding of the general business culture severely limit these businesses' potential market. Korean immigrants are often found catering to the needs of mostly other Koreans. The geographic and market-specific oversupply in certain fields of businesses leads to sometimes fierce competition between Korean shop owners, which eventually cuts into their meager profits. Especially in primarily non-Korean inhabited neighborhoods, these handicaps also lead to otherwise unnecessary conflicts between the Korean shop owner and his or her customers. Observe from the data cited above on the Koreans' language fluency that most of those surveyed found verbal communication in English to be most difficult. Yet, this is just the skill that a retail store owner needs most. It is sometimes difficult even for native-born Americans to understand the variety of dialects spoken in the Los Angeles area. Not surprisingly then, most Korean shop owners are at a complete loss when a customer with a Brooklyn accent asks questions in rapid English. Add to this the great difference between their cultural backgrounds and social dispositions, and it is not difficult to imagine where the conflicts and misunderstandings come from.[16]

The severe limitations imposed upon a Korean American immigrant small-business owner compels him to cut his cost of doing business at any price. The price he should really pay to

---

[15] Ibid., pp. 201-204.
[16] Ibid., pp. 160-167.

achieve efficiency, he can seldom afford. For that would mean recourse to the best counsel in legal and financial matters, sufficient capitalization, work force, technology, etc. One way in which he can cut costs is to locate his business in a neighborhood where operational expenses are cheap. Unfortunately, these neighborhoods mean high risk in terms of customer-base, property price appreciation, accessibility, and— a major issue in Los Angeles—safety. The prices the small-business owner has to charge to reach a break-even point are often above what normal market prices are in other neighborhoods. But, given the lack of supply in these high-risk areas, the shop owner can still charge these somewhat higher-than-market prices. This has led to further misunderstandings between the owners and their customers. Because of this, and because residents could easily do their shopping in other areas, the price markup that the owners may hope to receive in return for the higher risk, is severely limited. Another way of cost cutting is the employment of unpaid or underpaid family-labor. This usually involves the spouse of the owner and, quite frequently, the children, at least on a part-time basis. Such an employment structure has extensive impacts upon the Korean American family. [17]

We have referred to Korean immigrant families as young, nuclear families. Almost 75 percent of Korean families have children of 18 years or younger. Within their families, only 4 percent of Korean immigrants speak English as their only language; 67 percent of them do not speak English at all in their home; and 19.1 percent speak English only occasionally. Between parents and children, 63.2 percent of them converse in English occasionally. (English is spoken in 31.4 percent of Japanese American families, in 12.5 percent of Chinese American families, and in 13 percent of Filipino American families.) [18]

The first-generation-centered family life typical of Korean families results in a lack of communication and dialogue

---

[17] Takaki, pp. 442-443.
[18] Yi, pp. 222-224.

between parents and children. Immigrant parents are engaged in long hours of work in their small businesses and they find little time to talk with their children. The lack of dialogue between parents and children leads sometimes to delinquency on the part of the children, a worsening problem in the Korean American community. Another result of the lack of communication, particularly in English, is the poor verbal skills of their children.[19]

In nearly all cases, Korean immigrants cite better opportunities for their children's education as their motive to immigrate to America. Ironically, once in America, their hard immigrant life seldom allows these parents to address themselves to the needs of their children's education. One survey found that 54 percent of parents held jobs outside their homes; 67 percent of the women were working mothers. Naturally, parents cannot afford the time to talk to their children, much less help each other cope with the problems of adjustment, assimilation and racial discrimination. Parents seldom visit their children's school or attend PTA meetings to understand the problems their children face at school.[20]

Apart from their lack of practical involvement, Korean immigrants' enthusiasm for their children's education is intense. Often they may force their children onto a path to realize the dreams the parents themselves could not attain. They want their children to attend first-rate schools and become doctors, lawyers, and engineers. Following their parents' wishes—and because of their lack of strong verbal skills in English—Korean immigrant youths prefer majoring in business administration (30%), engineering (29.4%), and the sciences (15%). Only the minority takes up majors in the social sciences (13.2%) and humanities (5.8%). Consequently, in their professions they prefer careers in business, medicine, legal fields, and engineering.[21]

Those children that emigrated to America at an early age, at about age 10, are often referred to as belonging to the "1.5

[19] Kim, pp. 8-9.

[20] Yi, pp. 222-223.

[21] Ibid., p. 223.

generation." They are easily "Americanized," indoctrinated with American values as they go through public education. They acquire a good command of English, often at the cost of neglecting Korean. Children thus brought up, however, often face identity crises: they are torn between their parents' Korean culture and the American culture they have learned. They lack a useful frame of reference for their identity. This is a clear indication of the fact that neither the Korean nor the American cultures, as they are now understood and taught, can offer people the values required for man's existence. If one wonders why there is so much crime and delinquency among young people in America, it is because of the dominant culture's default in offering people, especially young people, the path that leads to their fulfilment and happiness in life. America guarantees its citizens the right to the "pursuit of happiness," but it offers no clue as to the path upon which happiness can be pursued. It was not always the case in America, and perhaps the time has come to return to the age and its cultural values that had brought about the creation of the American republic. We must add also that neither do other traditional cultures offer a system of values that may lead people to happiness—and if one doubts that, one can only be reminded of the mysticism prevalent in many historical cultures that declare man's inability to achieve happiness on earth. No more eloquent sign is needed to indicate their bankruptcy.[22]

Turning to the social life of Korean immigrants in southern California, in their interpersonal relations we find that they form closely-knit groups, such as those of close relatives, alumni, hometown friends, and business associates. Almost 75 percent of the respondents to a survey in Los Angeles claimed that they had close relatives living nearby, such as brothers, sisters, parents or children. As many as 50 percent meet once a week, 80 percent of them, once a month. As neighbors, 75 percent of Korean immigrants had Korean friends; 12.7 percent had both Korean and non-Korean neighbors as friends; 9.2 percent had

---

[22] Takaki, pp. 286-293.

only White neighbor friends, while only 3.3 percent counted ethnic neighbors as friends. Among Los Angeles Korean immigrants, 93.6 percent of male respondents stated they had friends; the number is 89.8 percent for women. [23]

The Korean American community in southern California has witnessed a proliferation of clubs and organizations for socialization and participation in social activities. Among them are alumni associations, veterans' organizations, churches, and so forth. As many as 73 high school alumni associations and 46 college alumni associations were listed in the *Korean Directory for Southern California*.[24]

Christian Churches play an integral role in the life of Korean immigrants. Their sheer number is astounding. A 1985 survey counted 1,500 Korean Christian churches in America. This means that there was a church for every 450 Korean immigrants in America. Southern California alone had over 300 churches. A study reveals that Korean churches are often established as "pioneer" churches because of the split of existing churches. Of the Los Angeles area Christian churches, denominational breakdowns were as follows: Presbyterian (51.35%), Catholic (10%), Methodist (9.1%), and Baptist (4.9%). The size of congregations varies, from as little as 19 members to as many as several thousand. The median size Korean congregation in southern California is 70 members. The annual receipt of donations from the congregation varies from less than $10,000 to over a million dollars. A 1986 survey revealed that 69.9 percent of the respondents listed themselves as churchgoers, and 51.3 percent of them had been Christians already before coming to America. [25]

Korean immigrant churchgoers are quite devoted: 82 percent of them say they go to church once every week, while 26 percent of them do so twice a week. When questioned, they said they go to church for worship and to receive counsel for

[23] Yi., pp. 113-114.

[24] Korea Central Daily News, *Korean Business Directory, 1993-1994* (Los Angeles: Korea Central Daily News, 1993.), pp. 6-43.

[25] Yi, pp. 146-147.

social problems. In a Los Angeles survey, as many as 24.4 percent of churchgoers said they go to church for "peace of mind," 22.4 percent for religion, and 14.2 percent for listening to sermons. Thus, the Korean churches meet both the religious needs and the social and psychological needs of Korean immigrants. Given their number, size, membership, and revenue, Korean churches in America and in southern California are the most important and influential public institutions in the life of the Korean Americans with religious, educational, social, psychological, and many other functions.[26]

Another institution that plays a significant role in the life of Korean immigrants is the mass media. In southern California, seven daily Korean-language newspapers (including major Seoul dailies), several weekly newspapers, and many television stations are available for the news hungry. A study showed that 78 percent of the respondents subscribe to Korean-language newspapers, and 22 percent subscribe to English-language papers. In the latter group, 63.6 percent were interested in ads, 60.4 percent in city news, and 55.1 percent in politics. Men are more interested in the economic and sports pages, while women read more about culture and home. Korean immigrants, particularly the first generation, show a strong Korea-oriented tendency.[27]

What emerges form this overview of the Korean American community in southern California is a vibrant, fast-growing, and somewhat self-contained ethnic minority community. However, in spite of the images of the successful minority, it has its share of problems.

First generation immigrants usually go through a stage-by-stage adaptation, from "sojourner mentality" to "settler mentality," mostly on their own. Their children, on the other hand, are on the fast track to become Americanized. The lack of dialogue between the first and second generations, as was pointed out, often leads to alienation and delinquency on the

---

[26] Ibid., p. 147.
[27] Ibid., pp. 116-122.

part of the second generation. The second generation, who listen to their parents, appears to be part of an "educational elite" group. They comply with the strong demands from their parents and have respect for education, professional degrees, and scholarship.[28]

Before the Korean American community becomes a fully integral part of society, it has to adapt to the American system. This requires the use of its resources and power. The Korean American community is an economically successful one; this is a source of power as well as a cause of friction with other minorities, notably Blacks and Latinos. The economic power notwithstanding, because of the lack of cohesion and leadership in the community, this resource has not been fully utilized in adapting to the American system. We have referred to a large number of community institutions with self-proclaimed leaders; yet, they lack cohesion and leadership. The Korean American community is divisive at times. For instance, during the 1992 civil unrest in Los Angeles, the community was without strong leadership and a united voice in coping with the crises. The lack of cohesion in the Korean American community shows itself in the form of factions. This poses a serious problem, and there is no easy solution for it.[29]

As many in the first-generation Korean immigrants came here to escape authoritarian regimes, they have not gone through stages of leadership training. Thus, some of these unqualified first generation leaders vie for leadership in the community. As they have not been trained in written and verbal communication in English with an outside audience, have not learned the ropes of the American political process, and have not had experience in coordinating community issues, they lack the vision necessary for convincing and effective leadership. The second generation has the advantage of being able to speak English, but this skill alone is not enough. Leadership would require involvement in community affairs, understanding

---

[28] Takaki, pp. 286-293.
[29] Yi, pp. 160-162.

community issues, relating the second generation children to the first generation parents. Fortunately, in Los Angeles we do find some young Korean Americans successfully going through the stages of training themselves for leadership.[30]

The need for strong leadership and a united voice in the Korean American community in southern California is a political necessity. With the community's resources—mainly its economic power—the Korean American community will find its proper place in the American political process. In other words, it has to develop political clout not only for the benefit of its own community but also for the larger society. The recent election of several Korean Americans to Congress, state assembly, and city council, is an encouraging sign. Such forms of representation are especially important considering the Korean community's frictions with other minority groups.[31]

Coming from the racially and ethnically homogeneous society of Korea, Korean immigrants generally lack experience in multiethnic living. It is also difficult for them to understand the principles of equality and diversity in race relations in America. The Korean American community in Southern California appears to be learning race relations the hard way, especially since the time of the civil unrest in 1992. The Korean American business community and the Afro-American residents of South Central Los Angeles had not developed mutually acceptable relations. The properties of Korean American business owners were brutally damaged and their presence there endangered. Although these business people played the traditional "middleman role" there, the way they played it was not acceptable to many residents in these areas. It is noteworthy that Korean American business, community and religious leaders have since taken the initiative to develop forums for dialogue and mutual understanding.[32]

---

[30] Ibid., pp. 122-135.

[31] Yong Mok Kim, "Imin" (Korean Emigration), in Korean Committee of the International Historical Conference, ed. *Hanmi Sugyo Paengnyonsa* (A Hundred Years History of Korean-American Relations), (Seoul: Korean Committee of International Historical Conference, 1982), pp. 568-571.

[32] Ibid., p. 571.

How the Korean American community deals with the majority group is as important as its relations with other minorities. We have mentioned the educational elitist view of the first and second—but not the one-and-a-half—generations. This can be explained as a way of integration into the majority group. This strategy is effectively working, as Korean Americans are moving fast upward. Another strategy for integration is the use of the community's financial strength in the pursuit of a certain political clout. This has not produced fast results, perhaps because for many Koreans the political process is difficult to fathom and join.[33]

The measure of the Korean American community's success in integration can be gauged from the way the majority accepts Koreans. To some degree, Korean Americans have been accepted by the majority as a "model minority" group, chiefly because of their economic success, their willingness to work hard, their active role in Christian churches, and their eagerness to adapt to the American system. Whether Korean Americans will balance this acceptance with a degree of cultural pluralism, remains to be seen.[34]

REFERENCES

Chungan Ilbo (Korean Central Daily News) Los Angeles edition, Los Angeles, 1983-1993.

Hankook Ilbo (Korea Daily News) Los Angeles edition, Los Angeles, 1970-1993.

Hundley, Morris, Jr., ed. *The Asian Americans: The Historical Experience.* Santa Barbara, CA: ABC Clio Press, 1976.

Kim, Ilsoo. *New Urban Immigrants.* Princeton, NJ: Princeton University Press, 1981.

Korean American Historical Society, ed. *Immigrant Life in America.* Los Angles: Korean American Historical Society, 1979.

Korean Committee of the International Historical Conference, ed. *Hanmi Sugyo Paengnyonsa* (A Hundred Years History of Korean-

[33] Ibid., pp. 568-571.

[34] Harry Kitano, *Race Relations* (Englewood Cliffs, NJ: Prentice-Hall, 1980), pp. 69-84; 209-216.

American Relations). Seoul: Korean Committee of the International Historical Conference, 1982.

Kitano, Harry. *Race Relations.* Englewood Cliffs, NJ: Prentice-Hall, 1980.

Light, Ivan and Edna Bonacich. *Immigrant Entrepreneurs: Koreans in Los Angeles, 1965-1982.* Berkeley: University of California Press, 1988.

Son, Tae-kun. *Chaemi Hangugin* (Koreans in America). Seoul: Hanminjok, 1988.

Takaki, Ronald. *Strangers from a Different Shore: A History of Asian Americans.* Boston: Little, Brown, 1989.

Yi, Kwang-gyu. *Chaemi Hangugin* (Koreans in America). Seoul: Ilchogak, 1989.

IMMIGRANT MENTALITY

Chungmoo Choi
Professor of East Asian Languages and Cultures
University of California, Riverside

I am not directly involved with the Asian American or the Korean American community itself, but as a person who is studying Korean society, I believe the following insights may help us better understand the Korean American situation. These suggestions arc not intended to provide an immediate, new direction, but rather to encourage scholars and other interested parties to consider a long-term perspective.

Koreans' inability to establish harmonious relationships with other ethnic minorities or other racial groups is often mentioned as a major cause of tensions. Some people describe Korean Americans as a minority with an "immigrant mentality." We have not looked at this "immigrant mentality" in a larger historical context, and until we do so, it can be neither understood nor explained. According to some sources, in the riots of 1992, 97 percent of the Korean American victims were born in Korea, their stay in this country being less than 12 years; moreover, 87 percent of that group are not fluent in English. These facts alone show their deep-rootedness in the Korean situation. When we evaluate the behavior of these people, we should look at their background: How was their ideology and perception of America shaped back in Korea?

In looking at the Korean situation, the notion of colonialism and the Korean experience of colonialism are frequently recurring themes. By colonialism I mean not just the Japanese colonial rule, but the subsequent colonial situation in which Koreans were not allowed to think independently and were constantly under the surveillance of Cold War ideology. In this period of Korean history, the influence of America's image was of paramount influence in shaping the Korean mind. Prior to this period, which started with the end of the Korean War, Korea was a poor and mainly agricultural country. The rapid industrialization and concurrent social developments coincided with a marked increase in the influence of the United States, both politically and ideologically. It was in this atmosphere that Koreans formed their "American Dream"—or whatever they perceived as such.

The American Dream, however, was not a complete ideology: it was, in many ways, suggested and introduced into Korea by the various forms of American popular culture; its deep philosophical and cultural roots in the United States never reached Korea. Thus, when Koreans came to the United States as immigrants, they were often disappointed to find quite a different reality than what they had imagined. This, I am sure, is similar to the experiences of other ethnic groups as well.

There is another issue, however, which is specific to the Korean political situation in the last thirty years. In the name of the National Security Law, South Koreans were not supposed to criticize the United States, because criticizing the U.S. was, and has been, the official position of North Korea. This was clearly an issue, because of the massive American military presence in South Korea. The Korean government and the American government had a demonstrable agreement in which the Korean government was not capable of indicting any American personnel or government employee in South Korea. So some of the illegal and criminal actions of American service personnel stationed in Korea were totally buried from the public eye. Because of the strong images sent by and received from the American popular media, even many Koreans who did have direct contact with the American military could not construct the real picture for themselves. If you ask a Korean about

American military personnels' rape of Korean women, most would answer that those who committed such crimes belonged to American ethnic minorities, although in reality that may not have been so. There is, indeed, a somewhat distorted notion of race that has been imposed on the Korean mentality.

When Koreans come to this country, especially during the early period of their immigrant life, there is a vast disparity between the ideology that has been developed and the actual realities of life in America. It is puzzling and confusing to many people.

Therefore, I suggest that the issue of ethnic tension and its alleged cause, the "immigrant mentality," be examined within the context of Korean American foreign relations and the history of those relations throughout the past thirty to forty years.

Korea Times, L.A.

April 30th, 1992 3rd and New Hampshire

DO KOREAN AMERICAN FIRMS INHIBIT THE GROWTH OF AFRICAN AMERICAN BUSINESS?

Ivan Light
Professor of Sociology
University of California, Los Angeles

In the media's efforts to expose the multi-cultural aspects of the Los Angeles riots of 1992, it de-emphasized the economic substructure of the entire conflict. In so doing, the media, in essence, overlooked the root of the problem, leaving the public more confused than enlightened about the causes of the April 1992 unrest.

It is a truism of the conflict resolution literature that when there is a conflict, the sides tend to "demonize" each other. To demonize means to make the enemy worse than he actually is. When there are conflicts, people, be it one person, or an entire nation, get demonized by the opponent, depicted as worse than they actually are. Demonization, of course, makes the conflicts even more difficult to resolve. With the unrest of 1992, a good bit of demonization was applied to the conflicts, and the media's focus on cultural differences brought the demonizing to the forefront. If the demonization can be shunted aside, the true conflicts become more identifiable, and as a result, more manageable.

The path to clarity can best begin by distinguishing the economic from the non-economic issues. For example, it is frequently said that the Korean merchants don't put anything back into the community. What that remark stands for is money: they don't put any money back into the community. That is an economic objection. By contrast, if it is said that they are rude, that is a non-economic objection (and subject to cultural interpretation, as well).

Many conflicts, not just inter-ethnic conflicts, have an economic basis. One doesn't have to be a Marxist to realize that economic beliefs influence business ideologies. In looking at how African Americans view Korean merchants, there appears to be an exaggeration of the deleterious effects of Korean-owned and operated businesses upon the economic development of the African American community. If conflicts are to be resolved, this exaggeration must be examined and subjected to open and honest discussion. Unfortunately, the popular media has shied away from discussing the economic influences behind racial conflict, thus creating a situation in which there is no dialogue about economic realities. As a result, the public is once again left to ponder half truths, exaggerations, and, in some cases, outright falsehoods.

For example, consider the argument that Korean American merchants are harmful to the long-term economic development of the African American community. One interpretation is that Koreans soak up economic opportunities which otherwise would become available to African Americans. The basic objection would be: Here is a Korean merchant with a corner store on my block. If he or she wasn't there, there would be an opportunity for an African American to own that corner store. The conclusion from that premise is that, if Blacks drive Koreans out, make it very difficult for them to stay and prosper, then Blacks free up opportunities for Afro-American economic development. Admittedly, this is not all there is to the existing tensions, but it illustrates the ideology behind the objections to Korean owned and operated businesses in South Central Los Angeles.

The obvious problem is that this ideology is unfounded. In a more pragmatic vein, let us consider what will be required to increase African American economic development, a legitimate goal. The first step is to deepen the total resource base within the African American community: the base in knowledge and education, in money and finance, and in human resources. Currently, the total resource base in the African American community is thin. There are people who *are* capable of running small businesses, but there are not enough of them. Moreover, most of those people have found (and continue to find) good jobs in the wage and salary sector. If the total resource base were strengthened, more people would be available for entrepreneurship. That's the positive theory.

The negative theory decrees that opportunities for African Americans will automatically open simply by driving out the competition. The negative theory is a falsehood in and of itself. If the Korean merchants were to vanish tomorrow, the African American community still wouldn't have five more cents in the bank to finance business start-ups than it does today. The elimination of competition does not automatically convey the availability of financial resources to the survivor. The claim is often made that lack of capital is the primary inhibitor of African American entrepreneurship; and there is something to that claim. But getting rid of Koreans or any other competitor would not increase the knowledge and education base, nor the money and finance base, nor the human resources base. These areas must be strengthened from within, regardless of the presence or absence of socio-economic competition.

We must take care, however, not to confuse knowledge and education base with motivation base. In a multi-cultural study conducted in San Franciso and Washington, D.C. among young adults 18 to 25 years of age, African Americans were consistently the most entrepreneurial in their outlook. The problem is not that Blacks don't have the motivation, the problem is that they don't have the resources. And if the Koreans left tomorrow, they still wouldn't have the necessary resources. It is precisely the deepening of resources that must be done in order to improve long-term economic prospects for the African American community. Such deepening would be beneficial not only to Blacks, but to all members of the greater Los Angeles community, regardless of ethnic or racial origin.

The bottom line is that what affects African American business is not the presence or absence of immigrant merchants, but rather the condition of the resource base *within* the African American community itself. Los Angeles already has the largest concentration of African American-owned businesses in the United States. It also has the largest concentration of Korean American-owned businesses in the United States. In looking at the ethno-economic conditions of Los Angeles, one could immediately conclude that there is no evidence that Korean merchants retard the economic development of the African American community.

The time has come to stop demonizing the "enemy." Instead, we must face the problems squarely, recognize them and call them by name, and be willing to begin a constructive plan for economic growth and prosperity for one and all. Our failure to do this dooms us to continued violence, moral as well as economic poverty, and unrelenting miscommunication. The journey will be long, but our humanity depends on it, and our survival demands it.

KOREANS AND JEWS IN THE URBAN ENVIRONMENT

Neil Sandberg
Executive Director
American Jewish Committee, Los Angeles

Koreans and Jews are interacting more and more in spite of historic, linguistic and geographic factors that have tended to keep them on separate and distinct paths. Until recently, there was relatively little activity between them, and it might well have been expected that this pattern would continue into the future.

Dramatic changes in the cultural, political, demographic and economic circumstances of both peoples, especially in the twentieth century, have led to new and unprecedented levels of collaboration. Contacts between Jews and Koreans today focus largely on their collective involvements in the United States, although both are part of a larger Diaspora with millions of Jews and Koreans living in various parts of the world, sometimes in threatening circumstances. Both groups have been victimized throughout history, and they share the similarity of trying to survive in unfriendly, even hostile environments. For example, Koreans suffer from ongoing discrimination in Japan, and Jews are still persecuted in Russia. The experiences of Korea and Israel are particularly instructive as both have been attacked repeatedly by unfriendly neighbors.

As with Jews, the upward mobility of Koreans has bred hostility and resentment that occasionally flares into conflict, even violence. Today, Koreans who came to the United States seeking a better life for themselves and their children feel they are under attack. Their assumption had been that hard work would lead to financial success and family security, but the harsh realities of inter-group conflict have cast a pall on this dream. The question now is how they can defend themselves without causing more anger and friction.

The growing migration of Koreans to the United States and their settlement in large urban centers put them into direct contact with major Jewish populations. Jews came to America at an earlier time than did the Koreans, but both entered a profound new era marked by an abrupt and radical break with the past. Historical traditions were reshaped as they left a relatively isolated existence with a suddenness that challenged their past. The modern world opened up possibilities for economic growth and personal development, as well as new forms of self-expression, organization and adaptation. This process has been reinforced by the enormous freedom of America as Koreans and Jews experienced unprecedented opportunities for mobility and assimilation.

The ancient Jewish and Korean cultures provide a natural underpinning for association between these groups whose experiences are deep in a rich national heritage. Both are part of evolving civilizations which helped to shape their respective identities and which gave them an ongoing sense of peoplehood. Within each culture, one finds a commitment to group survival that stems from identification with others with whom there is a sharing of mutual concerns and values.

People with long and sophisticated cultures have a problem maintaining their traditions when they move to new places. This has been particularly difficult for Koreans and Jews in the United States faced with the challenges of an open and diverse society. There are special concerns for the children of Korean and Jewish immigrants who have had the problem of living in two cultures: the American environment where they are considered too foreign, and in the homes of their parents where they are seen as too American. The situation was very different for the immigrants who had a clearly defined way of life grounded in a relatively homogeneous culture, and who were largely concerned with economic survival and adjusting to a new environment. Most immigrants participated in holidays and festivals and continued more or less regular patterns of group involvement. This often led to a significant gap between the immigrant generation and their children, as well as between the children and their grandchildren. The traditions of both groups lost their hold on individuals as children were taught in the public schools and the media to look upon the culture of their parents as inferior by the standards of the larger society.

This has been a special problem for the large number of Koreans and Jews who conduct their business and professional activities in the diverse, multi-ethnic world of the United States. They often live in mixed residential areas, and many participate in activities outside the sphere of the Korean and Jewish communities. They tend to see their American and ethnic identities as separate. In most activities they act as Americans, and only on particular occasions do they act as members of ethnic groups.

Although the family has been undergoing substantial changes it is still one of the most important structures for the transmission of identity and continuity. But the modern family is in difficulty with new household configurations, including the two-career family that sometimes deprives children of adequate care, along with a denigration of the role and status of mothers and homemakers. The Jewish family has been undergoing substantial changes, but it is still one of the most important structures for the transmission of the Jewish identity and continuity. Koreans too place a high value on family life, and both communities continue to stress religious and cultural education for their youth. To deal with their concern for the family, Jews have conducted studies to find out how to strengthen the commitment of young people to the Jewish tradition. The responses always emphasize three important areas: education, the family, and the community.

Most Americans identify themselves with some kind of subgroup whether it is Jewish, Korean, ethnic or regional; but the marks of identification are sometimes symbols without much social content or distinction. Ethnicity is seen by some as a counter-rational, uncontrollable social force that leads to hatred and violence and is the enemy of enlightenment and liberalism. However, this view confuses nationalism or tribalism with cultural heritage and is not particularly sensitive to the varieties of people in our society. In reality, ethnicity is emerging as a new social category, as distinct as that of social class. The liberal expectation that distinguishing group characteristics were to lose their meaning in modern society, and the radical expectancy that class would become the main line of division, eliminating tribalism, is being challenged by the ways in which *ethnic groups* in the United States are behaving as *interest groups* who seek to shape their own lives in terms of their unique values and traditions.

The experience of minorities in America has demonstrated that ethnic cultures can develop in an open and plural society and that interplay of various groups does not prevent the preservation of particular forms of communal expression. The social contract has been rewritten from a commitment to give up ethnicity in order to facilitate entry into American culture with acceptance and encouragement of ethnic feelings as an aspect of American identity. Members of all groups are free to express themselves in ways that indicate personal choice rather than imposition. They are also able to adopt the notion that a sense of peoplehood connects them to those of similar background everywhere, as they participate fully and freely in American life.

In order to meet personal and communal needs, Jews developed a complex organizational culture to assure their physical, communal and religious survival. A good deal of what is done under the auspices of Jewish organizations is philanthropic and, to a great extent, the institutions themselves have become the "culture" of many Jews. This activity is reinforced by the sense of mutual responsibility developed in the many lands where historically Jews faced persecution and oppression. Jews decided for themselves freely and voluntarily whether they wanted to associate with Jewish religious or communal endeavors. Voluntary associations proliferated for purposes of mutual aid and assistance, and large numbers of Jewish organizations were founded including hospitals, fraternal groups, centers, and social clubs. Various institutions and facilities also were created to care for the aged, orphans, and consumptives, as well as to provide other social welfare services.

Today in the United States, collective efforts are given expression through the vast array of organizations serving local, national, and overseas Jewish concerns. An institutional system has developed that serves a multiplicity of needs in such areas as support for Israel, Jewish education and community relations, along with more specialized requirements in the areas of health and social welfare. Jewish organizations persist and thrive as places where opportunities are provided for associational involvements that reinforce ties among community members. At the same time, it is well to remember that Jews belong to more non-Jewish organizations than they do to those primarily concerned with Jewish issues. This is part of a tradition that suggests an obligation to the needs of all people and underscores a commitment to the larger society.

In their earlier immigrant experience, Jews faced problems of adjustment to a sometimes hostile environment. Indeed, many of the small stores and businesses now owned by Korean Americans were formerly places of Jewish entrepreneurship. As the second and third generation Jewish Americans moved on to professional and corporate careers, Koreans and others have replaced them in the inner cities in a form of ethnic succession.

While they sought to adapt and acculturate to a new language and differing cultural styles, Koreans have also had to deal with xenophobia, racism, and problems of urban crime. This has been particularly acute in places like New York, Chicago, and Los Angeles as Koreans have located their businesses in the central cities occupied by others. The hundreds of Korean churches and communal groups represent an important base from which needed forms of institutional development can evolve.

To deal with such challenges, a number of Jewish "defense" organizations were created in the United States to protect the civil and religious rights of Jews everywhere. Through legal and legislative action, programs of public education and political action, Jews became very involved in the process of seeking a framework for Jewish life in the context of political and cultural freedom. This included the quest for full civil rights for all people, and the strengthening of primary Jewish institutions. All of the Jewish organizations are united today in the belief that equality for Jews is tied to the availability of equal opportunity for all, a concept that led to the creation of the civil rights movement and its coalition of Jewish and other minorities. This suggests an area of possible cooperation in which Jews might share with Korean Americans the benefit of years of experience in dealing with other groups.

Jews continue to believe that anti-Semitism is associated with other forms of intolerance that can pose a threat to democratic life and institutions, and they act to defend the freedoms they enjoy along with the rights and liberties of others. This strategy has been very successful for Jews who have, by and large, prospered and thrived in the United States. They are less and less excluded from political, economic, and cultural life, and despite their anxiety about anti-Semitism, they feel that America has provided them with more security and liberty than they had ever known before in their Diaspora experience. This perception has been given substance by the large numbers of Jews across the country who have gained important places in artistic, intellectual, and political worlds, as well as in business. Moreover, recent studies suggest there is an overall decline of domestic anti-Semitism, with fewer than one-third of non-Jews willing to accept some negative anti-Semitic stereotype.

At the same time, it would be foolhardy to ignore the ongoing manifestations of prejudice and discrimination still facing Jews and others in the United States. Social discrimination and exclusion from the executive suites of some major corporations and banks, together with the activities of hate groups such as vandalism of Jewish property, swastika paintings, and the desecration of cemeteries and institutions continue to arouse deep concern among Jews.

In the early days of the American Jewish experience, there was a tendency to move cautiously in politics, and to work through friendly non-Jews to satisfy group interests. But the expanding and direct involvement of Jews in American politics is now reflected in a political cohesiveness that has carried a growing number of Jews into local and state legislatures as well as into the halls of Congress. Undergirding this movement into political life is the growth of a civic awareness and confidence based on the objective reality that there is no government sanction or political base for ant-Semitism in America, along with a greater acceptance of Jews in all walks of life.

The growth of Jewish political expression stems from a recognition of distinct group needs that have a political dimension. Jews recall with anguish their passivity of many centuries that culminated in the slaughter of six million in the Holocaust. A desire to control their own destiny has influenced the vigorous political activity of Jews who are determined that never again will they be left defenseless victims of political terror. The mindset of Jews in the United States and around the world changed radically as Jews in Israel fought to defend themselves and Diaspora Jews rallied around them. Jewish political power was maximized on behalf of freedom for Russian Jews, and aid for Israel grew significantly through American and worldwide efforts to shape a Jewish future. Today, Jewish political activity contributes to Jewish identity by mobilizing individual and group support for Israel and other Jewish needs. This assertiveness is also manifested in programs of Jewish and public education aimed at strengthening awareness of what transpired during the Holocaust as a means of assuring that such monstrous behavior will never happen again. Jews are trying to remember those who perished and to impress on the minds of non-Jews the historical lesson that indifference can contribute to group hatred and genocide.

Israel is the most powerful indicator of Jewish identity today, and while most Jews have never been to Israel, they are deeply committed to its security and well-being. The question of Israel's survival is of profound concern to nearly all Jews, with most seeing Israel as a spiritual and cultural center as well as a place where Jews can decide their own destiny. Concern with Israel's future has become a major focus of the activities of individuals and organizations in the Jewish community. Their ideas converge on the unity of the Jewish people and the belief that Jews are linked not only to those who live in the same community, but to Jews everywhere.

Educators in Korea have expressed interest in the content and processes of Jewish education in the United States in terms of how these impact the maintenance of Jewish identity and commitment. The Korean Ministry of Education has been examining Jewish efforts in the American Diaspora to see how the survival of Jewish culture and tradition are addressed when a group lives as a minority in a larger, diverse society. Their hope is that a strong sense of historical and cultural identification can be maintained as Koreans emigrate in large numbers to the U.S. where they are also subject to the pushes and pulls of assimilatory processes.

It is clear today that the maintenance of ethnic continuity in America depends to a great extent on in-group processes that link friends and kin in formal and informal relationships. As neighborhoods change and mobility increases, people are finding new ways to maintain historic associations and group distinctiveness. Social relationships are important in identity formation so that ethnic identity can be measured through association with others within a group. Undergirding these changes, however, is a strong commitment to ethnic cultural expression, manifested by interest in the periodicals, books, music, language, and history of the group. There is also general acceptance of the view that children should have some cultural education that will help to shape their values and behavior as well as to influence the transmission of their heritage to future generations. For Jews, all of this is reinforced by the networks of associations between the Israeli and American Jewish communities in social, economic, religious, and cultural areas. This may also be the case for Koreans living in the Diaspora who may continue to be influenced by Korean culture and education.

The liberty both groups enjoy in the United States means they have a major stake in its future and feel a profound obligation to contribute to its well-being. It is here they have found political equality, religious liberty, and the opportunity to perpetuate their culture. This involves having the right to deepen an appreciation of their ancient traditions and homeland and to instill among their children those practices and beliefs that enhance the heritage of their respective communities. It also involves a sense of responsibility for the welfare of democratic society as a whole, including the strengthening of its institutions and a commitment to social justice and human rights.

Jews have had an important role to play in this position through their cosmopolitan understanding of blended cultures that has been an important characteristic of the Jewish leavening in the Western intellectual tradition. And Koreans are now enriching the pluralist character of America through their special qualities of language loyalty, religious enthusiasm, and creative effort. The dynamic environment of American pluralism creates a framework for cooperation and friendship in which the experiences of Jews and Koreans can be utilized for mutual benefit. A Korean-Jewish coalition, in the context of relationships with others, can advance the interests of both groups. This can be a major step forward in the process of enhancing cultural awareness and appreciation, as well as a further commitment to new areas of collaboration between our groups.

REFERENCES

Bock, Geoffrey E. "Does Jewish schooling matter?" *Jewish Education and Jewish Identity Colloquium Papers.* New York: American Jewish Committee, January, 1977.

Dashefsky, David and Howard Shapiro. *Ethnic Identification Among American Jews*. Lexington, MA: Lexington Books, Heath, 1974.

Erikson, Erik H. "The problem of ego identity," *Identity and Anxiety*. M.R. Stein, A.J. Vidich and D.M. White, eds. Glencoe, IL: Free Press, 1960.

Goldstein, Sidney and Calvin Goldscheider. *Jewish Americans: Three Generations in a Jewish Community*. Englewood Cliffs, NJ: Prentice-Hall, 1968.

Kelman, Herbert C. *The Place of Jewish Identity in the Development of Personal Identity. A Report*. Cambridge, MA: Harvard University, 1980.

Ritterband, Paul and Steven M. Cohen. *The Jewish Population of Greater New York. A Profile*. New York: Federation of Jewish Philanthropies of New York, 1984.

Rosenfield, Geraldine. "The polls: Attitudes toward American Jews," *Public Opinion Quarterly,* 46 (1982).

Sandberg, Neil C. *Jewish Life in Los Angeles*. Lanham, MD: University Press of America, 1986.

———*Ethnic Identity and Assimilation: The Polish-American Community*. New York: Praeger Publishers, 1974.

Silberman, Charles E. *A Certain People*. New York: Summit Books, 1985.

Waxman, Chaim. "The fourth generation grown up: The contemporary American Jewish Community," *Annals of the American Academy of Political and Social Science* 454 (March, 1981).

Weisberg, Harold. "Ideologies of American Jews," *The American Jew*, ed. by Oscar I. Janowsky. Philadelphia: Jewish Publication Society of America, 1964.

Woocher, Jonathan S. "The 'Civil Judaism' of Communal Leaders," *American Jewish Yearbook* (1981).

REFLECTIONS ON THE KOREAN AMERICAN IDENTITY

David Hyun
Architect of Little Tokyo Village Plaza,
Los Angeles

The devastating loss of life, livelihood and property which resulted from the riots of April 1992 has motivated the Los Angeles Korean American community to seek new directions and affect the changes necessary to reestablish its identity. Before change can be affected, however, there first must be an understanding and reaffirmation of the cultural heritage unique to the Korean people. For to understand where one is going, one must first know where one has been.

Modern Korean American identity is a carefully blended amalgamation of three distinct and independent histories: the Korean, the American and the Korean American. For better or worse, contemporary Koreans inherit, and are the custodians of, a 4,000-year-old Korean culture. This inheritance is far more than a series of ancient temples and palaces; it is a life-force of enormous vitality. Korean culture enabled Koreans to bear the pain and destruction of forty years of Japanese colonial exploitation that began in 1905, to survive the Korean War, and to overcome the bitter poverty which followed those events. The force and energy of Korean culture enabled its people to recover and to transform Korea from an agricultural nation into a world-class industrial power in the span of one generation. This stupendous achievement required the Korean people to restore education from ground zero and to develop the technology, organization and society that were needed by modern industry. But the very forces which caused the need for such improvements also left their own footprints on Korea and the Korean people.

Without a doubt, today's Koreans have also inherited the American culture—a culture with a global significance rooted in the proposition that all men are created equal with regard to life, liberty, and the pursuit of happiness. Korean American acculturation actually began in 1896 when Dr. Philip Jaisohn returned to Korea from America and founded the Independence Club—the club which gave Koreans their first vision of America. The American inheritance spread quickly throughout Korea, especially after President Woodrow Wilson announced the "Self-determination of Nations," the doctrine which ultimately inspired the Korean Declaration of Independence and the March First Demonstrations of 1919. Koreans thus inherit American traditions through adoption and adaptation by their parents as much as by United States citizenship.

Koreans are also inheritors of their own Korean American history. They inherit the vision of the first Korean visitors to America in the 1880s and the sacrifice of the first wave of immigrants who, starting in 1903, suffered unbelievable exploitation in the sugar cane fields of Hawaii. Koreans earned among the lowest wages, suffered restricted liberties and were forced to live in segregated camps. I remember those days very well. As a ten-year-old plantation laborer, I was lucky, because I could earn thirty cents a day while my friends earned only twenty-five. Something had to be done to stop the atrocities in Korea by the Japanese occupiers and it was up to the Korean people to do it. As quickly as they could afford, these first-wave immigrants donated one dollar, for many the equivalent of four days labor, to the Korean Provisional government in Shanghai in support of the Korean Independence movement.

The children of the first wave were an invisible population of two thousand who had neither political representation in Hawaii nor support from any Korean government at home. Yet these descendants, and I am one myself, achieved in spite of prejudice. It wasn't easy. Consider that when two-time Olympic diving champion Sammy Lee was a boy, he was refused entry into a public swimming pool. Undaunted, Sammy fought his way in. He won with the help of one other Korean: his father. When former California State Senator Alfred H. Song became the first Asian elected to the legislature, he had only two Korean votes, his own and his wife's! When Colonel Young Oak Kim was assigned to the famous 100/442 Japanese American regiment during World War II, he was given permission to reassign because he was a Korean. Instead, Col. Kim responded, "Sir, I prefer to stay. We are all Americans." Indeed, Young Oak Kim remains a leader in the Japanese American community to this day. As for myself, I became a developer of the Japanese Village Plaza, a shopping center in the Little Tokyo section of Los Angeles, the heartland of the Japanese American community. I won this opportunity because of my respect for my equal rights as an American.

The Korean people's three histories, alone or interwoven, create an energizing life-force, but the simple *identification* of the three histories is not enough; we must press further and ask, What do the three histories teach? What lessons can be learned that will enable us, the Korean people, to use our heritage to guide our new directions? Perhaps the most important lesson is that we Korean Americans are not alone. Our ancestors are with us each day and we are further accompanied by the diverse peoples which compose our three histories. In finding new directions for the Korean American community, however, a few cautions should be taken.

The rhetoric of racial prejudice should not be allowed to cloud the issues. It is not only White people who are prejudiced. We are all prejudiced, we all prefer our own. The prejudice of racism can be overcome, not by complaint and confrontation but, much better, by friendship and cooperation. Do not be led into believing that prejudice against Asian Americans is rising in the United States today. This is nonsense. Prejudice was much worse in the past. Even as recently as 1947, I could not rent a hotel room in Monterey, California. My family of four slept in a $3.50 roadside motel room. In 1947, Asians were not hired in Los Angeles architectural offices. Like Sammy Lee, the first Korean American Olympic diving champion, I fought my way in and pioneered the employment of Asians as architects. Compared to 1947, opportunities for Asian Americans are expanding by leaps and bounds.

The media reporting of the Soon Ja Du incident poisoned relations between African Americans and Korean Americans. The media summary repeated that Latasha Harlins, a Black teenager of South Central Los Angeles, was shot in the back of her head by Soon Ja Du, a Korean woman merchant, in a dispute over a bottle of soda pop. This summary is racist, misleading and provocative. A less provocative and more accurate statement is: "Soon Ja Du, a merchant in South Central Los Angeles who was felled to the floor four times by blows from Latasha Harlins, shot and accidentally killed her assailant, a suspected shoplifter."

Do not believe that prejudice by the White community is reserved only for non-White minorities. Prejudice by White residents against White immigrants is legendary. In 1856, Abraham Lincoln in talking about the "Know Nothing" political party said, "As a nation, we began by declaring 'All men are created equal.' When the Know Nothings get control, it will read 'All men are created equal except Negroes, foreigners, and Catholics.'"

After the attack on Pearl Harbor on December 7, 1941, the United States government issued the now infamous Executive Order 9066. This Order required that all Japanese American men, women and children in the United States, its territories and possessions, be rounded up and locked behind barbed wire fences. The United States government reasoned that because these people were of Japanese ancestry, their loyalty to the United States in the face of war with Japan was questionable. I share the Japanese American experience of World War II, but I also know that discrimination did not begin with Pearl Harbor. Before, during and for several years after World War II, Asian college graduates could not get work in factories or in the professions. They did gardening and the work of laborers. Yet, in spite of the racial prejudice against them, Japanese American men fought for and won the right to defend America in the war against Japan. They volunteered from behind barbed wire fences to form the 100/442 Combat Regiment. This regiment became the most decorated combat unit in American military history. The terrible injustice of Executive Order 9066 was transformed into an opportunity to reverse the prejudice against Japanese Americans and to increase civil liberties for all Asian Americans. The catastrophic devastation of the riots of 1992 can likewise be transformed into an opportunity to reverse the prejudice against Korean Americans and thereby further increase civil liberties for one and all.

In the United States, the Japanese American National Museum is a showcase and source of pride for the Japanese American community, a central resource for information, referrals, history, business and culture. The 800,000 Korean Americans in the United States need a national focus as well; and the creation of a Korean American National Museum, similar to the Japanese American National Museum, would be an excellent beginning.

We Korean Americans face the future with our identity formed and fortified by our three great histories. We do not walk alone. We are accompanied by the spirits of the great peoples of our past. They have given us a historic responsibility to find new directions for our Korean American community. Let us accept this responsibility. Let us persevere. Let us endure until we succeed as did those pioneers who came before us. We truly are what we are: we are Americans.

The Korea Central Daily

May 1st, 1992 11 AM at Vermont Ave. in Koreatown

II

TRANSFORMING THE URBAN LANDSCAPE
Los Angeles and Korean Americans
on the Eve of the Riots

April 30th, 1992   162 N. Vermont Ave.

Korea Times, L.A.

RIOT, REBELLION OR CIVIL UNREST?
THE KOREAN AMERICAN AND AFRICAN AMERICAN BUSINESS COMMUNITIES IN LOS ANGELES*

Nadine Koch
Professor of Political Science
California State University, Los Angeles

H. Eric Schockman
Professor of Political Science
University of Southern California

Ethnic tensions around the world seem to be spinning off from the centrificial forces of the post-Cold War epoch. Intra-ethnic conflicts within the United States seem to be not only intensifying, but to be dominating the discussion of our national urban agenda.

Urban America today can no longer be characterized as the Kerner Commission's report does, emphasizing that we are developing into two ethnic societies—one Black and one White—separate and unequal. Immigration has returned the city to an older, multiethnic demography. Latinos are the fastest growing ethnic group in big cities, and in some cities, especially on the West Coast, the Asian Pacific population has been growing rapidly. At the same time, in a few central cities such as Los Angeles, the African American proportion of the population has been declining between 1980 and 1990.

---

* This paper and our research is dedicated to the memory of Professor Byran O. Jackson who sacrificed so much of himself to his students, colleagues and community. Adapting T.S. Eliot, we assert: "A philosophy of life which involves no sacrifice turns out in the end to be merely an excuse for a hollow being, the sort of person one should never become."

California and its urban enclaves, for example, are one of the most ethnically diverse regions in the world. "With a total population of slightly less than 30 million people, it is rapidly approaching a non-White majority. By the year 2000, approximately 29 percent of all Californians will be of Hispanic origin while 13 percent will be Asian, and 7 percent will be of African American descent. Unlike the immigration occurring during the turn of this century, which was primarily European, 40 percent of new immigrants are coming from Asian countries...another 40 percent are coming from countries in Northern and Central America and the Caribbean" (Jackson and Preston, 1991:3).

California (and Los Angeles) was supposed to be on the way to becoming the world's first successful poly-racial society. But a new Darwinian dynamic of social tension (or perhaps a rehashed one) has witnessed different minority ethnic groups colliding with one another in economic and political competition. *Time* magazine's feature article (April 9, 1990) predicted that "the browning of America will alter everything in society, from politics and education to industry, values and culture."

One "sub-conflict" that has been receiving quite a lot of attention, but little real analysis, is the struggle between the Korean American and African American communities. From boycotts of Korean American grocers in New York City to the Soon Ja Du/Latasha Harlins case, Korean American merchants have been clashing with African American customers in impoverished neighborhoods, sometimes violently.[1] Some

---

[1] See for example, some of contemporary press stories covering Korean-Black relations, like: John H. Lee, "Prejudice Message Hits Home," *Los Angeles Times*, March 29, 1990; John H. Lee and John J. Goldman, "Boycott Puts Korean Stores at Center of New York Race Strife," *Los Angeles Times*, May 20, 1990; Miraya Navarro, "Ties of Need and Mistrust," *New York Times*, May 17, 1990; John Dillin, "Immigrant Influx Is Reshaping U.S.," *The Christian Science Monitor*, January 2, 1990; Stewart Kwoh, "Reject Scapegoating to Stop the Bashing," *Los Angeles Times*, February 21, 1992; Stephanie Chavez, "Mediators Work To Defuse Escalating Racial Tensions," *Los Angeles Times*, April 19, 1992.

argue that Black anti-Koreanism has an economic and ideological base; cultural and social differences add fuel to the already explosive situation. Others argue that a "clash of ideologies" is one of the major root causes of Korean-Black conflicts (see Cheng, 1990).

Tensions between Korean Americans and African Americans have been evident throughout Los Angeles County for roughly a decade. As early as April 1, 1983, the Los Angeles County Commission on Human Rights (LACCHR) conducted hearings on intergroup relations in the South Central Los Angeles area which uncovered mounting tensions between Korean American merchants and local residents. By July 1986, with the death of four Korean grocers and growing violence between Korean shop owners and Black clients, Los Angeles City Councilman Michael K. Woo (not Korean, but a Chinese American) and Congressman Julian Dixon called together leaders from the Black and Asian communities to build an on-going dialogue and interchange. Under the rubric of the LACCHR, a "Black-Korean Alliance" (BKA) was established in 1986, incorporated as a non-profit organization in 1987, and died a quiet death in the aftermath of the 1992 unrest. During its tenure, BKA served as a novel, neutral inter-ethnic testing ground for the "elite" membership of each respective community to work on dispute resolution, cultural and religious exchanges and, most importantly, joint ventures for promoting economic development. Yet, economic woes abound. In bemoaning promoting its extinction, Ms. Jai Lee Wong, a staff consultant who works for the LACCHR, accused the County of Los Angeles of not providing resources and leadership to the BKA to sustain its valuable community role (Interview, 1992). Indeed, the entire budget of the LACCHR, which is approximately $1.6 million, supports a staff of about 50-60 human relations managers spread thinly over the entire county (Note: the county itself is larger than 42 states of the 50 United States). All told, to "heal" human relations, the County of Los Angeles invests approximately 1/8 of 1 percent of the total county budget. The City of Los Angeles is no better, budgetarily committed to fund only one executive director and one secretarial position to administer the City's entire Human Relations Commission.

The changing ethnic patterns are directly associated with the changing demographic and socio-economic conditions in the region. The Los Angeles County Asian Pacific population increased 92 percent from 1970 to 1980 and has continued to grow into the 1990s. Los Angeles County is the port of entry for the largest number of Korean immigrants and the home of the largest Korean community outside of Korea. U.S. census figures tell us that there are 143,672 Koreans living in the county, while Eui-Young Yu estimates there are approximately 81,000 Koreans living within the boundaries of the City of Los Angeles (Yu, 1990:2).

In the last 20 years, since the urban riots of the '60s, the socio-economic conditions within inner city African American communities have gone from bad to worse. According to the 1990 Census, African Americans continue to have in Los Angeles County the lowest per capita income of all ethnic groups ($12,018), while Asian/Pacific Islanders have one of the highest ($20,650). There exists the erroneous perception that Asians are a monolithic population group with a uniformly high standard of living. This, however, is not the case: median incomes for the various sub-groups within the Asian population vary widely, with Filipinos at the highest end, on down to Vietnamese, who have the lowest overall income of any minority group in Los Angeles County.

South Central Los Angeles has a population base of 1,090,185 persons and constitutes 11 percent of the population of Los Angeles County. The most recent data of the ethnic breakdown of South Central compared to the overall county ethnic breakdown looks like this:

	SOUTH CENTRAL	*LOS ANGELES COUNTY*
African American	49.2%	10.5%
Latino	44.8%	37.8%
Anglo	3.6%	40.8%
Asian or Pacific Islander	1.8%	10.2%

Perhaps what is critical in analyzing these data is the high ratio of Latino residents (not necessarily citizens and/or voters) and the extremely low ratio of Asian or Pacific Islander population that reside in the South Central area.

In a 1988 study conducted by the Claritas Corporation and reported by Stuart Silverstein and Nancy Rivera Brooks in the *Los Angeles Times* (1991), the revealing socio-economic statistics paint the backdrop to this situation:

Number of Stores: In South Central the number was 2,411. Based on the population in the 1990 Census, that would be one store for every 415 residents. Countywide, the ratio is one store for every 203 residents.

Number of Service Businesses: In South Central, the number was 3,454 or one for every 290 residents. Countywide, the ratio is one service business for every 103 residents.

Median Household Income: For South Central, the 1990 figure was $20,820. That is 33% less than the countywide median of $30,525.

Access to Credit: Median bank credit card limit for a South Central resident was $4,881, versus $7,064 countywide.

Credit Problems: For South Central households, 53.7% of the households have at least one "derogatory indicator" in their credit files, versus 33.5% for households countywide.

In the depressed economy of South Central Los Angeles, Korean American merchants have acquired a multitude of small businesses, commonly referred to as "mom and pop" stores— from grocery markets and liquor stores to auto repair shops and gas stations. Desirability of concentration in this area is great: (1) there is little competition from the large chain stores which proportionally abandoned this area after the Watts Riot; (2) low rents and overhead; (3) access to the *kye*[2] system for

---

[2] Like the Chinese and Japanese, Koreans rely on the rotating credit association, known as the *kye* in Korean, to finance business venture capital. These are essentially a group of families or friends who regularly pool their investment money and act as an informal banking system. Thus by circumventing the traditional American credit and banking system, many Korean merchants have found valuable capital resources in areas traditionally "redlined" by major financial institutions. This in itself has

capitalization of their enterprises; (4) relative ease in skirting state labor enforcement laws by the high utilization of unpaid family labor and labor intensive, low-wage immigrant workers. Furthermore, Korean merchants have traditionally been "absentee owners," not in a laboring sense, but in that they usually do not live in the community where they operate their businesses, and generally are not involved in civic activities. Only a small proportion of Koreans actually live in South Central, yet there is a high proportion of home ownership among Koreans, geographically scattered around Southern California. Home ownership among Koreans overall has increased from 41.8 percent in 1978 to 49.8 percent in 1989. The median price of homes owned by Koreans is approximately $280,000, which is higher than the median price of homes in Los Angeles County. Also, while Koreatown is the epicenter for Koreans of citizen status, it is interesting to note that home ownership is relatively low (16%) among Koreans in Koreatown, meaning it attracts mostly elderly, single persons and new immigrants (Yu, 1990).

Given the media hype and misperceptions of the general public, one would be led to believe that patrons of Korean businesses are mostly Black. Eui-Young Yu's community profile study gives us a very different analysis of an ethnically diverse client base (Yu, 1990). In actuality Anglos constitute a majority of the customers for 48 percent of the Korean business establishments in his study. Koreans follow next at 22 percent of the clientele. Latinos and Blacks follow lastly at 17 percent and 10 percent of the business clientele respectively. Finally, one additional research note that Yu's data raise is the perplexing reality that Latinos and Blacks may as an aggregate support Korean businesses because they may be less discriminatory than White-owned business establishments,

caused further resentment between the African American and Korean American communities, in that Blacks often suspect Korean merchants have accumulated money in devious ways or through some hidden government program aimed at assisting newly arrived immigrants (Light and Bonacich, 1988; Cheng and Espiritu, 1989).

placing the magnitude of rupture at a much diminished scale. According to Yu:

> Korean businesses serving Hispanics and Blacks are the best income-wise. Sixty-three percent of the Korean establishments doing business mainly with Hispanics make more than $50,000 a year. The corresponding figures are 50 percent with Blacks, 42 percent with other Koreans, and 37 percent with Whites. Despite the recent reported conflicts between Korean merchants and Black customers, it appears that Blacks and Hispanics are actually less discrimatory against Korean shop owners than Whites. Competition with White-owned business establishments may be severe when customers are mainly White (Yu, 1990:10).

All these substratum developments seem to have come to an apex during the civil unrest in Los Angeles during April-May of 1992. It has been estimated that around 2500 Korean-owned businesses in Los Angeles were looted and/or destroyed, costing nearly $400 million dollars in damage, and the majority of the destruction was in the predominantly Black area of South Central Los Angeles (ABC News, 1992). But this was more politically complex than just Watts II, circa 1992. Arrest data from the Los Angeles Police Department suggest that the lawbreakers were poly-ethnic; and as the mobs moved up the "Vermont Street Corridor" spreading into Koreatown, Hollywood and beyond, shops owned by Korean Americans seemed to be the main target of reprisals.

While indeed Latino and Black businesses were destroyed, the African American community's stake in Black capitalism was handicapped back in the late 1970s as major industrial employers, such as General Motors, Goodyear, and Firestone, began to close down their aging factories, thereby laying the foundation for future civil unrest. By 1991 for example, the jobless rate in Compton was 18.4 percent compared to the overall jobless rate in Los Angeles County which was 9.3 percent. Developments during the later stages of the Tom Bradley regime sought to produce a "neo-Renaissance of Black Capitalism" with lack luster, mixed results. Baldwin Hills-Crenshaw Plaza failed to win the loyalty of affluent African Americans. Further, due in part to the recession of the late

1980s-early 1990s, approximately 60 percent of the 120 plaza stores were occupied. A *Los Angeles Times* marketing survey ranked the Plaza 46th out of 59 in retail sales volume.

The results? To many people the trial and verdict of Rodney King was the opening of the Pandora's box—once again Black justice was denied; Black capitalism truncated; social and political delivery services denied. Politically, the unwritten civic culture of those in the biracial liberal coalition under a Black mayor translated to the dicta: "Don't Embarrass the Mayor." Scholars have long chronicled this phenomenon in the dilemmas facing Black mayors in many metropolitan areas (Browning, Marshall, Tabb, 1990; Preston, Henderson, Puryear, 1987; Eisinger, 1976). The Bradley regime seems to have been the victim of these warnings.

This analysis of course raises many conceptual and pragmatic questions about the future of governing inter-racial coalitions in Los Angeles, as the twilight of the biracial liberal Bradley coalition flickers in its final hours. In our conclusionary section we will return to this important point about the future of a governing multi-ethnic coalition and what our data supports. Suffice to say here that in their 1984 book *Protest Is Not Enough*, Browning, Marshall and Tabb suggest that biracial coalitions are powerful tools for achieving minority incorporation in certain cities (Browning, Marshall, Tabb, 1984). Yet, we believe that it is Raphael J. Sonensheim's analysis that brings us one step closer to understanding what structural impediments can be overcome—like sharing a common ideological vision through an articulated leader—to transform a biracial or multiracial coalition into a true "governing rainbow coalition" (Sonensheim, 1990). Thus, as we move through this study and examine the points of contention and conflict between the Korean and Black communities, we wish to postulate about the future of racial politics and electoral coalitions providing a linkage for minority communities in Los Angeles.

THE SCOPE OF THIS STUDY

The foundational precursors discussed above set in a large measure the intellectual parameters for this study. Conceptually we set out to research the "political ethos" and the politics of ethnic coalitions of African Americans and Korean Americans in the prelude and aftermath periods of the L.A. riot\rebellion\civil unrest of 1992. This task was of no easy measure, especially for two social scientists who directly experienced these events and whose research on the matter must ensure objectivity and protect against any bias overlays.

Methodologically, we use two empirical tools designed to quantitatively measure the inter-racial political/social relations between these two communities. On an "elite-stratum axis" we designed an extensive closed and open-ended mailing questionnaire administered to a randomly sampled universe of business elites from both the Korean American and African American communities. During the course of events of 1992, it also became evident to the authors that the "dysfunctional leadership" or "non-leadership" in both communities had lost to some extent the political followership of many in each respective community. Thus, to study inter-racial conflict and cooperation on the political elite level may be only a slice of reality. To develop a "mass-stratum axis" we did extensive analysis of the official incidents motivated by hatred/prejudice (a.k.a. hate crimes) in the City of Los Angeles from 1990 to 1992, specifically between Koreans and Blacks. Our objective was to question whether there was "systemic hatred" between the African American and Korean American communities in Los Angeles and to what degree can political conflict and cooperation be expected in the future governing of Los Angeles.

REVIEW OF THE LITERATURE

Existing theories on inter-ethnic relations have been principally oriented to explaining the relationship between the

White majority and African American minority, and tend to be preoccupied with the elite power stratum. Inter-ethnic conflicts on the political elite level are well presented in the literature (Coser, 1956; Dahrendorf, 1959; Schattschneider, 1960). Peter K. Eisinger's topology of conflictual patterns of inter-racial politics in his study of the city of Milwaukee is emblematic of this thrust.

Korean Americans are often compared with the Jewish community as "model minorities" in their economic (and ultimately political) assimilation patterns. However, as George M. Frederickson (1981) and Hubert M. Blalock (1967) point out, class and race differences must be examined more deeply. When Black interests came into conflict with those of White liberals, as Sonensheim (1990) suggests is the case in New York City, liberal ideology is not enough to keep the governing coalition on course and non-conflictual. In the case of New York, conflict has resulted in tensions between the ultra-religious segment of the Jewish community, and a mass base of the Black population. These scholars would put the Black-Jewish conflict as a "vertical conflict," involving elements of domination and subordination characteristic of the historical developments between Blacks and Whites (Bonacich, 1987; Henry and Nunoz, 1991). While the structural dominating relationship may have switched from the Jewish landlord and store owner, the class and economic interests of Jews along with their cultural idiosyncrasies put them in direct opposition with the masses of Black people. At the same time, as Chang (1990) has pointed out, Jews have experienced a long history of discrimination in the United States and were linked to Blacks (and other minorities) by their early strong support for civil rights. Thus, at times, they may be susceptible to the more grandiose liberal ideological appeals, subordinating their own class interests for a more macro-minority agenda.

Chang goes on to develop what he terms is a more appropriate "horizontal relationship model," examining the tensions and conflicts between "intra-Third World communities," such as the Korean-Black relationship. We agree strongly with his analysis that, viewed from a horizontal perspective, Korean Americans have a greater affinity towards Blacks than do Jews. Chang asserts that Korean immigrants are not White, and have not been part of the historic White domination of Black communities. Korean businesses are more marginal than Jews; they have less political power than Blacks at this particular juncture of time. Korean immigrants tend to be fundamentalist Christians and, as in the Black community, Korean immigrant churches play a powerful role in maintaining a strong ethnic identity and in integrating and sustaining a community.[3] Parenthetically, two important pieces of scholarship provide a balanced assessment of Korean American churches. Hyung-chan Kim's "History and Role of the Church in the Korean American Community" (in his edited work, *The Korean Diaspora*, 1977) emphasizes the political significance of Korean churches in the Korean national independence movement prior to 1945. Steve Shim (1977) deals with the socio-economic development of Korean immigrant churches in Southern California between 1945 and the 1970s.

The problems of analysis along this horizontal perspective, however, are also apparent. Koreans (most of whom arrived post-1965) have no first-hand experience of the struggle for civil rights; there are obvious cultural differences; and furthermore political ideologies tend to be antithetical in comparison with one another.[4]

---

[3] Our polling data later discussed in this paper confirm a high proportion of both communities are church members--75 percent in the Korean American community; 72 percent in the African American community. Although we observed a noticeable difference when further asked whether churches should be involved in community politics and race relations. Only 58 percent of the Korean sample agree/strongly agree with this statement compared with 86 percent of the Black sample. This is perhaps an indication of the role that black churches have played in fighting for civil rights and continue to play in fighting for social justice issues.

[4] For example, our polling data reveal that for Koreans, 44 percent call themselves Republicans; 20 percent call themselves Democrats; 34 percent "don't belong to any political party." The percentages respectively for Blacks were 10, 72, 14.

Other scholars have been researching in the fields of sociological and psychological inquiry, developing structural theories emphasizing the social, political and economic structures of host societies and the role of minority immigrants in small business as "middleman minorities," and the underlying sociological reasons for the tensions between Korean merchants and the Black community. Current structural theses can be divided into five areas: (1) the status gap thesis, (2) the traditional society thesis, (3) Bonacich's Marxist split labor market thesis, (4) Min's status consistency theory and mobility theory of entrepreneurship, and (5) the immigrant hypothesis.

(1) The Status Gap Thesis (Rinder, 1959; Loewen, 1971; Blalock, 1967; Shibutani and Kwan 1965; Wong, 1977) argues that historically, minorities involved in trade have existed to fill the gap between the elite elements of society and the lower classes. Middleman minorities are brought or moved into a society to bridge the status and economic gap. We believe the status gap between Blacks and Whites in the United States explains the concentration of Iraqi, Jewish or Vietnamese small businesses in Black ghettos.

(2) The Traditional Society Thesis (Becker, 1956; Foster, 1974; Hamilton, 1978; Coser, 1972) asserts that ethnic minorities specialize in trade and commerce in "traditional societies" because such activities were considered stigmatizing and debasing to the general populace, thus best left to "outsiders," whose ethnicity became their advantage for success, as well as their point of political vulnerability. Coser in particular develops the notion that these middleman minorities are politically dependent on the elites (as the 18th century Jews in Spain were), and an example of "servants of power." Hamilton argues that "pariah capitalism" is an attempt to promote a "stranger" group's success rather than trade falling into the hands of another powerful indigenous group.

(3) The Split Labor Market Thesis (Bonacich, 1979, 1980; Bonacich, Light and Wong 1977; Light, 1972) focuses specifically on Korean small business, and Bonacich posits that "Korean small business is not business per se, but a form of

utilization of cheap immigrant labor by American capitalism"(1979:49). Large corporations use Korean small businesses to fill in the marketing gaps in the economy, especially in blighted ghetto areas. Bonacich, et al., view immigrant entrepreneurs as being both *oppressed* by large corporations whose products they sell, and *oppressive*, especially against the underclasses which their businesses usually serve. Bonacich applies the term "middleman minorities" to those immigrant entrepreneurs who are in the middle of the race/ethnic caste: they do not enjoy full privileges or recognition of the elite, but they do have more resources and are on higher social and economic strata than other minorities. According to Bonacich, "middleman minorities" can be utilized as scapegoats to the underclasses, by the elite. At the same time, these immigrant entrepreneurs are presented to other minorities as being "model minorities," who show that the American Dream is valid for all and everyone can succeed if they work hard enough" (Bonacich, 1987:462).

(4) Min's Status Consistency Theory and Mobility Theory of Entrepreneurship (Min, 1984a, 1984b) turns his focus from the structural forces that influence Koreans to start small businesses to the situational/immediate reasons Koreans go into business. He looks at middleman minority theories that examine the situational framework of why Korean immigrants go into small business. He looks at the "sojourning theory," developed by Bonacich, which argues that certain ethnic groups are merely sojourners rather than settlers in this country. They plan to go back to their home country, and are simply interested in making as much money as possible in as little time as possible. However, Min criticized the theory for not taking into account middleman minorities who have permanently settled here, such as Jews. Min also finds it inadequate on the grounds that most recent Korean immigrants do come to the United States to settle permanently. Min also looks at the "discrimination theory," which claims that middleman minorities seek a niche to avoid host discrimination and direct competition in the labor market with native born laborers and professionals, and find that niche

in small business. The "disadvantage theory" says that all the disadvantages of the labor market (discrimination, poverty, unemployment, etc.) make self-employment attractive to immigrants.

There are also two theories of stratification which Min pays close attention to: status consistency theory and mobility theory of entrepreneurship. The first refers to the inconsistency of Koreans' social and occupational status. Often, Korean immigrants are highly educated and held white-collar or professional occupations before immigrating. However, due to problems of adjusting to the American labor market, they often end up in low-wage, low-status jobs that do not match their educational level. The latter theory asserts that certain individuals become entrepreneurs in order to gain upward mobility, especially when it appears that other avenues of social advancement are closed to them. Thus, Min comes up with four hypotheses as to why Koreans decide to go into small business (Min, 1984a:337):

1) The situation of Koreans as sojourners is not one of the major factors which lead them to enter small business;

2) Host discrimination in the labor market is not one of the major factors which lead Korean immigrants to enter small business;

3) Disadvantages in the American job market is one of the major reasons why Korean immigrants turn to small business;

4) Korean immigrants' inability to find desirable white-collar occupations in this country leads them to enter business to achieve economic and social mobility.

To test these hypotheses, Min uses the same data from surveys from his earlier research. He then analyzes the respondents' answers to questions concerning their desire (or lack of) to settle in the U.S. permanently, their experiences with employment discrimination, their reasons for starting a small business, and their status-inconsistency. In the area of sojourning, Min finds that 84 percent of the interviewees desire to stay in the U.S. permanently, and only 4 percent want to go back to Korea. Only 3.1 percent said the opportunity to quickly gain enough money and return to Korea was *part* of the reason they started in small business, but no one said that was the main reason. These findings appear to support Min's first hypothesis.

In the area of discrimination, approximately 57 percent of the respondents believed they had experienced some discrimination in the job market. Of those, over 80 percent stated that they would have started their own business whether they were discriminated against or not. This finding does not substantiate Min's second hypothesis, thus he rejects the hypothesis. As for disadvantages in the job market leading to immigrant entrepreneurship, Min finds that over 90 percent of the respondents found their disadvantages in the labor market, particularly in white-collar professions, to be a leading motive for turning to small businesses, which does substantiate his third hypothesis. Finally, Min turns to status inconsistency and mobility. In his findings, 54.5 percent of college-educated Korean immigrants were working at blue-collar jobs prior to starting their own business. Of those who held white-collar jobs prior to immigrating, almost 72 percent were in blue-collar jobs before becoming self-employed. Additionally, 67 percent responded that they started a business for economic reasons, and 54 percent said that their inability to find a white-collar position was a reason for establishing a small business, all of which support Min's fourth hypothesis. Min concludes that the most dominant and immediate reasons Koreans start their own businesses are to avoid the disadvantages of the labor market, and to become economically mobile.

(5) The Immigrant Hypothesis (Cheng and Espiritu, 1989) starts from the assumption that Koreans own a significant portion of small businesses, such as gas stations, small markets, and liquor stores, in large urban areas, particularly New York, Chicago, and Los Angeles. These businesses tend to be concentrated in poor Black and Latino neighborhoods. While there have been well-publicized clashes between Korean merchants and Blacks, both as customers and merchants, there hasn't been the same overt hostility between Koreans and Latinos, despite occasional labor disputes.

Cheng and Espiritu examine some of the socio-psychological explanations that have been previously given for the conflict between Koreans and Blacks. The first theory they look at is the "prejudice theory." The prejudice theory focuses on how the two ethnic groups feel about the other, culturally. They point out that some cultural characteristics Koreans have, such as lack of eye contact with strangers, lead to "misunderstanding and disapproval by Blacks" (1989:525) and that Black hostility towards Koreans may be long-standing, going as far back as the Korean War. On the other hand, it is also posited that Korean society is homogeneous and does not equip Korean immigrants to live in a multi-racial, multi-ethnic society. If so, perhaps Koreans learned racial prejudice and negative stereotyping against Blacks during the Korean War, along with other characteristics of American mass culture. Those stereotypes are then reinforced with every unpleasant experience a Korean may have with a Black person. However, Cheng and Espiritu find the prejudice theory inadequate, since the hostility is the cause of tension, rather than a mere symptom of it.

Cheng and Espiritu also explore another socio-psychological "scapegoating theory," which holds that "less-powerful groups assuage their powerlessness by scapegoating their problems upon an identifiable but relatively harmless object" (1989:526). In applying the scapegoating theory to Black and Korean relations, the authors examine the lack of economic opportunities in poor Black neighborhoods and how that leads the Blacks who live within these areas to blame Koreans. Blacks would prefer to blame Whites, but do not have access to them. The authors also note that the economic stagnation in Black neighborhoods is what allows Korean immigrants to set up businesses at a relatively low cost.

The authors then turn their focus to a "resource competition" explanation, which looks at the conflict stemming strictly from an economic focus. Blacks and Koreans are competing in the same economic area, but as Blacks find it difficult to secure loans from banks, Korean businesses expand.

Cheng and Espiritu also point out that Koreans are insular in both their social and their business dealings, as part of their role of "middleman minorities," which intensifies negative feelings by Blacks towards them.

The authors find that neither set of theories fully explain the reasons for the conflict between Koreans and Blacks, and why there's not the same acrimony between Korean merchants and Latinos. Thus, they attempt to integrate the two explanations into the immigrant hypothesis: "immigrants have a frame of reference different from that held by native-born Americans" (1989:528). Because the Latino population and the Korean population both have significant numbers of immigrants, there is an immigrant ideology present that allows Latino customers and merchants to relate better to Korean merchants than Black residents and customers.

In evaluating this hypothesis, Cheng and Espititu assert that immigrants have a specific ideology that emphasizes the American dream and upward mobility through hard, even menial, work, while "Blacks appear to have largely rejected this dream" (1989:528). According to the authors, Blacks accused Korean merchants of being foreigners who take over their communities. Also, Black merchants face more competition from the immigrant entrepreneurs than any other segment of non-immigrant business owners. The authors also suggest that both Koreans and Latinos have developed a monopoly on certain small businesses in Black neighborhoods, such as the aforementioned gas stations, small markets and liquor stores, which heightens the animosity between the residents and the store owners. However, according to their findings, there is competition in Latino neighborhoods, which influences how the store owners are perceived by Latino customers and merchants, and how the customers are, in turn, perceived. Cheng and Espiritu conclude that their immigrant hypothesis best explains the animosity between Blacks and Koreans, and why the conflict is limited to between those two groups.

MASS STRATUM AXIS: HATE CRIMES BETWEEN AFRICAN AND KOREAN AMERICANS

Methodology

According to an internal Los Angeles Police Department (LAPD) memo on investigation of incidents motivated by hatred/prejudice, a "hate crime" is defined as:

> any malicious or offensive act directed against an individual or group based upon their race, religion, culture, disability, ethnic background, lifestyle, sexual orientation, and similar incidents against other groups that may be singled out for acts of hatred or prejudice (LAPD, n.d.).

A hate crime is what we consider a "high crime" because it tears at the basic fabric of society and is considered a crime against all people who live in a free and democratic society.

The two largest vesting agencies that are officially charged with keeping hate crime data for the region are the LAPD and the Los Angeles County Hate Crime Task Force under the Los Angeles County Commission on Human Relations (LACCHR). The data sets we examined on the county level had both structural and reporting flaws, although the catchment area is much larger and takes in urban, suburban and rural populations. The LAPD's reporting data prior to 1990 are collectively viewed both inside and outside the Department as unreliable, thus the authors have limited their time scope to the data from January, 1990 to June, 1992.

Collection of hate crime data by the LAPD starts in the field and is centralized for analysis within the Criminal Conspiracy Section of LAPD's Detective Support Division, which prepares quarterly and year-end statistical reports. These reports are disseminated to the Department, the media, and forwarded to the LACCHR.

In each of the LAPD's 18 divisional geographic areas, the commanding officer is charged with the responsibility of an intensive follow-up investigation and evaluating the social impact on the immediate community. A police unit, usually the assigned neighborhood Basic Car, will interview the hate crime victim and liaison with the detective assigned within each division as a hate crime specialist.

The authors scanned the LAPD's PACMUS central computer system that stores and sorts all reported city hate crimes at the Criminal Conspiracy Section. Particularly for the purposes of this study, we were interested in the following variables retrievable from the raw hate crime data:

1. Did this incident meet the definition of a hate crime?
2. Date of occurrence
3. LAPD Division reporting
4. Location of incident (residence, business, street, house of worship, school).
5. Victim's race
6. Victim's national origin
7. Suspect's race
8. M.O. (Modus Operandi)

Data Analysis and Hypothesis

Our main hypothesis in this sub-study was to test, on a mass stratum, the magnitude, depth and trend of "systemic hatred" in the City of Los Angeles, between Korean Americans and African Americans. According to A.H. Maslow, safety needs are primal human needs; they refer essentially to the avoidance of pain and physical damage through external forces (Maslow, 1971). Our secondary hypothesis was to test hate crimes between Koreans and Blacks and to determine in fact if they followed the "standard" aggregate patterns of all hate crimes.

The authors fully understand the built-in limitations inherent in hate crime analysis. Hate crime is not all crime and has a difficult threshold for classification.[5] Hate crimes overall are dramatically under-reported to police authorities, especially by

---

[5] There is an interesting behind-the-scenes struggle going on now between the LAPD and the LACCHR regarding the reporting of incidents during the civil unrest. The LAPD feels each case needs to meet a tough definition and be evaluated separately. While the civil unrest may have reflected intergroup tensions, they are not considered hate crimes because they were not aimed at a specific target.

victims who are newly arrived immigrants. Hate crime tabulation and documentation are highly subjective, starting with the individual patrol officer and the standard of training and sensitivity he or she might have received. Lastly, hate crimes targeting Koreans may be difficult to ascertain in the overall anti-Asian hatred incidents. With much of the Japan bashing of the early 1990s, we must suspect some cases of hate crimes may be smudged together based on mistaken identity.

Despite these structural limitations, we feel this data bank and subsequent analysis lend themselves to "a snapshot of inter-ethnic relations" in one of the most diverse regions in the United States. Recent empowering state/municipal legislation has meant greater prosecution of hate crimes (and we expect greater reporting). In 1991, for example, the Los Angeles County District Attorney's Office took 21 hate crime cases to court.

Findings

Measuring specifically the data based on the victim's race/national origin and on the suspect's race we identified up to 30 hate crime cases where Koreans were the victims and the suspect was Black. The total number of cases peaked in 1991. In no case could we locate any documentation of the reversed hate crime: (Black/victim; Korean/suspect). We were also curious to examine along the lines of Cheng and Espiritu's (1989) immigrant hypothesis the reported hate crimes between Latinos and Koreans. For the period we examined, we could not locate any case that met this criterion, thus supporting in the abstract Cheng and Espiritu's hypothesis. Graph #1 charts the Annual Hate Crime Growth of this selected universe, and what is interesting to note is that the trend of Korean-Black hate crimes is actually *decreasing*. End-of-the-year analysis for 1992 conducted by the LAPD, confirms in their aggregate data that national origin incidents of hate crimes (Korea in particular) have decreased 28 percent overall from 1991 totals.

Graph 1

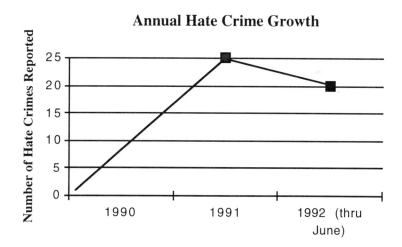

Annual Hate Crime Growth

In examining the actual number of hate crime cases over the months of 1990-92 some interesting observations occurred. From March 1990 to March 1991, no cases were documented. (See Graph #2) We theorize that two societal forces were going on at the time that might have turned attention elsewhere: the Persian Gulf Crisis and an economy that was shaky but not fully smashed.

On Graph #3, we observed that starting in April 1991 an explosion of hate crimes erupted between these two communities. After a partial content analysis of the news stories emanating at this juncture, we theorize from the data that the episodical nature of the reported hate crimes are media-driven and media-hyped. In other words, each rise on the graph appears to be associated with some celebrity case or media exposé covered extensively in the local press and ethnic media.[6]

---

[6] In our survey for this paper we found "high reliability" quotations in the information people received from television news, radio and newspapers--Korean-Americans had a 93 percent "very reliable/somewhat reliable" rating; African-Americans had a 91 percent.

On March 16, 1991, the Latasha Harlins case broke and within the African American and Korean American communities leaders appealed for reason and reduction of anger. In the next three months hate crimes took off.

Graph 2

1990 Hate Crimes Per Month

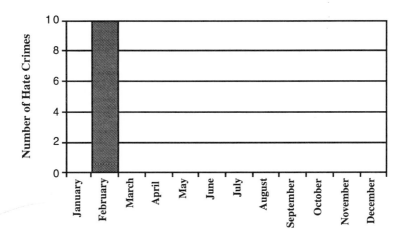

On June 4, 1991, the killing of Arthur Mitchell, an African American, during a robbery attempt of a Korean liquor store was covered widely in the media. On June 14, 1991, Mayor Tom Bradley and Councilman Robert Farrell, both of whom are African Americans, called a press conference with the LACCHR urging the Commission develop a strategy in a 60-day period which explored the basic issues related to intercultural conflict. On June 17, 1991, Danny Bakewell (Brotherhood Crusade), Mothers in Action and the Bethel A.M.E. Church, all African American activist organizations, held a press conference and demonstration criticizing the killing and raising the issue of the treatment of the African American community by Korean and other small store owners. They announced an intent to maintain the demonstration for 90 days.

Graph 3

1991 Hate Crimes Per Month

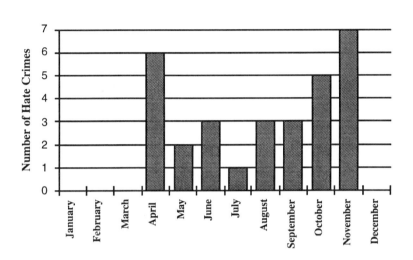

Graph 4

1992 Hate Crimes Per Month

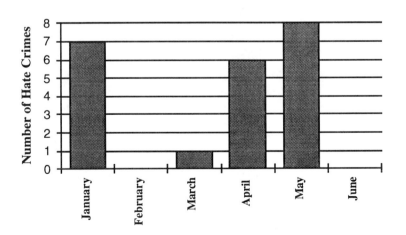

On June 18, 1991, flammable liquid and molotov cocktails were thrown at the liquor store where Mitchell was killed resulting in minimal property damage and no injuries. The June 20, 1991, edition of *The Sentinel*, a Black-owned newspaper, ran a headline story on the liquor store boycott concluding with the language "Leaders Urge Calm." Simultaneously, hate cases went up for the month of June.

November 1991, registered seven new hate crime cases that month, a record high from the previous tracking months. The media was reporting (and sensationalizing) two major events that we theorize fed into this escalation. First was the trial and sentencing of Soon Ja Du, the Korean store owner who killed African American Latasha Harlins. She was given probation and community service time instead of any jail sentencing. (The District Attorney, Ira Reiner, took the case to appeal and lost in January, 1992. Hate crime data rose simultaneously in that month.) Second was the controversy regarding the protest against Black rap artist Ice Cube's new album entitled, "Death Certificate." Led by the Korean American Grocers Association (KAGRO) of Southern California, a group of Korean leaders attacked the album because "its violent and derogatory lyrics promote racial hatred and violence, particularly against Korean store owners" (KAGRO Press Release, 1991). The lyrics of one of the tracks, *Black Korea* goes as follows:

Group:　　Ice Cube
Album:　　Death Certificate
Track:　　*BLACK KOREA*

[Sounds from the Spike Lee film, "Do The Right Thing" are used in the background. Black Korea uses the scene of a conflict between a Black customer and a Korean merchant and his wife in the beginning, end, and in between choruses.]

Lyrics:
Everytime I wanna go get a fucking brew
I gotta go down to the store with a tool
Oriental ones (can you count) mother fuckers
They make a niggar mad enough to cause a little ruckus
Thinking every brother in the world's on the take

So they watch every damn move that I make
They hope I don't pull out a gat and try to rob
Their funky little store, but bitch I got a job
So don't follow me, up and down your market
Or your little chop-suey ass will be a target
of the nationwide boycott
Choose with the people
That's what the boy got
So pay respect to the Black fist
or we'll burn your store, right down to a crisp
And then we'll see ya
Cause you can't turn the ghetto into Black Korea...
(KAGRO, Ibid).

Graph 5

1991 Location of Hate Crime

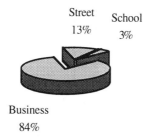

Street
13%

School
3%

Business
84%

Finally, we note the April-May 1992 (Graph #4) rise in hate crimes associated with the civil unrest and compare this with the later released *Webster Commission* report which in part admonished the media for more responsible journalism during times of domestic civil unrest. Local Chanel 9's portrayal by one reporter was the statement (obviously referring to race relations): "There's a war going on down here."[7]

---

[7] The Southern Christian Leadership Conference has tried in the past to instill a "Code of Ethics for Media Reporting," especially in coverage of minority communities. Their efforts in this field have produced meagre results to date.

Graph 6

1992 Location of Hate Crimes

Street   Other
31.8%   4.6%

Business
63.6%

Graph 7

1991 Hate Crimes by LAPD Area

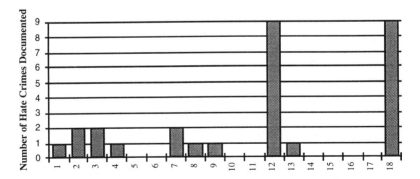

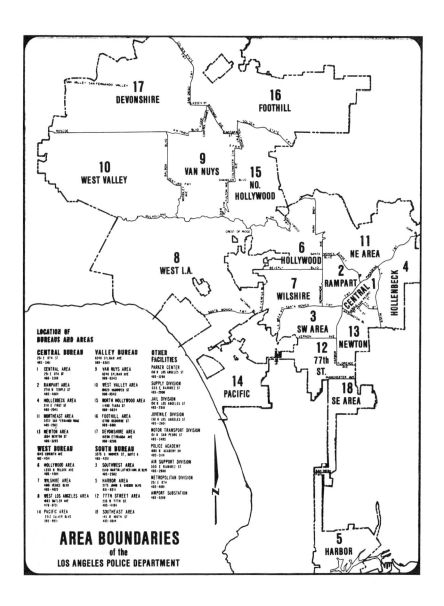

AREA BOUNDARIES
of the
LOS ANGELES POLICE DEPARTMENT

In exploring our secondary hypothesis, we noted that the location and sites of hate crimes between Koreans and Blacks during 1991 and 1992 show an amazing contradiction with the "normal" aggregate patterns of hate crimes (in all categories—including religious hate, racial hate and sexual orientation hate). The LACCHR date for racial crimes of hate from 1981-89 mentions that the preferred target site 71 percent of the time has been at *residences*. For the same period only 13.8 percent has happened at businesses (LACCHR, 1990:10). In the county data, as well as in the tracking done by the LAPD, the profile of hate crimes (in all categories) in the '90's continue to register residences for the greatest number of hate crime sites, with some movement recently towards greater attacks in public places. Business sites continue to register only a fraction of the aggregate total. For example, LACCHR'S "Hate Crime in Los Angeles County 1991" reports as total percentages: 43.1 percent at residences; 24.5 percent at public places; 20.1 percent at businesses (LACCHR, 1992).

Graph 8

1992 (thru June) Hate Crimes by LAPD Area

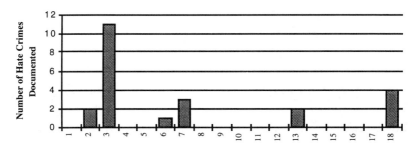

Graphs #5 and #6 based on our research demonstrate that most hate crimes between Koreans and Blacks happen at *business establishments*, not in *residences*. In 1991, 83.3 percent were in businesses compared to just 3.3 percent occurring at places of residence. By 1992, more hate crimes between these two populations shifted to the streets/public places (with 31.8 percent), however the vast majority (63.6 percent) remained tied to business establishment venues.

Lastly, we were curious about the spread and distribution of hate crimes between Korean Americans and African Americans based on geographic divisional reporting districts of the LAPD. Graphs #7 and 8 report our results. In 1991, the majority of the hate crime cases were confined to the 77th Street Area and the Southeast Area Divisions (District 12, 18). By 1992 (through June) a northernly pattern was moving into more territorially defined Koreatown and its perimeter business establishments. New LAPD area jurisdictions were impacted, with the Southwest Area (District 3) picking up the bulk, followed by Southeast Area (District 18); Wilshire Area (District 7); Newton Area (District 13); Hollywood Area (District 6); and Rampart Area (District 2).

Hypothesis

Reexamining our main and secondary hypotheses *vis-á-vis* the hate crime data we dissected in this section, we conclude that there is *no* support to sustain an analysis of "systemic hatred" existing between the African American and Korean American communities in Los Angeles. To us, systemic hatred would connote an all-pervasive, ever-present pattern of sustaining tensions leading to the overt manifestations of hate crimes. While further methodological research is needed in this area we have observed the following:

(1) Despite the general impression that the pre- and post-civil unrest period has produced greater amounts of hate crimes, the trend is actually in decline.

(2) Hate crimes between Koreans and Blacks are episodic and appear to have some correlation with media-driven exposés about tension/flare-ups between the two communities. If this was truly a pattern of "systemic hatred" the researchers would have expected to see a higher number of cases, spread consistently over the months and years.

(3) Hate crimes we believe between Koreans and Blacks are based on *economics*, not systemic racial hatred. We deduce this position by reexamining the unusual patterns of where hate crimes take place—at businesses. If again this was truly a pattern of systemic hatred, we would expect to see Korean merchants, etc., victimized at their residences, perhaps having been followed home for harassment and further victimization.

(4) Hate crimes, while diminishing between these two populations, are spreading out of the traditional epicenter into new parts of Los Angeles.

ELITE STRATUM AXIS: SURVEY QUESTIONNAIRE AND ANALYSIS

Methodology

Members of both the Korean American and African American business communities were interviewed. Both groups were mailed questionnaires consisting of open and closed-ended questions. Respondents were randomly selected from published business directories within each business community. Approximately 600 businesses were sampled in each community. The response rates for the Korean American and African American business establishments were nearly identical, with approximately 120 responses from each, resulting in a response rate of 20 percent.

Questionnaires were first mailed to respondents during November-December 1992. A second mailing was sent in January 1993. The Korean American questionnaire was bilingual and bilingual coders were used to code the open-ended responses.

Data Analysis and Hypotheses

This sub-study will first compare the responses of Korean American and African American business owners on a number of variables relating to their perceptions of conditions in their respective communities, life in Los Angeles, inter-racial relations, and other relevant issues. The second part of the analysis will test some hypotheses relating specifically to the Korean American business community, their role in the community, and their relationships with other ethnic groups. The following hypotheses will be tested:

1. According to Min (1984), Korean Americans who become minority business middlemen do not conform to the sojourner model of immigrant business owners as proposed by Bonacich (1987). Korean Americans are permanent settlers and are not sojourners who plan to return to their native homeland.

2. Most Korean American business owners are highly educated and received their degrees and advanced training in Korea. Labor market discrimination and other factors force these highly qualified professionals into small businesses.

3. According to Cheng and Espiritu's (1989) immigrant hypothesis, Korean Americans would feel closer to Latinos and other immigrant groups than to African Americans who don't share the immigrants frame of reference.

Findings

When asked how they believed things were going in their respective communities, both Korean Americans and African Americans responded negatively, with 68 percent of the Korean Americans and 55 percent of the African Americans responding "pretty badly" or "badly." When asked about the quality of political leadership in their communities one local leader stood out for his high evaluations: Michael Woo. He received an "excellent" or "good" rating from 68 percent of the Korean Americans and a 77 percent rating from African Americans. No other local leader came close to his approval ratings. In fact, when asked about the upcoming mayoral contest, Michael Woo had a majority of support from both communities with 70 percent of the Korean Americans and 53 percent of the African Americans supporting him. He was the front runner. Evaluations of Mayor Bradley were predictable with nearly 80 percent of the Korean Americans giving the Mayor a "fair" or "poor" evaluation, while 51 percent of the African Americans gave him an "excellent" or "good" rating. Former District Attorney Ira Reiner received negative evaluations from both groups. Eighty-six percent of Korean Americans rated him negatively as did 57 percent of African Americans.

Respondents were asked about the involvement of the various levels of government in responding to the social and economic problems confronting Los Angeles. An overwhelming majority of respondents from both communities believed that city/county involvement was warranted (Korean Americans 81 percent; African Americans 77 percent). Nearly two-thirds of both groups wanted an active role taken by state government. However, only 44 percent of Korean Americans wanted active involvement by the federal government, whereas 63 percent of African Americans supported federal involvement.

Questions were included to measure the opinions of the respondents' attitudes toward the Los Angeles Police Department and the local judicial system. When asked if the passage of the police reform measure, Charter Amendment F, and the hiring of a new Police Chief increased their confidence in the LAPD, almost three times as many African Americans as Korean Americans responded in the affirmative (58 percent to 21 percent). Respondents were asked their opinions on two extremely controversial court cases: the Latisha Harlins case and the Reginald Denny case. When asked if they supported the judge's sentencing in the Harlins' case, where a Korean American grocery store owner was sentenced to probation in the killing of a teenage African American girl, it was not surprising to find 84 percent of Korean Americans agreeing or strongly agreeing with the sentence, with only 6 percent of African Americans indicating support.

Only the African American sample was asked questions relating to the Denny case. Denny, a White truck driver, had been dragged from his truck and brutally beaten during the 1992 riot. Live television coverage of the incident had a tremendous impact on the viewing audience. Only 30 percent supported the way the District Attorney's office handled the case of those accused of assaulting Denny, while 61 percent disapproved. Respondents were asked to indicate if they believed those accused of assaulting Denny were "political martyrs," "criminal thugs," or "something else." Thirteen percent thought them to be martyrs, 39 percent viewed them as thugs, with the remainder seeing them as something else or offering a "don't know" response.

A surprising finding was the similarity in response to the trust in government question. Nearly identical percentages responded one could "always" trust City Hall (2 percent Korean American; 3 percent African American), 14 percent Korean Americans responded one could trust government "most of the time" with 12 percent African American offering the same opinion. About 80 percent of both groups thought one could trust government only "some of the time." More African Americans than Korean Americans thought city government is run by a "few big interests" (57 percent compared to 42 percent). Differences between the two communities were also evident in a question concerning the treatment of criminals by local courts. There is nearly unanimous consensus in the Korean American community that the courts are not harsh enough with criminals (89 percent) while only about half as many African Americans hold that view (46 percent). In fact, almost one-fifth of the African Americans thought the courts were too harsh with criminals compared to only 1 percent of Korean Americans taking that position.

The Korean American sample was asked questions about hate crimes directed at members of their ethnic group. Forty-nine percent responded that they or an immediate family member had been a victim of a hate crime during the last year, and 80 percent reported they believed there has been an increase in the frequency of such crimes over the past few years.

Both groups were asked questions relating to their feelings of closeness to various ethnic groups. The findings suggest that members of the African American business community feel closer to the Korean American community than vice versa. Seventy-two percent of the Korean Americans reported feeling not very close to African Americans (22 percent reported feeling very or somewhat close), while slightly over a majority (52 percent) of the African Americans reported feeling not very close to Korean Americans (47 percent felt very or somewhat close). Unfortunately, majorities in both communities do not have friendly feelings toward the other. Korean Americans and African Americans had different feelings about other ethnic groups in Los Angeles. Korean Americans and African Americans reported feeling "very" or "somewhat close" to these groups at the following percentages: Jewish Americans (37 percent and 69 percent), Japanese Americans (65 percent and 40 percent), Latinos (51 percent and 80 percent), Chinese Americans (84 percent and 47 percent), and Anglos (52 percent and 67 percent).

Questions attempting to measure the impact of the civic unrest on Korean Americans' perceptions of African Americans and vice versa were asked. In addition, Koreans who were not native to the United States were asked about their attitudes towards African Americans prior to their immigrating to the U.S. While living in Korea, 53 percent reported having "very positive" or "positive" feelings toward African Americans. Since living in the U.S. 13 percent reported their feelings have become more positive, 30 percent reported no change in their feelings, and a majority (57 percent) reported more negative feelings. The upheaval of last year left Korean Americans with a more negative feeling (66 percent) toward African Americans with only 17 percent African Americans reporting an increase in negative feelings, 30 percent reporting no change, and 32 percent reporting an increase in positive feelings toward Korean Americans.

A series of questions about the rebuilding of Los Angeles was asked of respondents. Again, this is an area where there are some expected differences. Eighty percent of Korean Americans were opposed to the meeting last fall between the Korean American Grocers Association and the Bloods and the Crips while nearly as many (76 percent) African Americans supported that meeting. When asked whether or not it was important for Korean Americans to invest in South Central Los Angeles, only 14 percent of Korean Americans indicated it was important compared to 73 percent of the African Americans. Within the Korean American community there was no consensus as to the type of investment that should be made in the community. African Americans preferred job training programs (27 percent), Korean Americans preferred joint partnerships (13 percent); as for manufacturing jobs and grocery stores and other service industries, they were the same (10 percent each). In fact, three-quarters of the African Americans want to see Asian banks involved in the South Central community development.

Both groups indicated support for giving all racial groups a chance at getting jobs in the Rebuild L.A. reconstruction projects (Korean Americans 82 percent, African Americans 89 percent). Both groups also supported hiring quotas based on race (51 percent and 77 percent). Yet, when asked if Rebuild L.A. would revitalize the economically depressed areas only 32 percent of the Korean Americans and 49 percent of the African Americans answered affirmatively. More suprising was the finding that only 9 percent of the Korean Americans thought reconstruction projects would ultimately result in more economic equality in Los Angeles while a majority of African Americans (53 percent) thought it would. The question of community zoning hearings for liquor stores found both communities on opposite sides with 95 percent of Korean Americans believing it would hurt the Korean American store owner and 87 percent African Americans supporting such hearings.

Hypotheses

The first hypothesis claimed that Korean American business owners were not minority middleman sojourners. Min's theory that Korean Americans are part of the permanent business class was tested. Of our Korean American sample only 2 percent were born in the United States. Thirty-eight percent have lived here for only ten or fewer years. When asked if they plan on moving from the Los Angeles area, only 9 percent reported they would likely move, 30 percent reported a move was somewhat likely, and 48 percent indicated they had no plans to move. For those who indicated a move might be in their future plans, only 7 percent said they would move back to Korea. Forty percent would move within the state of California, and 50 percent would move out of state. It is interesting to note that of the 28 percent of the African Americans who indicated they might consider moving from Los Angeles, only 27 percent would remain in California and two-thirds would move out of state. Therefore, Min's theory that Korean Americans are not members of the sojourner class was supported.

The second hypothesis claims that members of the Korean American business community are highly educated and many received advanced professional training in Korea. Although our data does not include information on whether or not labor market discrimination forced these highly educated and trained individuals into the minority middleman class, the findings indicate that 62 percent of the sample has a college degree and 22 percent has a post graduate education. Korean American and African American business owners have the same percentage of high school graduates (11 percent). African Americans have a higher percentage of "some" college (41 percent) than Korean Americans (5 percent) with 48 percent of African Americans having a college or post graduate level of education compared to 84 percent of the Korean Americans. Fifty-seven percent of

Korean Americans reported completing their highest level of education in Korea. It appears that the data support previous findings that Korean American business owners are highly educated and may have entered into small business ownership due to professional discrimination.

Cheng and Espiritu's hypothesis that Korean Americans would feel closer to other immigrant groups such as Latinos was tested. The data partially supported their hypothesis. The data indicate that Korean Americans feel especially close to other Asian groups, possibly identifying with the immigrant frame of reference. Korean Americans reported feeling "very" or "somewhat" close to Japanese Americans (65 percent) and Chinese Americans (84 percent). They feel "very" or "somewhat" close to Jewish American (37 percent), Latinos (51 percent), and Anglos (52 percent) at lower rates. We postulate that race might be more of a factor related to closeness than is the immigrant experience. Latinos and Anglos received approximately the same closeness ratings and Anglos are obviously not part of the immigrant class and Latinos are. The data does not support Cheng and Espiritu's hypothesis, which we feel is an important point since it opens the door to possible future political coalitions between Blacks and Koreans. It is interesting to note that African Americans feel closest to Anglos (67 percent), Jewish Americans (69 percent) and Latinos (80 percent) and least close to Korean Americans (47 percent), Japanese Americans (40 percent), and Chinese Americans (47 percent).

CONCLUSION

This paper and its various methodological pursuits covered a wide expanse in the analyses of inter-racial relations between the African American and the Korean American communities in Los Angeles. We initally titled our paper "Riot, Rebellion or Civil Unrest?" Perhaps the musings of a pair of frustrated social scientists trying to cover all bases. So what did happen? What do we call "it"? And what is the future of race relations in Los

Angeles? We tend to offer the reader different iterations based
on *Webster's Ninth Collegiate Dictionary* to more
constructively suit the analysis at hand. According to Webster:
(1) a *riot* is: a public violence, or disorder; a disturbance of the
public peace by 3 or more persons assembled together and
acting with common intent; a random or disorderly profusion;
(2) a *rebellion* is: opposition to one in authority or dominance;
open armed and usually unsuccessful defiance of or resistance
to an established government; (3) lastly, we could not find,
interestingly, a definition for civil unrest, so we took it apart
and it is defined as, *civil*: relating to or based on civil law, and
unrest: a disturbance or uneasy state; turmoil.

Korean Americans commonly call this period *Sa-i-gu* (4-29)
or April 29. In South Korea important events are known for the
day they occur. For the authors, April 29 was both a
continuation of the political forces leading up to this period as
well as a sharp intellectual departure into new paradigm shifts
we conclude from the data sets.

Will the tensions and political differences between African
Americans and Korean Americans ever be bridged in forming a
multiethnic ruling coalition to lead Los Angeles in the 1990s?
Will these two communities become full-fledged members of
the dominant *Gemeinschaft* rather than "underdogs fighting
underdogs"?

Drawing upon the analysis of the hate crime data we see no
residual structural, permanent "systemic hatred" dividing these
communities. From our perspective, the key motivating factor is
economic disparity and the present lack of ethnic leadership in
each respective group to chart a cogent vision of new immigrant
economies in synergy with established economic needs of older
ethnic communities. Historically, census figures show that
African Americans have a lower rate of business start-ups than
Asian Americans or Latinos (Lee, 1992:A17). In field
interviews for this paper we learned of three Black-owned Los
Angeles financial institutions—Family Saving Bank, Broadway
Federal Savings & Loan and Founders National Bank—have
joined forces to form a revolving credit pool, analogous to the

kye that exist in Korean American neighborhoods. This example of ethnic economic self-help strategies cross-fertilized between communities hold great promise.

One particular mayoral candidate, Mike Woo may be the great unifying force, pressing a plan for joint Asian-African Development Banks, that speaks to this synergy of ethnic economics and multiethnic politics. Our data demonstrated resoundingly that Mr. Woo has strong loyal support in both communities.

What is perhaps most exciting about our data analyses is the pre-movement indicies away from traditional ethnic voting patterns (e.g., Blacks only vote for Blacks) towards a "candidate-centered" vote. We term Mr. Woo, based on this early shifting, a "transcendent politician" and the forerunner in constituting a neo-multiethnic liberal governing coalition as the changing dialectic of Los Angeles transpires.

Additionally, on the point of ethnic coalition building, we found African Americans still holding onto the remanants of the "old Bradley coalition," especially in their stronger feelings for Jewish Americans (by 69 percent), Anglos (by 67 percent), and Latinos (by 80 percent). This was surprising, especially given the "wedge" between Jews and Blacks over two Jesse Jackson Presidential attempts and other divisive issues. Furthermore we question the strong sentiments with the Latino population. The 1990 reapportionment process of Los Angeles might have left great scars between Blacks and Latinos, had not Mr. Woo declared his mayoral run, thus putting the 13th Council District as a "Latino-leading" seat and acting as a safety valve. We conclude however that for our Korean sample, we denote a new pan-Asian solidarity (perhaps moving into a solidified coalition) with strong feelings towards Japanese Americans (by 65 percent) and Chinese Americans (by 84 percent). Ultimately the logic of coalition behavior is centered around the conflicts within the existing political arena. Coalition building theory is formulated under a set of 3 general requirements: (1) individual rationality (2) collective rationality (3) and the possibility of greater pay off. All three conditions have various shades of applicability in our study between our sample populations.

Lastly, we conclude in offering an alternative hypothesis that has either been overlooked in past research or is a new phenomenon emanating out of the post-civil unrest that warrants further study. We term this hypothesis a "victimological syndrome" and literally, as a mad chemist finds by accident a new formula, did we stumble onto this hypothesis in our study and analysis of the Korean American community in Los Angeles.

Time constraints hinder an in-depth, more comprehensive examination; however, the rudiments of this hypothesis find their causality in the Korean business elite that we sampled, viewing themselves as what Richard A. Ball calls victims of an "institutionalized resignation to fate." (Ball, 1976.) For Ball, fatalism contributes to victimization by precluding adaptive and constructive responses. Mutual victimization produces reciprocal self-distructive responses and Ball argues this sets off "victimological cycles" which are mutally reinforcing.

The concept of victim is a new socio-pathology and politically de-empowering phenomenon adapted to segments of the Korean American community. Ball's victimological cycle can easily be overlaid on the research this study and others are beginning to show. "Korean immigrants were victimized first by the rioters, then by a combination of their unfamilarity with the American institutions and the ignorance and insensitivity of bureaucrats," claims Mr. Yeong S. Jyoo, a researcher who just released a study on people who lost businesses in the civil unrest, conducted by the Korean American Inter-Agency Council (as reported in Kang, 1993). Jyoo's survey found only 28 percent of the businesses destroyed have reopened, and only 29 percent of the "victims" say they were optimistic. Two-thirds of the respondents said they have not recovered from the riots, and 49 percent said they were pessimistic about their future and viewed the rebuilding process as a "hopeless cause" (Kang, 1992).

This "victimological syndrome" also makes a case for the notion of victim compensation which traditionally has been a politically marginalized, poorly run, government program. This is due to the fact that most crime victims in this society are lower-class people who have interests and characteristics that are unrepresented in the political systsem. One could argue that through government negligence, or social obligation theory, or even Jeremy Bentham's claim that compensation should be awarded because the social contract between "victim" and his government has been broken. Whatever the legal/moral/ humanitarian rationale applied, Korean "victims" of the civil unrest deserve due reparations. Mr. Tyson B. Park, counsel for the 1,600 member "Association of Korean American Victims of the L.A. Riot," wrote recently about the dual-victimization of City Hall's non-responsiveness and the removal of constitutional due process in preventing some merchants from rebuilding their liquor stores in South Central. His concluding remarks are worth noting:

> It saddens me to see the troubles of people in my community lumped into a basket, labeled as mere "Korean problems," and on that basis ignored. Like African Americans, Irish Americans, Mexican Americans, Italian Americans, Jewish Americans, and every other racial group that ever found itself the unlucky whipping boy of popular public sentiment, Korean Americans feel the pain that comes with being the victims of injustice, racial stereotyping and discrimination. We came seeking the American Dream. We work hard. We contribute. Are we not worth some small consideration? (Park, 1992)

We find evidence of this victimological syndrome hypothesis extrapolated out of our survey analysis. When directly asked whether you or a member of your immediate family have ever been a victim of a "hate crime" (i.e., a criminal act against you or your personal property solely because of your race or ethnicity), *almost half* of the respondents answered yes. Even more revealing (especially since hate crimes against Korean Americans had been declining), we asked if in their opinion have hate crimes against Koreans increased, decreased, or remained the same over the past few years? *Eighty percent* felt they have increased, which we believe further operationalizes Ball's thesis.

Moreover, other indicies in comparison with the African American community underscore this hypothesis even further. Korean respondents thought things are going pretty badly/very badly by a ratio 67.8 percent to Blacks 55 percent. Perhaps this is the onset a general malaise. Koreans tend to be more removed from trust in government or governmental agencies than Blacks. For example, confidence in the LAPD increased 58 percent for Blacks and only 21 percent for Koreans with the passage of Proposition F and the hiring of a new police chief (who happens to be an African American). Koreans seem to know they are politically weak and can't do much about it. For example, a specific question to the Korean sample was "Did you support the dividing up of Koreatown into several council districts during reapportionment?" Over two-thirds opposed the new district plan, with 89 percent agreeing the split was due to lack of Korean American leadership. Finally, Koreans seem less involved in the Rebuild L.A. revitalization process than Blacks, with 32 percent affirming these projects will help compared to 49 percent of the Black respondents.

Politically, we end on a note of caution. The victimological syndrome concerns we raise in this paper may also prove to be an insurmountable political liability, especially if "victim constituencies" ramify from those who view themselves as victims of the civil unrest. Victim constituencies are persons who identify with the victims and who can imagine the same injury being done to them. On the one hand, the message can be one of political fatalism. Or, on the other hand, as the Jewish American victimization experience has proven, the message can be one of political empowerment through progressive coalition for one's own survival interests. The Jewish philosopher Hillel's questions still apply: "If I am not for myself, who will be for me? If I am only for myself, what am I? And if not now, when?"

REFERENCES

ABC News, "World News Tonight," September 13, 1992. [Transcript from Lexis Nexis.]

An, Rosario. *Korean Immigrants in Atlanta*. Chicago, IL: Asian American Mental Health Research Center, 1979.

Ball, Richard A. "The Victimological Cycle." Paper presented at the 2nd International Symposium on Victimology, Boston, MA. 1976.

Becker, H. *Men in Reciprocity*. New York: Frederick Prager, 1956.

Blalock, Hubert M. *Toward a Theory of Minority Group Relations*. New York: Wiley and Sons, 1967.

Bonacich, Edna. "Making It in America," *Sociological Perspective*, Vol. 30, No. 4 (October, 1987):446-465.

――― , "Middleman Minorities and Advanced Capitalism," *Ethnic Groups* 2, (1980):211-19.

―――, "The Present, Past, and Future of Split Labor Market Theory," *Research in Race and Ethnic Relations* 1 (1979):16-64.

―――, I. Light, and C.C. Wong. "Koreans in Business," *Society*, 4, (1977):54-59.

Browning, Rufus, P., Dale R. Marshall, and David H. Tabb. *Racial Politics in American Cities*. New York: Langman, 1990.

――― , *Protest Is Not Enough*. Berkeley: University of California Press, 1984.

Cha, Marn J. "An Ethnic Political Orientation as a Function of Assimilation: With Reference to Koreans in Los Angeles." *Journal of Korean Affairs*, Vol. 5, No. 3 (Oct., 1975):14-25.

――― , "An Ethnic Political Orientation as a Function of Assimilation: With Reference to Koreans in Los Angeles." In *The Korean Diaspora*, Hyung-chan Kim, ed., Santa Barbara, CA: Clio Press, 1977.

Chang, Edward T. "New Urban Crisis: Korean-Black Conflicts in Los Angeles," Ph.D. Dissertation, UC Berkeley, 1990.

―――, "The Politics of the Korean Community in Los Angeles: Kwangju Uprising and Its Impact." Thesis, UCLA, 1984.

Chang, Won Ho. "Communication and Acculteration: A Case Study of Korean Ethnic Groups in Los Angeles." Thesis, University of Iowa, 1972.

Cheng, Lucie and Yen Espiritu. "Korean Businesses in Black and Hispanic Neighborhoods: A Study of Intergroup Relations." *Sociological Perspectives*, Vol. 32, No. 4, 1989.

Choy, Bong-youn. *Koreans in America.* Chicago, IL: Nelson-Hall, 1979.

Coser, Lewis. *The Functions of Social Conflict.* London: Rutledge and Kegan Paul, 1956.

————, "The Alien As a Servant of Power: Court Jews and Christian Renegades." *American Sociological Review* 37, (1972):575-80.

Dahrendorf, Ralf. *Class Conflict in Industrial Society.* Stanford, CA: Stanford University Press, 1959.

Eisinger, Peter K. *Patterns of Inter-Racial Politics: Conflict and Cooperation in the City.* New York: Academic Press, 1976.

Foster, B.L. "Ethnicity and Commerce." *American Ethnologist,* 1 (1974):437-48.

Frederickson, George M. *White Supremacy.* New York: Oxford University Press, 1981.

Gellene, Denise. "Black Builders Want Fair Share of Construction." *Los Angeles Times,* Tuesday, May 5, 1992:DI.

Hamilton, G. "Pariah Capitalism: A Paradox of Power and Dependence." *Ethnic Groups* 2 (1978):1-15.

Henderson, William L. and Larry C. Ledebur. *Economic Disparity: Problems and Strategies for Black America.* New York: The Free Press, 1970.

Hong, Lawrence K. "Perception of Community Problems Among Koreans in the Los Angeles Area." In *Koreans in Los Angeles: Prospects and Promises,* 1982.

Hurh, Won Moo. *Assimilation of the Korean Minority in the United States.* The Philip Jaisohn Memorial Foundation, 1977.

———— and Kwang C. Kim. "Methodological Problems in the Study of Korean Immigrants: Conceptual, Interactional, Sampling and Interviewer Training Difficulties." Paper presented at the 1979 annual meeting of the Midwest Sociological Society, 1979.

————. *Korean Immigrants in America: A Structural Analysis of Ethnic Confinement and Adhesive Adaptation.* London & Toronto: Associated University Press, 1984.

Jackson, Byran O. and Michael B. Preston, eds. *Racial and Ethnic Politics in California.* Berkeley: Institute of Governmental Studies, University of California at Berkeley, 1991.

Kang, Connie K. "Korean Riot Victims Suffer Stress Disorder." *Los Angeles Times,* March 3, 1992.

Kim, David S. and Charles Choy Wong. "Business Development in Koreatown, Los Angeles." In *The Korean Diaspora*, Hyung-chan Kim, ed. Santa Barbara, CA: Clio Press, 1977.

Kim, Hyung-chan, ed. *The Korean Diaspora.* Santa Barbara: CA: ABC Clio Press, 1977.

——— and Wayne Patterson, eds. *The Koreans in America (1882-1974).* New York: Oceana Publications, Inc. 1974.

Kim, Illsoo. *New Urban Immigrants.* Princeton, NJ: Princeton University Press, 1981.

Kim, Jin Keon. "Communication Factors in Acculturation: The Case of Korean Immigrants in Southern California." Ph.D. Dissertation, University of Iowa, 1978.

Kim, Kenneth Kong-On, Kapson Lee, and Tai-Yul Kim. *Korean Americans in Los Angeles: Their Concerns and Language Maintenance.* Los Alamitos, CA: National Center for Bilingual Research, 1981.

Kim, Kwang Chung. "Intra-and Inter-Ethnic Group Conflicts: The Case of Korean Small Business in the United States." In Harold H. Sunoo, and Dong Soo Kim, eds. *Korean Women in a Struggle for Humanization.* Memphis, TN: Association of Korean Christian Scholars in North America, Inc., 1978, pp. 201-232.

Kim, Woong-Min. "History and Ministerial Roles of Korean Churches in the Los Angeles Area." D. Min. Dissertation, School of Theology at Claremont, 1981.

Kitano, Harry H.L. "Asian-Americans: The Chinese, Japanese, Korean, Philipino and Southeast Asians." *The Annals of the American Academy of Political and Social Science*, Vol. 454 (March, 1981):125-138.

——— and Roger Daniels. *Asian Americans: Emerging Minorities.* Englewood Cliffs, NJ: Prentice-Hall, Inc., 1988.

Korean American Grocers Association (KAGRO), Press Release, November 4, 1991.

Lee, Kyung. "Settlement Patterns of Los Angeles Koreans." Master's Thesis, University of California, Los Angeles, 1969.

Lee, Patrick. "Blacks Seek to Nurture an Entrepreneurial Class." *Los Angeles Times*, June 8, 1992.

Light, Ivan. *Ethnic Enterprise in America: Business and Welfare Among Chinese, Japanese, and Blacks.* Berkeley: University of California Press, 1972.

————, and E. Bonacich. *Immigrant Entrepreneurs: Koreans in Los Angeles, 1965-1982*. Berkeley: University of California Press, 1988.

Loewen, J.W. *The Mississippi Chinese: Between Black and White*. Cambridge, MA: Harvard University Press, 1971.

Los Angeles County Commission on Human Relations (LACCHR). "Hate Crimes in the 1980's: A Decade of Bigotry. A Report to the Los Angeles County Board of Supervisors." February, 1990.

————. "Hate Crimes in Los Angeles County 1991. A Report to the Los Angeles County Board of Supervisors." March, 1992.

Los Angeles Police Department Internal Memo, "Investigation of Incidents Motivated by Hatred/Prejudice," n.d.

Maslow, A.H. *The Farther Reaches of Human Nature*. New York: Viking, 1971.

Melendy, H. Brett. *Asians in America: Filipinos, Koreans, and East Indians*. Boston, MA: Twayne Publishers, 1977.

Min, Pyong-Gap. "From White-Collar Occupations to Small Business: Korean Immigrants' Occupational Adjustment." *The Sociological Quarterly*, Vol. 25, (Summer 1984a).

————. "A Structural Analysis of Korean Businesses in The United States." *Ethnic Groups*, Vol. 6, (1984b).

Oh, David M. *An Analysis of the Korean Community in the Mid-Wilshire Area, Part I*. Los Angeles: Office of Economic Opportunity, State of California, Mid-Wilshire Research Center Corp., 1983.

————. *An Analysis of Korean Firms in the Los Angeles Area*. Los Angeles: Office of Economic Opportunity, State of California, Mid-Wilshire Community Research Center Corp., 1983.

Park, Gary Wanki. "Koreans in Transition: The Development of the Los Angeles Korean Community from 1965 to the Present." (A paper submitted to the Department of History in partial fulfillment of the Master Degree, University of California, Los Angeles, 1989.)

Park, Jong Sam. "A Three Generational Study: Traditional Korean Value Systems and Psychosocial Adjustment of Korean Immigrants in Los Angeles." D.S.W. Dissertation, University of Southern California, 1975.

Park, Tyson B. "Why Punish The Victims?" *Los Angeles Times*, July 15, 1992.

Preston, Michael B., Lenneal J. Henderson, Jr., Paul L. Puryear, eds. *The New Black Politics: The Search for Political Power*. New York: Longman, 1987.

Rinder, I.D. "Strangers in the Land: Social Relations in the Status Gap." *Social Problems* 8 (1959):253-61.

Schattschneider, E.E. *The Semisovereign People: A Realist's View of Democracy in America*. New York: Holt, Rinehart, and Winston, 1960.

Shibutani, T., and K. Kwan. *Ethnic Stratification: A Comparative Approach*. New York: The Macmillan Company, 1965.

Shim, Steve S. *Korean Immigrant Churches in Southern California Today*. San Francisco: R & E Research Associates, 1977.

Silverstein, Stuart and Nancy Rivera Brooks. "Shoppers in Need of Stores." *Los Angeles Times*, November 24, 1991.

Sonensheim, Raphael. "Biracial Coalitions in Big Cities: Why They Succeed, Why They Fail," in Browning, Marshall and Tabb, *Racial Politics in American Cities*. New York: Longman, 1990.

Wong, C.C. "Black and Chinese Grocery Stores in Los Angeles Black Ghettos." *Urban Life* 5, (1977):439-64.

Yancy, Robert J. *Federal Government Policy and Black Business Enterprise*. Cambridge, MA: Ballinger Publishing Co., 1974.

Yoo, Jay Kun. *The Koreans in Seattle*. Elkins Park, PA: Philip Jaisohn Memorial Papers, 1979.

Yu, Eui-Young. *Korean Community Profile: Life and Consumer Patterns*. Los Angeles: The Korea Times/Hankook Ilbo, 1990.

Looters ravage the Jons Market at 8th St. and Normandie on April 30th.

THE CIVIL UPRISING AND INTRA-URBAN GOVERNANCE

Harlan Hahn
Professor of Political Science
University of Southern California

One of the most significant developments in the second half of the twentieth century has been the emergence of intensified efforts to modify public policies and institutions through movements that reflect a sense of political identity based on personal characteristics. In fact, the attempts by disadvantaged groups to build the foundations of a new social order by translating attributes such as race, ethnicity, gender, sexual orientation, age, and disability into a positive sense of pride has served to become the major impetus for social change during this era.

This phenomenon has crucial implications especially for the future of urban America. As the principal site of social heterogeneity, the capacity of cities to accommodate the political aspirations of these groups may constitute a critical test of a society based multicultural diversity. Increasing evidence has revealed the inadequacy of the traditional model of assimilation, which is commonly described as "the myth of the melting pot," implying that a uniform social identity might eventually submerge the divergent elements of America's population. But this paradigm could be replaced by continued oppression, pluralistic harmony, distinctive community structures, or waning enclaves. The creation of local institutions capable of reconciling the interests and goals of disadvantaged groups, therefore, may have a decisive impact on the fate of an urbanized society. This analysis focuses on the strategies adopted by such groups to fulfill these objectives and on the remedies and reforms implied by the use of various tactics. By conducting the investigation at a conceptual level, valuable insights also might be gained about relatively specific issues, such as the relationship between the Korean American and African American communities in Los Angeles.

Although the strategies chosen by minority groups to achieve their political ambitions have been varied, they seem to reflect a spectrum that ranges from relatively conventional tactics such as voting, litigation and interest groups activity to somewhat unconventional methods including protests, demonstrations, and collective violence. Almost all of these groups defined by race, ethnicity, gender, sexual orientation, age, and disability have pursued their aims through conventional political activities, and most of them have also engaged in protests and demonstrations. No major segment of the population have participated in attempted coups or revolutionary action. Perhaps the most significant remaining activity, of course, consists of incidents of collective violence that are usually labeled with relatively apolitical words like riots, disorders, or disturbances, rather than by terms such as uprisings or revolts. As events that reflect both the most extreme manifestations of popular discontent and the most serious repercussions for the continued operation of the political system, these uprisings have crucial implications for the future of urban areas that deserve careful scrutiny. And, of course, their relevance for the fate of Los Angeles was clearly demonstrated by the nations's most devastating outbreak of collective violence in the spring of 1992.

The history of violence in America has disclosed many occasions on which destructive force, exerted or condoned by government officials, has been imposed on oppressed groups including racial or ethnic minorities. Perhaps the most revealing evidence about the use of violence for political purposes, however, can be gained from the troubled history of White and

Black Americans. During the first half of the twentieth century, violence was almost always instigated by Whites against African Americans as punishment for real or imagined breaches of the "color line" that separated these communities. Subsequently, however, in a trend that extended from Watts in 1965 to Newark and Detroit in 1967 and to many US cities after the assassination of Martin Luther King, Jr., in 1968, collective violence began to assume a new pattern that revolved about issues of political authority. These issues seemed to promise to introduce different concepts and an innovative vocabulary into speculation about the future of local government; but, unfortunately, the investigations of social scientists were largely ignored by policy-makers and political leaders in the formulation of proposed solutions to the problems that triggered these occurrences. Thus, a comparison of urban violence in the 1960s and the 1992 uprising in Los Angeles revealed that almost nothing had changed, except perhaps the responses to these events. In order to explore new and creative remedies for the tensions that continue to plague Los Angeles and other cities, therefore, it is necessary to review briefly the major features of collective violence in the second half of the twentieth century.

This analysis is divided into two parts. The initial portion examines the issues of political authority implicit in the principal patterns of urban violence that extend at least from 1965 to 1992. The second segment presents conjecture derived from the preceding analysis about institutional remedies for the problems that spawned the violence. The methods used especially in the first section rely upon published studies, structured and unstructured interviews, personal observations in Detroit in 1967 and in Los Angeles in 1992, and, most importantly, knowledgeable informants who lived in the neighborhoods where the violence erupted. Because I have become increasingly convinced that evidence must disclose a situated viewpoint based on the relationship between the observer and the observed, I must also acknowledge that I have, insofar as possible, attempted to utilize information in the analysis that reflects the perspective of local residents who experienced the violence. These data are often markedly different from media reports and from the conclusions of supposedly impartial investigations; but I am convinced that they embody greater authenticity as a foundation for policy recommendations than alternative sources.

THE CIVIL UPRISING: A COMPARATIVE ANALYSIS

Perhaps one of the most striking and invariable features of the urban violence that exploded during the 1960s was the role of hostile or abrasive contacts between ghetto residents and the police in the precipitating incident, or the situation that triggered subsequent developments. Although these encounters often reflected a legacy of animosity between these groups, promoted perhaps in part by law enforcement policies of "preventive patrolling," the direct and nearly ubiquitous involvement of the police in precipitating events appeared to introduce questions of political authority as a natural starting point for any analysis of ghetto violence. For most people, government authority is reflected and symbolized more by the cop on the beat than by impersonal institutions and officeholders. Hence, opposition to existing authority is also more likely to be directed at local police, who are immediate tangible personifications of official power, than at distant capitols or civic structures. The reaction to the failure of a jury trial to convict four police officers accused in the beating of Rodney King that precipitated the 1992 uprising in Los Angeles and the response to the assassination of Martin Luther King, Jr., might appear to be exceptions to this general pattern; but, in both of these circumstances, African Americans were expressing a sense of injustice about the inadequacy of the entire legal system that clearly involves issues of political authority. The slogan "No Justice, No Peace" that began to appear on the streets of Los Angeles in 1992, therefore, may still be a prophetic warning to political leaders who fail to heed growing resistance to official power in ghetto neighborhoods.

Soon after the precipitating incident, a new normative order quickly emerged to govern the conduct of local residents in the communities that experienced ghetto revolts during the 1960s or later. This pattern was consistent with the view that episodes of collective violence are defined by the deliberate repudiation of rules that ordinarily regulate social behavior and the continuing defiance of efforts to reimpose those rules upon the community. Most reports by the mass media and public officials of these events were devoted to condemnation of the expropriation or destruction of private property represented by looting or other attacks on business establishments. Relatively little attention was directed at aspects of this normative consensus which often supported the protection of innocent bystanders and the observance of the "Soul Brother" or other signs that designated stores owned or operated by African Americans. As a result, the general public missed the basic point: that the outbreak of these ghetto revolts fundamentally represented the replacement of the existing social order by a new constellation of social and political values. Whereas the established order is ultimately predicated upon the protection of property as a paramount objective, the normative order that emerged during these uprisings assigned a higher priority not only to the frustrated needs of low-income residents but also to the formation of a sense of community that respected both the commercial activities of members of their own group and the legitimate rights of outsiders. In many respects, the effect of the new order may have only slightly been different from the harm inflicted on the community by the personal violence and illegal acts that occur when the police are technically in control of the area.

Perhaps the most pervasive misconceptions about ghetto violence, however, have revolved about the identification of the businesses that become the targets of looting or destruction during the uprisings. The predominant content of both media and official accounts of the so-called "riots" has tended to portray such actions as random, senseless, and purposeless. Yet neither wanton vandalism nor the destruction of residential property has ever been a major feature of ghetto revolts.

Furthermore, in Detroit and Los Angeles, personal observation informed by knowledgeable residents of the neighborhoods where the violence started disclosed a complex, though clearly detectable pattern on the day following the uprisings. In general, the designation of the stores that became the objects of looting or burning appeared to be determined primarily by the nature of the merchandize sold, the race or ethnicity of the owner or employees, and the reputation or relationship of the business with the community. None of these factors seemed to be decisive. Sometimes one element, such as the race or ethnicity of the owner, appeared to overshadow all other considerations. But there were cases in which the businesses of Latino or Asian American merchants had been spared apparently because of the favorable relationship they had with the surrounding community. And there were also instances in which the stores of African Americans had been damaged due to the attitude that they had displayed toward shoppers. Perhaps most significant, however, was the finding that these patterns were explainable. They were not necessarily the product of spontaneous, chaotic, or aimless behavior. The violence was selective; and, while the activities revealed no evidence of planning in advance, they were organized or structured in terms of discernable social and political objectives.

The transfer of political control that occurred through the creation of a new normative order was, of course, temporary instead of permanent. For a relatively brief period of time before the "normal" social order was restored, however, authoritative decision-making for the community was effectively exercised by crowds on the streets rather than by politicians in government offices. During this interval of what might be called "street violence," many ordinary people in these neighborhoods experienced the exhilarating sense of becoming the masters of their own destiny. A basic theme of the ghetto violence, therefore, was reflected in the perennial quest of people throughout the world for the right to govern themselves. Power was forcibly seized from the government agencies and rested in local residents. Although people were obviously aware that this type of self-government could not continue indefinitely, the dynamism of modern forms of collective violence indicate that the desire to achieve this goal seemed to be an intrinsic aspect of these events. As a result, they can be interpreted as representing an evident, if futile, effort to promote the principles of community autonomy that deserves the designation of "uprisings" or "revolts" instead of mere "riots" or "disorders." And, although the violence frequently spread to nearby cities, they never became part of a national political movement. They remained focused on local conditions and institutions. Hence, they may be appropriately referred to as "civil uprisings."

INTRA-URBAN GOVERNANCE

Although the defining characteristics of the urban violence of the 1960s and the Los Angeles uprisings of 1992 were remarkably similar, the responses to the events revealed marked and significant differences. In the late sixties, the ghetto revolts promoted a vigorous discussion—at least among social scientists—of the concept of community control. In almost all major respects, this proposal was a natural and logical recommendation derived from the principal objectives of the uprisings. Since these incidents disclosed a strong desire by ghetto residents for self-government and for increased participation in decisions affecting their lives, advocates of this concept sought to decentralize political authority to allow many government programs to be placed under the jurisdiction of community assemblies, town meetings, local councils, or other groups at the neighborhood level. Limited attempts to implement these suggestions were made in various cities especially in the 1970s; but these plans floundered largely because the partial decentralization of authority was never accompanied by a commensurate delegation of the resources necessary to make real and important changes in people's lives. Perhaps even more significantly, the principle of community control was hardly ever mentioned by anyone in the aftermath of the Los Angeles revolt of 1992. Instead, attention was concentrated almost exclusively on the private sector and on the effort to rebuild the businesses that had been destroyed during the violence in the hope of restoring needed jobs and economic stimulation to disadvantaged areas of the city.

The difference between the responses to urban violence in the 1960s and in 1992 seemed to reflect a major shift in the parameters of public debate that had occurred between those years. Policy proposals appeared to narrow down traditional liberal-conservative lines and to exclude many recommendations that had been considered previously. In 1992, there were few endorsements of a "Marshall Plan" for American cities that had been prominently supported in the sixties. Liberals focused primarily on attempts to promote economic growth; and the principal difference between them and their opponents was marked by the relative emphasis placed on job training or implements of reduced taxes in the pursuit of this goal. Former Vice-President Dan Quayle's attempt to link the Los Angeles uprising with the pregnancy of Murphy Brown, an unmarried television character, represented a reserved conservative attempt to blame the violence on personal or cultural characteristics that supposedly were not—and would not be—mediated by changes in public policy. Thus the debate about appropriate responses to the Los Angeles uprising has tended to revolve almost exclusively about competing theories of economic growth and a controversy about the efficacy of policy intervention. Such disputes may be an appropriate response to protests or demonstrations, but violence seems to demand the assessment of institutional change. Conspicuously absent form this discussion has been any consideration of proposals to increase political participation by restructuring local government. Yet, because the major characteristics and problems related to the Los Angeles uprising of 1992 had not changed appreciably since the ghetto revolts of the 1960s, there appear to be ample—and compelling—reasons to revive the consideration of alternative forms of community control in the development of a new system of intra-urban governance.

The technique of restructuring local institutions to allow distinct segments of the population to fulfill their objectives is not a new concept in American politics. The device has been used most successfully and extensively by Whites who have sought to preserve their lifestyles and values from the feared influx of social and ethnic minorities by creating a suburban ring on the fungus of the center city. The major effects of suburbanization, of course, were the increased isolation of Whites who left the inner city as a "hollow cow" or an "empty prize" to be captured by a minority leadership that was simultaneously deprived of the tax revenues needed to cope with growing urban problems.

Yet the principles of community control can also be adopted to meet the demands of disadvantaged groups through a variety of arrangements including metropolitan confederations, multiple tiers within city government or other vehicles that would give them greater representation and increased participation in the policy-making process. This approach is consistent with the principal themes expressed in civic uprisings, and it may be necessary to avert further violence; but community control must be explored with considerable caution. Extensive experience, for example, has tended to confirm a basic axiom of local politics: while the decentralization of authority usually inspires increased political participation, the centralization of power improves the likelihood of adopting and implementing programs that can produce significant changes in people's lives. The task is to find a means of resolving the paradox. Although the accomplishment of such an endeavor lies beyond the scope of this analysis, a few relevant considerations may be examined briefly.

First, the creation of decentralized political institutions within urbanized areas might be appropriately based on the principle that they should reflect real and meaningful divisions in the electorate. Thus, it may be necessary to modify the practice of defining governmental jurisdictions exclusively by arbitrary geographic boundaries. As an alternative to this procedure, particular attention could be devoted to the representation of disadvantaged groups that have launched important social movements on the base of ethnicity, gender, sexual orientation, age, and disability. Hardly any of these groups have been able to achieve equitable representation in prominent government positions through existing methods of apportionment. Moreover, while racial or ethnic minorities have often been geographically confined by housing segregation, women are segregated primarily in the workplace rather than by place of residence; and disabled citizens are frequently separated from their non-disabled counterparts by lack of access to public facilities or accommodations. Hence, delegations to higher levels of government from neighborhood jurisdictions within cities could be supplemented by methods such as proportional representation, cumulative voting, or minority vetoes, and by selections from spokespersons from designated "non-geographic" constituencies of disadvantaged groups. The purpose of such a plan for intra-urban governance is, of course, to give an increased voice to the Other, the outsider whose opinions and perspectives are usually neglected or ignored by powerful social or political leaders. Since there are few grounds for the optimistic belief that campaigns in districts containing a preponderance of dominant groups will ever produce an adequate representation of disadvantaged segments of the electorate, some institutional mechanism must be found to ensure that their viewpoints receive appropriate consideration in major decision-making councils of government.

This proposal is based on the assumption that the visible differences between significant segments of the urban population may continue to overshadow their similarities for some time. Perhaps the major unifying feature of groups forming social movements in the second half of the twentieth century is that most of them possess salient physical characteristics which permit them to be differentiated from other portions of society and which have been used as a basis for discrimination for centuries. While some forms of prejudice seem highly resistant to change, other types of bias can be mitigated through public policies. One study comparing African

Americans and Asian Americans, for example, has suggested that the different experience of the latter groups could be attributed at least in part to immigration laws and to their capacity to find a stable niche in specific occupational categories. Until a comprehensive means can be discovered to eradicate the effects of racism, sexism, and physicalism from American society, it would seem prudent to acknowledge the social significance of the physical differences of disadvantage groups and to grant them appropriate recognition in the political process instead of indulging in the pretense that these differences are either inconspicuous or inconsequential.

Second, any system of intra-urban governance must take into account the distinctive social attributes of groups seeking representation. Perhaps a new approach to this issue is indicated by the conservative emphasis on "family values" and by the feminist perspective that "the personal is political." Important segments of the population can be arranged along a continuum of lifestyles including extended families and single parents that provide various levels of services and support. They also reflect different historical or cultural legacies regarding capital accumulation and entrepreneurial activity. Each of these characteristics can be modified by public policy. Yet there is no reason to prescribe any single form of neighborhood government or system of designated representation for all groups. By dismantling a rigid distinction between public and private spheres of activity, local institutions can be adapted to fit the differences in family structures, cultural traditions, and policy impacts experienced by the groups they serve.

Finally, the design of a system of intra-urban governance must consider the nature of the issues to be decided by different levels of government. Regardless of the extent to which civic authority is decentralized, increases in political participation may never be anticipated as long as public debates are confined primarily to the lexicon of incumbent politicians and to the controversy over contrasting philosophies of economic growth. Numerous surveys have revealed that the daily concerns of ordinary people are dominated by worries about their jobs, their health, and their families. To stimulate expanded political involvement, some method must be found to translate policy issues into a vocabulary that is relevant to such everyday problems. The pluralist vision of a world in which the needs of everyone—including disadvantaged groups—can be satisfied through conventional politics and interest group activity may be a futile dream. In addition to a restructuring of local political institutions, new proposals need to be placed on the public agenda. In particular, changes in the capacities of various layers of government to raise necessary tax revenues may be required; and politicians could be compelled to shift from discussion about how to allocate the proceeds of economic growth to a consideration of redistributive policies, in which the needs of disadvantaged groups are met in part by reducing the prior benefits that have been conferred upon privileged segments of society.

Despite the limitation imposed by the existing issues and institutional configurations, there are indicators even in conventional political activity that disadvantaged groups have begun to form important new coalitions and alliances. Significantly, in spite of the tensions between these communities, both Asian Americans and African Americans gave a majority of their ballots to City Councilman Michael Woo in his unsuccessful bid to become Mayor of Los Angeles in 1993. Perhaps even more significant, at both the local and the national levels, citizens who are disadvantaged on the basis of race or ethnicity, gender, sexual orientation, age, or disability, form a majority of the electorate. If appropriate issues and institutional vehicles can be found to stimulate increased participation among a unified bloc of these voters, there is little doubt that they could produce significant and enduring changes in American politics.

CONCLUSION

The American system of federalism provides unusual opportunities for innovation and experimentation. Originally conceived as a method of promoting political stability, the federal principle can also be employed as a device to foster social change. As both the ghetto revolts of the 1960s and the Los Angeles uprising of 1992 indicated, there seems to be a persistent and possibly growing demand for a new form of intra-urban governance based on the decentralization of political authority. Moreover, the same concept can be adopted to satisfy the aspirations of many other groups that have been disadvantaged on the basis of race or ethnicity, gender, sexual orientation, age, or disability. As a result, there appear to be ample grounds for the revival of increased public consideration of these concepts.

Perhaps the greatest danger is that Americans will retreat from the exploration of unfamiliar or creative proposals. In June of 1993, President Bill Clinton exercised a subtle form of censorship by withdrawing Lani Guinier from consideration as Assistant Attorney General because of her discussion of many of the ideas presented in this analysis. He indicated that such thoughts were outside the mainstream of American politics. In the context of civic uprisings, however, increased experimentation with these proposals, especially by disadvantaged groups, may be a crucial means of preserving the democratic process—not only from violent upheavals—but from the gradual erosion of public trust and confidence.

A scene of South Central Los Angeles on April 30th.

The Korea Central Daily

PERIPHERAL EFFECTS: INTERMARRIAGE

Harry H. L. Kitano
Professor of Sociology and Social Welfare
University of California, Los Angeles

Yuko Kawanishi
Postdoctoral Fellow
University of California, Los Angeles

The publicized effects of any dramatic event concentrate on the center of the conflict. For example, the center of an earthquake, where the damage is the greatest, attracts the media; the further away from the epicenter, the less the attention.

Similarly, the coverage of the Los Angeles riots have focused on the minority communities where the damage was the greatest. Broken buildings, looters, uncontrolled fires, and confrontations provided vivid images of the riot, so that an indelible picture of the aftermath of the first Rodney King trial was that of the conflict between rioters and their victims. Major concerns included business losses, deaths and injuries, lack of insurance coverage and the lingering conflict between minority groups who were at the center of the riot.

But, there are also peripheral effects of the riots. One such effect may be on the marital practices of the Korean American community. Specifically, will intermarriage between Koreans and other groups in Los Angeles be affected? Let us examine specific data regarding the marital practices of Koreans in Los Angeles, along with a hypothesis of the effect of the Los Angeles riots of 1992 on these practices.

DEFINITIONS

The term *inmarriage* is used whenever a Korean marries another Korean, whereas when a Korean marries a non-Korean,

Community in Crisis

it is viewed as an *outmarriage*. *Interracial marriage* is used when a Korean outmarries, and the marriage is to a non-Asian.

TABLE 1

Outmarriage Rates of Chinese, Filipino, Japanese, Korean, and Vietnamese, Total and by Gender for 1975, 1977, 1979, 1984, and 1989, Los Angeles County

			Outmarriages		Percent of Outmarriage by Gender	
Ethnicity	Year	Marriages	#	%	Women	Men
Chinese	1989	1,836	622	33.9	63.0	37.0
	1984	1,881	564	30.0	56.6	43.4
	1979	716	295	41.2	56.3	43.7
	1977	650	323	49.7	56.3	43.7
	1975	596	250	44.0	62.2	37.8
Filipino [a]	1989	1,384	565	40.8	74.2	25.8
Japanese	1989	1,134	588	51.9	58.3	41.7
	1984	1,404	719	51.2	60.2	39.8
	1979	764	463	60.6	52.7	47.3
	1977	750	477	63.1	60.6	39.4
	1975	664	364	54.8	53.6	46.4
Korean	1989	1,372	151	11.0	74.8	25.2
	1984	543	47	8.7	78.6	21.4
	1979	334	92	27.6	79.6	20.4
	1977	232	79	34.1	73.4	26.6
	1975	250	65	26.0	63.1	36.9
Vietnamese [b]	1989	555	147	26.5	54.4	45.6
	1984	560	34	6.0	74.7	25.3

[a]Data for the Filipinos is limited to 1989.
[b]Data for the Vietnamese is limited to 1984 and 1989.

Source: Los Angeles County Marriage License Bureau

EARLY STUDIES

Early data from Hawaii indicates that there was a low degree of outmarriage by Koreans up to 1920, followed by a rapid increase starting in the 1920-30 decade which has continued to the present time. Between 1980-89, 76 percent of the Korean females were married to non-Koreans, compared to 47.3 percent of the males (Kitano, et al. 1994).

Harvey and Chung (1980) found that in the 1960s, 80 percent of the Koreans outmarried, in comparison to 40 percent outmarriage rates for Hawaii's other ethnic groups. They explained that a scattered, small ethnic community, with little cohesion, would be forced to look for marital partners outside of their own ethnic group. Further, there was a tolerant racial climate in the state, and the Korean emphasis on education and entering the professions meant heightened interaction with the larger community.

Kitano and Chai (1982) studied outmarriage among Koreans in Los Angeles and found that their rates of outmarriage in the 1970s was consistently in the high 20 percent level. The majority of outmarriages was by Korean females.

Los Angeles County

Table I shows the outmarriage rates of Chinese, Japanese, Filipinos, Koreans and Vietnamese by gender for the years 1975, 1977, 1979, 1984, and 1989. The data are from Los Angeles County and indicate that each group shows different patterns.

The Chinese show an increasing trend in total marriages, starting with 596 in 1975 up to 1,836 in 1989. They also show an increasing trend in the number of outmarriages, with 250 in 1975, and 622 in 1989. However, because of the increased number of total marriages, the actual number of total out marriages has decreased from 44 percent in 1975, to 33.9 percent in 1989. Women outmarry more than men.

The Japanese also show an increase in total marriages, from 664 in 1975 to a high of 1,404 in 1984, and a drop to 1,134 in 1989. The percentage of outmarriages is the highest of any of the Asian groups, ranging from about 51 percent, in 1984 and 1989, to a high of 63.1 percent in 1977. Again, women outmarry more than men.

The Koreans also show an increasing trend in total marriage, starting with 250 in 1975 to 1,372 in 1989. The total number of outmarriages reached a high of 151 in 1989, however, compared to the other Asian groups, the percent who outmarried was still extremely low with rates of only 8.7 percent and 11 percent in the 1980s. As with the Chinese and Japanese, Korean females outmarried more than did Korean males.

The information on both Filipinos and Vietnamese is new and indicates a relatively high rate of outmarriage for relatively new groups.

KOREANS IN 1989

A further analysis of Korean marital practices by gender, age, generation, education and number of marriages in Los Angeles in 1989 is shown on Table II. Generation was the most powerful predictor of outmarriage; for the 15 third-generation females who were married, 100 percent chose non-Korean partners. Similarly for men, outmarriage was significantly related to generation. There were no significant differences in marital practices by age, education, and the number of marriages.

Table II

Mean Age, Education, Generation, and Number of Marriages Between In- and Out-Married Koreans by Gender in Los Angeles County, 1989

	Female		Male	
	Inmarriage	Outmarriage	Inmarriage	Outmarriage
1st Generation (N.%)	608 (86.7)	93 (13.3)*	599 (96.3)	23 (3.7)*
2d Generation (N.%)	3 (37.5)	5 (62.5)	4 (66.7)	2 (33.3)
3rd Generation (N.%)	0 (00.0)	15 (100.0)*	6 (31.6)	13 (68.4)
Age ($\underline{M}$)	28.8	30.0	31.5	28.6
Education[a] ($\underline{M}$)	14.6	14.6	15.3	15.6
# of Marriages[b] ($\underline{M}$)	1.22	1.34	1.24	1.21

[a]Education refers to the number of years of education completed.

[b]Number of Marriages refers to the total number of marriages, including the marriage presently being applied for.

*To control for simultaneous alpha rate, $p < .001$ is used as the significance criterion.

For variables testing proportions as denoted by percentages, test for significance of difference between two proportions is used. For variables testing means, t-test is used.

Generation is related to length of time spent in America and the effects of acculturation. The longer one lives in America, the higher the probability of taking on American ways, especially in the adolescent and post-adolescent years. High school exposes one to the values, language, and life styles of the majority group, and it is difficult for parents to halt the trend towards "Americanization."

Children also grow up in an interracial society, so that there is constant exposure to other groups. In addition, parents, including the mother, often have to work long hours, so that family influence and control over dating and marriage may be lessening.

In summary, the following factors are related to current Korean marital practices:

1. There are no longer anti-miscegenation laws preventing the mixing of "races." Although there remain prejudice and discrimination, the direction is to lessen the barriers in interracial contact.

2. There has been a breakup of the "ghetto," and more integration and mobility in housing. Integration in housing leads to more interracial and inter-ethnic contact. Other areas creating more equal status contact include education and occupation.

3. Traditional Asian perspectives concerning family influences in dating and marriage have changed. Acculturation means following the American model of more freedom of choice.

4. There is a higher degree of tolerance towards outmarriage among younger generations in both the majority and the minority communities.

CONSEQUENCES OF THE LOS ANGELES RIOTS

There are a number of interactive effects concerning the riots and Korean marital practices. One pertains to the supply of new Korean residents—Los Angeles has lost its attractiveness as a place to live. Population growth may be affected for a number of years which will be reflected in a diminishing number of Koreans who will marry in Los Angeles.

However, those Koreans already residents of Los Angeles will continue to acculturate. In addition, generational changes will occur so that the ratio of a descending number of total marriages, continued acculturation and generational changes will be reflected in increasing rates of outmarriage. Therefore, the ratio of outmarriages to total marriages will change, so that it is our hypothesis that one of the peripheral effects of the Los Angeles riots will be increased rates of outmarriage.

There are several factors which may alter the proposed rise in outmarriages. One will be the ability of the Korean community to provide ample opportunities for social contact among young adults of marriageable age. Churches and other organizations that foster social contact between members of the ethnic community provide opportunities for the young to date and marry within the group.

Coupled with increased intra-ethnic social contact will be the ability of parents to play a major role in choosing marital partners, and in helping children achieve and maintain a strong ethnic identity. Increased migration of Koreans will also provide more opportunities for inmarriage.

Perhaps the greatest impetus for staying within the group will be prejudice and discrimination from the dominant society. It was not that long ago that there were anti-miscegenation laws (Kitano, et al., 1994), and restrictions on occupation, education and housing. Hopefully, the changes towards the acceptance of the Korean minority will continue, although one should also realize that increased acceptance will be related to higher rates of outmarriage.

REFERENCES

Harvey, Y. S. L. and S. H. Chung. "The Koreans," in *People and Cultures of Hawaii*. J. McDermott, S. Teng and T. Maretzki, eds.. Honolulu: University of Hawaii Press, 1980, pp. 135-154.

Kitano, H. L., D. Fujino and Y. Takahashi. "Interracial marriage: Where are the Asian Americans and where are they going?" *Handbook of Asian American Psychology*. L. Lee and N. Zane, eds. Newbury Park, CA: Sage Publications, 1994 (in press).

——— and L. K. Chai. "Korean Interracial Marriage." *Journal of Marriage and the Family* 5:2 (1982): 75-89.

——— and W. T. Yeung. "Chinese Interracial Marriage." *Journal of Marriage and the Family* 5:2 (1982): 35-48.

RETHINKING LOS ANGELES

Stephen Toulmin
Henry R. Luce Professor of Multiethnic
and Transnational Studies
University of Southern California

The issues we set out to deal with when we planned the Center for Multiethnic and Transnational Studies are issues that no one can escape nowadays. Every time I turn on NPR, the BBC World Service, or *The MacNeil Lehrer Report*, or pick up a newspaper, I find something which falls directly into the center of our subject matter. We are living in a time that is both stressful and fascinating. For one thing, we have reached the limits of the value of organizing the world on the basis of separate nation states. Every day of our lives we are challenged by issues that require us to think beyond the kinds of political organizations we have been living with for the past two hundred years.

The contemporary city has to rethink its whole mode of operation. But the moment we start looking at how the contemporary multiethnic city works, we find that the problems stretch beyond the city, out across the world. In the situation that developed after April 1992, it was interesting to see where the different affected communities turned for the support they needed to develop and mobilize their own resources. For many people who had come to America—and I, though English, regard myself as a first generation American—it was clear that there was, and is, a continuing belief that, while we build up our networks of friendships, support, and alliance within our place here, there is always the knowledge that we have families and

institutions to which we can turn in critical moments. I know
that for many people in the Korean American community, the
question arose very actively as to where they should look for
support. For them, the option of reaching back to Seoul and
finding the support systems in their connections across the
Pacific gave them strength in a time of crises. It was in some
ways also a challenge, because it underlined one of the
questions central to our discussion: how to strengthen and make
more effective the institutions through which all minority
communities can build a prosperous future for themselves, here
on the ground where they live.

There have been multiethnic cities throughout the history of
the world, from Alexandria and Babylon, to Vienna and
Zanzibar. What is extraordinary about America is that here an
experiment was undertaken, the experiment of attempting to
insure that no one group among these multiethnic populations
would necessarily be permanently superior. And although
America has often stumbled in trying to keep the promises it
made to its immigrant communities, it has never fallen
completely. However much America has failed its immigrant
communities, the conscience of America is always there to be
brought to bear.

Two hundred and twenty years ago, when America's
Founding Fathers talked about the spirit in which the new
republic was to be founded, they understood how to organize a
political entity for a more or less homogeneous population. I
would not for a moment criticize the American Constitution,
which the Founding Fathers produced as a result; I only want to
say that it's fine as far as it goes, but it doesn't go far enough.
Today we live in a different world. We live in a world where
communities are increasingly inhomogeneous, where people of
all kinds come and live alongside one another and hope to be
treated with respect. We are in the process of discovering by
trial and error—and, hopefully, sometimes by success—what
additional institutions we need, what other means we need to
find, what further devices we need to create, which will allow a
very mixed group of people to live together in the same kind of

civic peace that the nation state provided for homogeneous populations between the late seventeenth century and the early twentieth century.

That is one of the intellectual challenges the Center for Multiethnic and Transnational Studies faces; a challenge that we seek to face because it compels us to consider how Los Angeles is not only going to be rebuilt, but rethought. The motto "Rethink LA" is just as important as the motto "Rebuild LA." Yes, we have to rethink it, but we also understand now that to rethink LA is also to rethink the entire world. In facing the new questions of Los Angeles' future, we are facing the questions which will arise again and again in cities around the globe. Hopefully this challenge will allow us to come forward with new ways of organizing our affairs which will fill the gaps in the United States Constitution, gaps which were not gaps in 1787, but become gaps since. Hopefully, it will allow us to complement all those Constitutional protections devised in the 1770s and 1780s with new ones that will insure that all the different kinds of people who make up this wonderful mosaic or rainbow, are able to live as citizens together, giving and receiving the mutual respect to which each and all are entitled.

In finding ways of defending our own interests, we are in an enterprise which requires us also to support and respect the activities of other people who are finding ways of defending their own interests. The defense of each of the constituent communities of a city such as Los Angeles is a defense of the interests of all those communities. It is a task which faces all communities equally, and they learn from alliance, from respecting each others' methods, and from supporting each others' efforts, because none of us fully knows what the governance of a multiethnic city is going to have to be. And in solving this problem for the Korean American community, we can help solve the problems of other communities which, at one time or another and for all kinds of reasons, feel threatened and need to have the assurance that the instruments they have chosen will protect them.

Korea Times, L.A.

May 3rd, 1992   Western and 86th St.

III

TRANSFORMING THE COMMUNITY

Responses to the Riots

Members of Korean Youth Association are positioned on a rooftop to protect a commercial building on 9th St. and Western Ave. on May 4th.

THE KOREAN AMERICAN BAR ASSOCIATION AND THE RIOT

John S. C. Kim, Kim & Andrews
Past President, Korean American Bar Association

Sung J. Hwang, Cromwell & Sullivan

The members of the Korean American Bar Association of Southern California (KABA) helplessly witnessed the tragic events of the L.A. riot, and the apparent hate crimes being inflicted upon their fellow Korean Americans, for three consecutive days. As trained legal professionals, we decided to mobilize our resources to help the Korean American victims in the best way we can—by providing legal assistance. Thus, on May 2, 1992, still in the midst of total chaos and fear, concerned members of KABA gathered at the Oriental Mission Church (OMC) to discuss how we as lawyers would provide legal assistance to the victims. It soon became apparent that the following services would be required of, or incumbent upon, us:

1. Providing a "walk-in" legal clinic to give legal advice on such questions as insurance coverage, lease termination, debtor's rights, and government assistance. KABA provided this service at OMC for about two weeks, commencing May 2, 1992.

2. Establishing a legal aid center for a sustained period of time to represent, or to make referral to a volunteer attorney who can represent, the victims in the more protracted matters (e.g., landlord/tenant dispute). KABA has worked with Public Counsel to establish Urban Recovery Legal Assistance (URLA), a free legal aid center for the victims, in the heart of Koreatown. URLA is still actively operating for the benefit of the victims.

3. Locating appropriate resources (attorneys with the needed expertise) in representing the victims on the larger issues that adversely affect the rights of the victims as a whole. KABA has been coordinating efforts with private and public interest law firms to advocate and/or preserve the rights of the victims in complex legal proceedings.

4. Advocating the concerns and issues of the victims in the mainstream media. For instance, Angela Oh, our then president-elect and now president, spoke forcefully on behalf of the victims and the Korean American community on "Nightline" hosted by Ted Koppel.

Nearly a year has passed since we implemented the above described services. While enormous efforts have been made by the KABA attorneys, having given thousands of *pro bono* hours for these efforts, we are disappointed that the benefits of this legal assistance were often limited because of adverse political forces.

AREAS OF LEGAL SERVICE

Insurance Issues:

It was apparent to us from advising the victims on insurance matters that only a few understood what risks they were insured against, what their coverage amount was, and whether their policies excluded coverage for damages from looting or riots. Actually, most KABA volunteers did not themselves understand insurance coverage law very well at the inception of the program. However, we had "experts" train the volunteer attorneys on the basics of insurance coverage law, and to the extent difficult questions arose, the experts were then consulted at the clinic.

KABA gave advice to some 600-800 victims on insurance coverage issues. We provided them with blank "notice of claim" forms in conjunction with rendering advice on coverage. We also provided them with sample letters to creditors and landlords seeking forbearance.

Most of the victims were under the mistaken belief (apparently due to an inaccurate article in a Korean newspaper) that fire damage caused by a "riot" was excluded from the coverage benefit. We assured them that under California law, at least with respect to fire policies, the carriers were not allowed to make such an exclusion for riot. Also, virtually all of the victim-tenants did not know that, if they had paid their proportionate share of the landlord's premium for the building's coverage, they may be entitled to receive compensation for or replacement of certain tenant improvements (fixtures and betterment). This compensation would be paid by the landlord's carrier.

To our great disappointment, of all the people whose insurance policies were reviewed, more than one-half were underinsured or insured by "offshore" insurance companies that were not licensed in California and were without sufficient assets to pay the claims of their insureds.

1. Inadequate Insurance Coverage

We found that most of the victims had purchased insurance based not on careful consideration of risks and a realistic valuation of their business assets, but on the amount of the insurance premium and the recommendation of their trusted (but later found to be irresponsible) insurance agents. For example, many businesses were insured for much less than the full value of the replacement cost of their insurable assets. Many policies also contained exclusions for risks a reasonably comprehensive insurance policy should insure against. For victims with such problems, KABA was not able to do much more than advise them of the deficiencies in their insurance policies and assist them in filing for government loan/grant programs.

KABA volunteers advised the victims about the feasibility of pursuing claims against the insurance brokers and agents who had: (1) told their victim-insureds that their policies were "comprehensive," (2) sold inadequate policies knowing that their clients did not fully understand that they were left exposed to significant risks, or (3) that the carriers were not licensed in

California. However, we also advised them that, to our knowledge, most brokers and agents who had sold such deficient policies were themselves not insured for professional "errors of omissions" liability.

2. Non-Admitted Offshore Carriers

Perhaps the biggest scandal exposed by the riot was that a substantial number of the Korean American victims were insured by offshore insurance companies that do not have sufficient assets to pay on the claims. Under the California Insurance Code, an insurance carrier that sells policies in California may either be licensed (i.e., "admitted") by the California Department of Insurance (DOI) or sell only limited types of insurance policies as unlicensed (i.e., "non-admitted") carriers. The admitted carriers are required to file reports with the DOI and are subject to the supervisory authority of the DOI. A state-guaranteed fund is set up to make payments on policies written by admitted carriers that become insolvent.

Non-admitted carriers, however, are not subject to the supervision of the DOI, nor are their policies guaranteed by a state fund, as there are no DOI reserve requirements for non-admitted carriers. To sell insurance in California, a carrier needs only to be duly organized in its home jurisdiction and qualified to do business in California. We were informed that the reason for allowing such companies to sell insurance is that admitted carriers were choosing not to write insurance in market segments considered to be high risk. Insurance sold by non-admitted carriers is referred to as "surplus line" because they were supposed to sell insurance only in market segments lacking appropriate coverage.

In practice, the surplus line system has turned out to be a disaster. First, because many admitted carriers have chosen to "redline" certain areas of California's inner cities, "surplus line" has come to include insurance, such as property damage and premises liability insurance for commercial enterprises, that should have been available from admitted carriers. Second, because the DOI does not require non-admitted carriers to meet any financial standards, many non-admitted carriers with inadequate capitalization or reserves have aggressively marketed their policies in California. The California Insurance Code specifically prohibits non-admitted carriers from selling insurance at rates lower than those offered by admitted carriers. However, because of a lack of supervision by the DOI and the unwillingness of the brokers and agents to comply with this rule, many non-admitted carriers marketed their policies with premium levels much lower than would be sufficient to support the risks they were underwriting.

Of course, not all non-admitted carriers were so reckless. Most non-admitted carriers that are incorporated in other states in the U.S. are subject to the supervision of insurance authorities of their home states with respect to capitalization and reserve requirements. Accordingly, such carriers did pay, or are expected to pay, the riot-related claims. Some off-shore carriers, such as Lloyd's of London, exercised prudent underwriting practices and were able to pay the claims. However, most non-admitted carriers that sold insurance in Koreatown and south central L.A. were organized in Caribbean jurisdictions and other parts of the world not subject to competent supervision by their respective governments.

Presently, KABA is working to assist the victims who were insured by fiscally irresponsible offshore carriers. On a *pro bono* basis, KABA is investigating the feasibility of a suit against such carriers, hoping to recover whatever compensation possible. KABA is aided in its efforts by a private law firm, by the Asian Pacific American Legal Center (APALC), and by URLA.

3. Redlining Practices of Admitted Carriers

We believe the underlying cause for the proliferation of non-admitted carriers in Koreatown and south central L.A. is the *de facto* "redlining" practiced by admitted carriers in those areas. A common complaint among the Korean American victims was that even those business owners who understood the difference between admitted versus non-admitted carriers were often unable to procure insurance from admitted carriers for their businesses. Many of the insurance agents in Koreatown confirmed that they were unable to procure insurance for businesses in Koreatown and south central L.A. because the admitted carriers simply refused to write insurance in those areas.

We believe that the DOI has the responsibility to prevent or reduce the now apparent hazards of the redlining practice. At the very least, the DOI has the responsibility to educate citizens within redlined areas about the risks involved in procuring insurance from non-admitted carriers.

LEASE TERMINATION ISSUES

The victims, with or without insurance alike, had concerns about their commercial leases, as the vast majority of them were tenants. We counseled them as to the rights and obligations of both tenant-victims and landlords. To the extent that workouts or amendments to the leases became necessary, KABA volunteers often took the matter to their respective offices on a *pro bono* basis. Generally, we found that most landlords were quite willing to ignore the automatic termination provisions in their leases in favor of helping the tenant-victims rebuild.

In those cases where landlords commenced unlawful detainer proceedings, URLA and/or outside volunteer attorneys successfully represented the tenant-victims being evicted. In other cases, the tenant-victims took the opportunity to cancel an unfavorable lease in hopes of relocating to a different location with more favorable terms.

DEBTOR'S RIGHTS ISSUES

The victims whose ability to meet their debt payments were suddenly cut off were devastated in the fear that they would lose their homes, cars, and other leveraged assets. While programs of the Federal Emergency Management Agency (FEMA), other government agencies, and private agencies provided temporary help, the victim-debtors were faced with financial collapse, and were rapidly losing their means of paying their debts.

We advised the victim-debtors of their rights as consumers with respect to debts or loans, particularly the protection and benefits they have under the anti-deficiency statutes relating to real property ownerships. Many of the victims received cooperation from their lenders, particularly from the Korean American community banks. However, we are now informed that a very significant number of the victims either have lost their properties by foreclosure or repossession, or are facing the same.

SBA AND FEMA

KABA, in conjunction with the Korean American CPA Society, generally assisted the victims in the preparation of their applications for programs of Small Business Administration (SBA) and/or FEMA. Currently, URLA is assisting the victims in the appeal of the SBA and/or FEMA rejections.

On a national level, KABA is coordinating efforts with certain private and public interest law firms throughout the county in the proposed action against FEMA as part of a class action with the victims of the Florida, Hawaii and Oakland disasters, alleging that FEMA has failed to perform its duties in a competent, nondiscriminatory manner.

LEGAL AID CENTER (URLA)

We learned from our experience at OMC that those victims who came to see us would need continued legal advice and representation not only in areas of insurance but also in areas of landlord-tenant relations, debtor's rights, land use regulations and other real estate issues. KABA concluded that the only way to effectively coordinate and meet the overwhelming demand for free legal services was to establish a legal aid center for the victims, to be staffed by attorneys who are bilingual or are willing to work with interpreters. KABA found a willing partner in this effort in Public Counsel, the most prominent public interest law firm in California. Accordingly, KABA and Public Counsel (along with certain other organizations) jointly set up URLA, a multicultural legal services center as the vehicle to meet the legal needs of victims of all colors for a sustained period of time.

Through URLA, KABA was able to place many Korean American victims with individual attorneys and law firms who had responded to the call for *pro bono* legal services. Many KABA volunteers each took on several of the victims as *pro bono* clients. APALC contributed to URLA a fully bilingual Korean American paralegal who coordinated the works of KABA volunteer attorneys and Korean American law student volunteers. KABA is deeply thankful to Public Counsel and APALC for their generous assistance in the legal relief efforts for the Korean American victims.

IMPACT ISSUES

Conditional Use Permits and Zoning Problems

There are many Korean Americans who own and operate grocery or liquor stores that sell alcoholic beverages for off-premises consumption in the south central Los Angeles area. The presence of Korean American merchants in areas predominantly populated by African Americans has long been a source of racial tension in Los Angeles. Stores in these neighborhoods were especially hard hit during the riot.

The stores that sell alcoholic beverages are regulated at three different levels. The State of California requires such stores to obtain a license from the California Department of Alcoholic Beverage Control (ABC). Such stores also must obtain a Conditional Use Permit from the City of Los Angeles and comply with the city zoning regulations.

State law requires that the holder of an ABC license surrender the license if the premises for which the license was issued is destroyed and reapply for the license upon reconstruction. There are certain timing requirements for both the surrender and the re-establishment of the license. KABA organized a workshop for the victims and invited officials from the ABC. The state officials were very cooperative in explaining the details of the surrender and re-application process for an ABC license and granted special waivers of deadline requirements for the victims.

Victims who owned businesses that required Conditional Use Permits from the City have had to reapply for their Conditional Use Permits for the re-establishment of their businesses. In order to rebuild their stores, the business owners were required to go through a series of public hearings that mandated them to prove that their stores were operating in conformity with the welfare of the neighborhood. Many KABA attorneys have advised and represented those store owners seeking to reestablish their businesses.

In theory, the requirement that any business establishment operate in conformity with the goals of the neighborhood's welfare is a sound one. In practice, however, KABA attorneys have found that the determination of "neighborhood welfare" has been made on subjective and political considerations rather than on objective criteria. As a result, many Korean American victims have found that, due to the political influence of community activists and certain elected officials (with whose opinion a substantial number of south central residents disagree), the City of Los Angeles is predisposed to imposing conditions on the re-establishment of their businesses so as to make them economically not viable. Some of the conditions are: (1) armed security guards during business hours, (2) a prohibition against selling ice, (3) restrictions on the hours of operation, and (4) a prohibition against selling individual containers of alcoholic beverages.

The merchant-victims who have had to go through the public hearing process found themselves being blamed for a host of problems in their neighborhoods, including crime, traffic congestion and, in some cases, unemployment. They have been accused by certain groups and politicians of being one of the causes of the riot. The effect of such accusations has been that many victims are discouraged from pursuing their vested rights to their property. Not only have KABA attorneys advised and represented victims through the public hearing process, but also have acted as public advocates to combat the distorted, negative perceptions some people have of Korean American store owners.

In addition, many of the stores that were destroyed were located in areas that were downzoned from "commercial" to "residential". The Los Angeles Zoning Department's position has been that each store owner needs to obtain a zoning variance in order to rebuild. Because it is a discretionary remedy on the part of the city, the decision to grant variance for a particular site is subject to a number of factors, including, as we found out during the process, political influence. In addition, KABA attorneys who have been advising and representing those applicants for variance believe that the Zoning Department is interpreting the relevant laws and regulations incorrectly. As a consequence, to date none of the Korean American applicants have been successful in obtaining the relief they requested.

LEGISLATIVE ISSUES

In July of 1992, a California assembly member from Los Angles introduced legislation (AB-40X) that would have made it very difficult for the ABC licensed owners of stores destroyed during the riot to reapply for their licenses by proposing procedural restrictions and numerical limits on ABC licenses. KABA attorneys advised and represented Korean American victims in their successful defeat of the proposed AB-40X.

KABA attorneys are also currently involved with a group of community organizations working to propose a bill in the state legislature to provide residential property tax relief to the victims. We thank all the elected officials, especially

Assemblyman Louis Caldera, State Senator Art Torres and those state representatives who have shown an interest in this issue.

CIVIL RIGHTS LAWSUIT

At the request of KABA, a northern California law firm undertook and completed comprehensive legal research into the issue of whether the victims can recover against the local governments for allegedly violating their civil rights (i.e., failing to provide police and fire protection or providing them in a discriminatory manner). The legal memorandum on the research was delivered to the victim groups for their consideration as to whether they desire to pursue the claims for such violation, including the violation of the fundamental rights under the Equal Protection Clause of the U.S. Constitution. The KABA attorneys have been actively involved in gathering and investigating the facts in preparation of the possible action.

FUTURE ACTIONS

To date, the *pro bono* activities of KABA have been largely on an individual, *ad hoc* basis. KABA is realizing that the magnitude of legal assistance still needed by the victims, as well as the complexities of the issues involved, requires a more concerted and systematic effort not only on the part of KABA attorneys but on the part of Korean American community and political organizations, as well. The following areas or issues will need continued legal assistance:

(i) Continue the legal assistance to the victims in their individual legal problems (i.e., the work currently being done by URLA);

(ii) Pursue possible remedies against non-admitted, offshore insurance carriers;

(iii) Continue coordinating efforts in pursuit of legal action against FEMA;

(iv) Pursue possible recourse against the City of Los Angeles for violations of the U.S. constitutional rights of the victims in being denied their right to rebuild their businesses, and incorrect interpretations of the city ordinance regarding zoning variances;

(v) Continue monitoring efforts to safeguard the interests of victims in matters before the California State Legislature;

(vi) Provide assistance to those victims pursuing their claims for damages resulting from the local government's violation of the victims' civil rights (Equal Protection Clause of the U.S. Constitution);

(vii) Continue to articulate to the mainstream media the concerns of, and issues affecting, the Korean American community in general and the riot victims in particular.

THE ROLE OF KOREAN CHURCHES IN THE COMMUNITY

Chung Keun Lee
Dean, World Mission Theological Seminary

In Asian culture, religion is understood as the supreme teaching, as *chongkyo* indicates. This understanding seems to be parallel in its essence with the definition of religion by Paul Tillich, a distinguished theologian of this century: "Religion is the state of ultimate concern, a concern which qualifies all other concerns as preliminary and which itself contains the answer to the question of the meaning of our life.... The predominant religious name for the content of such concern is God—a god or gods.[1]"

Tillich understands religion not only in terms of the ultimate concern, but also as the answer to the ultimate human problem. Buddhism, for example, began when Guatama searched for the answers to the basic human problems of life, aging, illness, and death. Although there are various theories on why religion has come about, one important motive was the search for the answer to the ultimate problems of human beings, individually and collectively. In any religion, it is believed that the supreme beings supply some supernatural power to solve these problems, especially during times of crises.

From a socio-cultural perspective, Christianity is taken as a religion. Christianity has also provided the answer to the

---

[1] Paul Tillich, *Christianity and the Encounter of the World Religions* (New York: Columbia University Press, 1963), 4-5.

fundamental problems of human beings, as individuals and as collective groups. Christianity responds positively to the physical, psychological and spiritual problems of individuals.

Moreover, Christianity has participated aggressively in solving community and national problems. From the outset of Christianity in Korea, for example, Christians have committed themselves to modernization, independence, and the unification of their nation. Christian churches have established schools, from which most of the national leaders have received their education, as well as hospitals, which have been the center for the Westernization of Korean society.

The Korean Independence Movement is a model in Korean history demonstrating the response of religions to national crises. During the Japanese occupation, Korea was suffering under immense hardships imposed by the Japanese Military Government. Consequently, independence and freedom were the primary goals of all Koreans. The Movement was led mainly by Christianity and Chontokyo, the latter being a mixture of Christianity and Korean religious ethics. Also there was strong support from Buddhism and Confucianism. Of the thirty-three signers of the Independence Declaration, fifteen were Christians, fifteen Chontokyo, and three Buddhists[2]. At that time, the number of church members in Korea was a little over one percent of the total population of twenty million. Christianity was a minority numerically, but a majority in its influence at the time of national crisis.

The response of Christianity to national challenges extended to the democratization and unification of Korea following World War II. In many ways, Christian churches and their leaders pioneered and steered these movements, sometimes in the face of severe punishment.

RELIGION IN THE RANKS OF KOREAN AMERICANS

Among the first immigrants from Korea to Hawaii in 1903, about half of the ninety-seven passengers were church

---

[2] Taikpoo Chun, *The History of Church Development in Korea* (in Korean; Seoul: The Christian Literature Society, 1987), 203. The number of Christians in 1919 was thought to be 234,703.

members[3]. Advertising was done through churches around the ports of Inchon. Also, Christians knew more about America than others. At the time, the ratio of Christians to the total population of Korea was less than 0.05 percent.

Korean American churches began with the Korean immigrants to America. The first church was founded for Korean laborers of the sugar cane fields in Hawaii on July 4, 1903[4]. Since the beginning, there have been churches wherever Korean Americans resided. A church was established in Los Angeles by Korean Americans in 1904, one in San Francisco in 1905, one in Chicago in 1919 and one in New York in 1921.

Since 1968, both the number of Korean churches and the number of Korean immigrants in America have increased considerably. In 1950, there were less than twenty Korean American local churches in the United States[5]. Today, it is estimated that there are about 2,700 local Korean churches in the United States and Canada, which amounts to one church for every 400 Korean Americans. According to estimates, one-third of the Korean American population of the local Korean churches of the United States and Canada resides in Southern California.

In the Korean American community, Christian churches have played various roles throughout their history. In addition to the proper roles of religion as discussed above, Korean American churches have served the members individually, and the community at large, by reinforcing their identity, educating them about Korean culture, especially the Korean language, introducing new immigrants to American culture, teaching English, providing needed services, disseminating information, counseling and job-placement, to name a few. To first-

---

[3] Soo Hoon Ahn, *History of the Development of the Korean Evangelical Church* (in Korean; Seoul: Council of the Korean Evangelical Church in America, 1981), 338-340.

[4] Warren Y. Kim, *The History of the Fifty Years of Koreans in America* (in Korean; Reedley, CA.: N/P, 1959), 40ff.

[5] Ibid., 46.

generation immigrants, every phase of American life is a crisis due to culture shock.

As the role of churches has been prominent from the outset of American history, Korean American churches have responded to the challenge aggressively. Before World War II, these churches had become the center of the struggle for liberation from the Japanese Military Government. Among other things, churches had convened prayer meetings, collected money for the financial support of freedom movements, encouraged their members to participate in the war as U.S. servicemen, and publicized the cause of Korean liberation. The churches have been an important seedbed for nurturing Korean national leaders, not only in politics but also in technology and the arts.

The Los Angeles riot, which occurred on April 29, 1992, brought a horrifying shock to Korean Americans. It was gravely serious to Korean Americans because it was the first experience of such civil unrest for most of them, and also because it was related to ethnic conflicts. Since Korea is a mono-racial society, most Korean Americans have not experienced living in a multi-ethnic context. Understandably, the riot and its aftermath had a serious psychological, economic, and social impact.

During the past year, Korean American churches have taken an active role in healing the trauma that resulted; helping to turn a crisis into an opportunity. "Consider it all joy, my brethren, when you encounter various trials" (James 1:2). "In the world you have tribulation, but take courage; I have overcome the world" (John 16:33b). "Love your enemies, and pray for those who persecute you" (Matthew 5:44). "Forgive your brother when he sins against you up to seventy times seven" (Matthew 18:21-22). These texts from the Bible are suitable for preaching.

The church leaders basically understand the riot as an opportunity to discipline ourselves, to love members of other ethnic groups, especially African Americans, to do more work for evangelizing other ethnic groups, and to become active in public-policy making. The mainstream of preaching within the church has been in line with this understanding.

Prayer and counseling have been a powerful avenue for healing psychological crises. Ministers and church members pray and encourage those members who lost their businesses.

Also, prayer and counseling are needed for all Korean Americans who harbor strong fear and panic caused by the riot.

The churches have financially supported the members who have lost their businesses, properties and jobs. The churches have collected money in each local church for their own members. However, there has been financial support from other Christian churches and organizations located in New York, in Seoul, Korea, and in other countries. Even Japanese churches in Southern California have sent financial assistance. This financial support helps not only within the realm of economics, but also in the recovery of morale.

Churches have performed other services, including providing documentation, information, translations, and distributing food. To soften the emotional conflict between African Americans and Asian Americans, the churches have carried out some challenging projects, including providing scholarships for African American students, employing African American youths as church staff, and providing travel to Korea for African American community leaders.

THE FUTURE

Now, a little more than one year after the riot, it is agreed that the most important task is to consider how to prevent such an event from recurring. Have we found the fundamental causes of the riot? Have we started to remove these causes? In the first section of this paper, it is suggested that religion is one way to answer ultimate problems.

The fundamental causes of the riot are listed below. (The order does not correspond to importance. These findings are not based on any scientific analysis, but are the results of surveying various articles on the riot):

1. Malfunction of police and city administration
2. Racial discrimination as in the Rodney King case
3. Poverty and unemployment
4. Gang activities and the high tide of crime
5. The keeping and bearing of arms (U. S. Constitution, Amendment II)
6. Low moral consciousness
7. Undocumented people

8. Emotional conflicts between African Americans and
   Asian Americans
9. Failure of value-free school education

Regarding the malfunction of police and city administration, poverty and unemployment, the keeping and bearing of arms, and undocumented people, churches do not have any tools for a direct solution. Churches may take the role of pressure groups in the policy-making process. When other organizations lead the way to abolish the freedom of keeping and bearing arms, churches can cooperate.

The major role expected from the community may be more related to reducing organized crime, promoting moral consciousness, softening emotional conflicts, and condemning racial discrimination. That role, however, cannot be effectively realized without cooperation from other communities.

In general, Korean American churches favor the integration movement of Martin Luther King, Jr., over the segregation movement of Malcolm X.[6] Reconciliation is the basic ideology in Christianity; churches in different communities can and must provide a common ground for the foundation of the visible Kingdom of God on the Earth, in which the wolf dwells with the lamb (Isiah 11:6). Churches are to be the stronghold for the removal of discrimination, prejudice, hate, conflict, and organized crime, and for the reinforcement and promotion of love, cooperation, moral consciousness, and education.

We are not optimistic concerning the solutions to the problems which were raised by the riot. However, the riot has awakened Korean American churches in that both their leaders and members are aware that it is very urgent to have both internal reformation and external reformation. For internal reformation, the churches proclaim repentance, consolation, reconciliation, and sanctification. For external reformation, the churches must actively lead moral-rearmament movements. To bring about a social reformation, it will be necessary to communicate and cooperate with the churches of other communities as well.

---

[6] James H. Cone. *Martin & Malcolm & America* (Maryknoll: Orbis 1991), 16.

KOREAN AMERICAN RIOT VICTIMS: A MENTAL HEALTH CENTER'S RESPONSE

Mikyong Kim-Goh, Ph.D., LCSW
Human Services Program
California State University, Fullerton

Theresa Kyunghoi Kim-Moon, M.D.
Riverside County Department of Mental Health

Jiun Shin, R.N., M.H.N.
Asian/Pacific Counseling & Treatment Center, Los Angeles

Chong Suh, Ph.D.
Asian/Pacific Counseling & Treatment Center, Los Angeles

In April 1992, Los Angeles experienced the worst urban disturbance in modern U.S. history. During the first five days of the riot, 53 people were killed and 2,393 people sustained bodily injury (*Los Angeles Times*, November 19, 1992). Aside from the more obvious need for assistance for practical matters such as food, housing, and financial aid, the Los Angeles civil disturbance created critical needs for various mental health services for victims. The overwhelming emotional trauma and psychological damages were so intense that government and community agencies immediately began to address the need for crisis mental health intervention services.

The Federal Emergency Management Agency (FEMA) granted the initial funds for crisis counseling. This, at the time, was the largest amount for crisis counseling ever issued by that agency. In fact, it was the first time that FEMA provided the funding for crisis counseling for the victims of a man-made disaster (*Los Angeles Times*, August 13, 1993).

While many ethnic groups suffered losses in the riot, one group, that of Korean American merchants, was impacted far out of proportion to their numbers in the general population. Although Korean Americans comprise less than 2 percent of the total population in Los Angeles County (U.S. Bureau of Census, 1990), this group alone incurred almost 40 percent of the total damages from the riot (Ong and Hee, 1993). More than 2,000 Korean American-owned businesses were destroyed, burned and/or looted, and approximately $360 million worth of damage was incurred by this group. In addressing the mental health services needs of the Korean American victims, tremendous difficulties have emerged in organizing and providing services for this specific group. While the number of Korean victims was disproportionately large, there were very few mental health professionals bilingual in Korean and English and/or bicultural. In addition, the Korean American community is a relatively new immigrant society which lacks resources and support service systems.

A recent review of reports on the mental health effects of disasters revealed that the impacts of human-made disasters tend to persist longer than those of natural disasters (Solomon and Green, 1992). Most stress reactions from natural disasters appear to abate by about 16 months (Bravo et al., 1990; Steinglass and Gerrity, 1990), whereas negative effects from human-made disasters often persist for years (Baum et al., 1983; Green et al., 1990). The literature on traumatic stress has increased dramatically since Post-Traumatic Stress Disorder (PTSD) was formally recognized in the DSM-III (American Psychiatric Association, 1980; Saigh, 1992).

However, the research on the phenomenology of human-induced PTSD has been limited primarily to Vietnam veterans (Birkhimer, DeVane, and Muniz, 1985; Lindy, Grace, and Green, 1984) and rape victims (Burgess and Holmstrom, 1974; Kilpatrick, 1983). In fact, despite the widespread and crosscultural scope of civil disturbances, only a handful of studies have examined the psychological effects of riots.

Some of the existing research has suggested that rioting does not lead to enduring psychological distress (Fishbain, Aldrich, Goldberg, and Duncan, 1991; Greenley, Gillespie, and Jacob, 1975). Greenley et al. (1975) compared symptom levels of 938 adults living in New Haven, Connecticut, where racial rioting occurred. They found that a decrease in distress was associated with the riot. Greenley et al. posited that the decreased symptom levels were due to an increase in social cohesion. More recently, Fishbain, Aldrich, Goldberg, and Duncan (1991) found no significant increase in requests for psychiatric emergency services after the riot.

The above findings may be partially due to a sampling bias in that the researchers did not differentiate people who were personally affected, e.g., sustaining financial loss or physical injury, from those who were indirectly affected by virtue of living in the riot-affected community. Inasmuch as a dose-response traumatization pattern, i.e., individual post-disaster psychiatric morbidity, is usually proportional to the amount of stress experienced as a result of a disaster (McFarlane, 1986), it is reasonable to assume that the directly affected victims will be more likely to experience severe psychiatric morbidity than the general community sample. In fact, a recent study of 202 Korean American victims of the L.A. riot indicated that the majority of them were severely distressed, and that 75 percent of the sample met the criteria for being diagnosed as suffering from PTSD (Kim-Goh, Suh, Blake, and Hiley-Young, 1993).

The objective of this paper is to describe the intense, collective efforts of Korean American mental health professionals and paraprofessional crisis workers to provide mental health services to the Korean American community and particularly to the directly impacted victims. The funding was provided by FEMA, but administered by the L.A. County Department of Mental Health as Project REBOUND, mentioned above. The setting for most of the activities described here was the Asian/Pacific Counseling and Treatment Center (APCTC), a multiethnic and multilingual mental health center serving the Asian/Pacific Islander and Indochinese communities of Los Angeles County. Located in the center of Koreatown, APCTC, with 15 years of history, is the largest Asian Pacific mental health agency in the country.

APCTC'S RESPONSE TO THE DISASTER

Immediately following the riot, two authors of this paper (Kim-Goh and Suh) helped mobilize the existing Korean American mental health workers in the community and graduate social work students from outside in order to organize volunteer efforts to help the victims deal with trauma. These volunteer workers were dispatched to the various disaster assistance centers primarily to provide debriefing and mental health referral services to the affected victims. With the funding from FEMA, APCTC was soon able to hire full-time crisis workers.

In total, 36 workers, including crisis counselors, community outreach workers, and psychiatrists were involved in the disaster counseling program at APCTC during the 18 month program period between May 1992 and November 1993. Although the majority of the staff were Korean Americans (95% of the clients were also Koreans), the disaster counseling staff were multiethnic, including Hispanic, White, and African American workers. Due to the shortage of bilingual/bicultural professionals, some of the Korean staff were recruited from San Diego and Riverside Counties.

In order to train and sensitize the workers about disaster counseling and the impact of trauma, the Center received support from other established disaster training groups. The Burlington Group, a private psychological consulting firm, offered staff training in debriefing and recording the general mental health impacts of the disaster. Another group of experts from the National Research Center on PTSD in Menlo Park provided an intensive two-day training session on various areas of disaster counseling including assessment, diagnostic criteria for PTSD, and brief treatment.

By the time Project REBOUND was terminated, the Center had served over 630 victims of the riot. Among them, 95 percent were Koreans and the remaining included Hispanic, Chinese, and Filipino clients. Forty-nine percent were male, 51 percent were female.

Traditionally, Koreans have a tendency not to seek psychiatric treatment in order to avoid being subjected to cultural bias and the stigma attached to mental illness. Provision of much information regarding PTSD symptoms by the crisis workers has encouraged the victims to get much needed mental help. The crisis workers made extensive outreach efforts to alert the victims to potential psychological impacts of trauma so that they could benefit from early intervention. They sent letters to all the identifiable victims, made telephone contacts with the victims, and informed Korean pastors in the community of the services available to the victims. On-site counseling was also provided for the victims who were not able to come to the Center due to lack of transportation, severe depression, or inability to be away from their business. The on-site counseling occurred in the victims' residence, business site, e.g., swapmeet, victims' association office, food distribution center, neighborhood school, or church. Community outreach services were also conducted using mass media such as various Korean and other ethnic radio, TV, and newspapers. Throughout the year, conferences focusing on the mental health needs of the victims were held for the various sectors of the community. They were participated in by religious leaders, leaders of victims' organizations, victims who were parents of small children, and Korean paraprofessionals who were working in various human services agencies.

CLINICAL ISSUES AND SOCIOCULTURAL CONSIDERATIONS IN TREATMENT

The victims of the riot reacted with rage, which came at the expense of their mental and physical health. During the first few months after the riot, anxiety symptoms related to hyperarousal were most prevalent. Almost every client who sought treatment suffered from nightmares, exaggerated startle responses, insomnia, and family dysfunction. Somatic symptoms, such as oppressive and heavy feelings in the throat, headaches, chest palpitations, and indigestion, were also common. By the time they were seen by a psychiatrist, many had already been on medication regimens. Some of them had also tried Oriental herbal medicine and acupuncture, but few had found relief.

The first group of clients, who sought treatment soon after the riot, were noted to be well informed and willing to utilize social resources to their benefit. Most of them were quite vocal about their suffering and anger. Ventilation of anger and frustration in a supportive group setting were most effective in acute emotional crisis resolution. As expected, this group of victims was very reluctant to take medication. Despite the immediate effectiveness of medication, most patients managed to stretch their small supply of medication for months. For them, one or two visits were often sufficient to meet their medication needs.

The second group of patients tended to have certain predispositions and risk factors, and because of that needed continuous follow-up individual sessions and medication treatment. Rigid and strict personality traits, excessive dependency needs, chronic lack of family support dating back to their childhood, and histories of previous victimization were good indicators among this group of psychopathology. Along with case management services, clinical intervention with couples or families was provided for this group.

The last group consisted of patients who were seeking mental health services for the first time several months after the riot. This group of patients was more likely to be suffering from delayed symptoms of PTSD. Although their symptoms were quite severe, the clients in this group typically denied their emotional needs and psychiatric symptoms.

Among Koreans and Korean Americans, there are certain cultural restraints in emotional expression. The higher one's social class, the more measures of "face saving" are expected.

No matter what type of crisis one is experiencing, the individual is expected to maintain proper mannerisms and perform well-defined roles.

However, these culturally reinforced Korean ways of restraining oneself and respecting authorities were not compatible with the skills necessary to cope with a major disaster such as the riot. As a result, the feelings of guilt and shame, as well as anger, were often expressed through various symptoms, such as anxiety attacks, alcohol abuse, or violent behavior.

Until the outbreak of the riot, many Korean Americans denied the dangers in doing business in the inner city. Most of them were willing to endure long hours, lack of social contact, and repetitious menial tasks in hopes of achieving the "American dream." However, the riot dissolved their usual defenses—denial and internal suppressions—in a most violent and degrading fashion, and the victims were left destitute and traumatized.

Many of the clients who were suffering from PTSD symptoms had already been victimized by the tumultuous history of their old country. These were powerless people whose lives were stained with personal losses and tragedies through the Japanese colonization of Korea, the Korean War, and oppression under the rule of the military government. They were not free to talk about their experiences, let alone their emotional pain, if they were to avoid systemic persecution. Direct or indirect exposure to the L.A. riot inevitably precipitated recurrent symptoms of PTSD among this group.

As the acute symptoms were alleviated, longer lasting behavioral tendencies emerged in some victims. Aloofness, emotional detachment, helplessness, extreme dependency, and avoidance of social interaction would further impair their personal, social, and occupational functioning. Many began to regret their decision to immigrate to the U.S. in the first place, and seriously considered returning to their native country for good.

Termination of the treatment program stirred mixed feelings among both the disaster workers and the clients. The workers, overwhelmed by heavy case loads and the intensity of the patients' feelings, were often at risk of overidentifying with the victims and thereby losing their sense of therapeutic objectivity. There was no ready solution to the predicaments that the victims were in, and a sense of hopelessness would prevail among the workers as well as the clients from time to time. However, the much described "burn-out syndrome" of crisis workers was not frequently observed. The daily debriefing sessions for the workers at the Center were thought to be extremely important and helpful in preventing it.

CONCLUSION

The Center's efforts to reduce the impact of the trauma through crisis intervention and clinical work have been largely well received by the Korean American community. The unique traditional qualities of Koreans, i.e., warm and close interpersonal relationships, interdependency, and perseverance, seemed to have played a significant role in helping the victims cope in times of crisis. Despite the healing process that took place after the riot, larger social and structural issues still remain and will continue to challenge mental health workers in providing services to the victims.

REFERENCES

American Psychiatric Association (1980). *Diagnostic and Statistical Manual of Mental Disorders.* 3rd ed. Washington, DC: American Psychiatric Association.

Baum, A., R. J. Gatchel, and M. A. Schaeffer (1983). "Emotional, Behavioral, and Phychological Effects of Chronic Stress at Three Mile Island." *Journal of Consulting and Clinical Psychology*, 51: 565-572.

Birkhimer, L.J., C. L. DeVane, and C. E. Muniz (1985). "Post- Traumatic Stress Disorder: Characteristics and Pharmacological Response in the Veteran Population." *Comprehensive Psychiatry*, 26: 304-310.

Bravo, M., M. Rubio-Stipec, G. L. Canino, M. A. Woodbury, and J. C. Ribera (1990). "The Psychological Sequelae of Disaster Stress Prospectively and Retrospectively Evaluated." *American Journal of Community Psychology*, 18: 661-680.

Burgess, A. W. and L. L. Holmstrom (1974). "Rape Trauma Syndrome." *American Journal of Psychiatry*, 131: 981-986.

Fishbain, D. A., T. E. Aldrich, M. Goldberg, and R. C. Duncan (1991). "Impact of a Human Made Disaster on the Utilization Pattern of a Psychiatric Emergency Service." *Journal of Nervous and Mental Disease*, 179: 162-166.

Green, B. L., M.C. Grace, J. D. Lindy, G. C. Glaser, A. C. Leonard, and P. L. Kramer (1990). "Buffalo Creek Survivals in the Second Decade: Comparison with Unexposed and Non-Litigant Groups." *Journal of Applied Social Psychology*, 20: 1039-1050.

Greenley, B. L., M. A. Gillespie, and J. L. Jacob (1975). "A Race Riot's Effect on Psychological Symptoms." *Archives of General Psychiatry*, 32: 1189-1195.

Kilpatrick, D. G. (1983). "Rape Victims: Detection, Assessment and Treatment." *Clinical Psychologist*, 36: 92-95.

Kim-Goh, M., C. Suh, D. Blake, and B. Hiley-Young (1993). "The Psychological Impact of the Los Angeles Riots on Korean American Victims and Implications for Treatment." Unpublished manuscript.

Lindy, J. D., M. C. Grace, and B. L. Green (1984). "Building a Conceptual Bridge between Civilian Trauma and War Trauma: Preliminary Psychological Findings from a Clinical Sample of Vietnam Veterans." In B. Der Kolk, ed., *Post-Traumatic Stress Disorder: Psychological and Biological Sequelae*, pp. 43-57. Washington, DC: American Psychiatric Press.

Los Angeles Times (November 19, 1992). "Understanding the Riots—Six Months Later," 2 (JJ).

Los Angeles Times (August 13, 1993). "Millions for Counseling Riot Victims Went Unspent," 1(A).

McFarlane, A. (1986) "Posttraumatic Morbidity of a Disaster." *Journal of Nervous and Mental Disease*, 174 (1): 4-1 Civil Unrest 4.

Ong, P. and S. Hee (1993). *Losses in the Los Angeles Civil Unrest April 29-May 1, 1992: Korean Merchants and the L. A.*

Riot/Rebellion. Los Angeles: The Center for Pacific Rim Studies, University of California, Los Angeles.

Saigh, P. A., ed. (1992). *Post-Traumatic Stress Disorder: A Behavioral Approach to Assessment and Treatment*. New York: Macmillan Publishing Co.

Solomon, S. D. and B. L. Green (1992). "Mental Health Effects of Natural and Human-Made Disasters." *PTSD Research Quarterly*, 3: 1-7.

Steinglass, P. and E. Gerrity (1990). "Natural Disasters and Post-Traumatic Stress Disorder: Short-Term versus Long-Term Recovery in Two Disaster-Affected Communities." *Journal of Applied Social Psychology*, 20: 1746-1765.

U. S. Bureau of the Census (1990). *The 1990 Census of the Population: Race and Hispanic Origin for the United States and Regions*. Washington, DC: U.S. Government Printing Office.

PSYCHONEUROIMMUNOLOGICAL IMPACT ON KOREAN AMERICANS[*]

Juna Byun
Ph.D. Candidate, Department of Anthropology
University of Florida, Gainesville

Leslie Sue Lieberman
Professor, Department of Anthropology
University of Florida, Gainesville

Michael J. Philip
Dean, Graduate School
University of Florida, Gainesville

ABSTRACT

In June 1992, six weeks after the riot, 194 Korean American victims were surveyed in Koreatown, Los Angeles. One hundred and twenty-six had had direct property damage and 68 were indirect victims of the riot violence. Standardized self-rating psychosocial instruments and psychoneuro-immunological profiles of saliva samples were employed to examine the relationship between psychological, neuro-immunological, and social components of distress associated with the riot. Results show that there is a significant group difference between the direct property-damaged victims and indirect victims in the frequency of stressful life-change events, in the frequency of somatization, in salivary cortisol levels, and in salivary secretory immunoglobulin A (s-IgA) levels. The

---

frequency of stressful life-change events was 4.65 times higher, and the frequency of somatization was 2.20 times higher for direct victims than for indirect victims. Cortisol levels were 2.08 times higher in direct victims and s-IgA levels were 2.18 times lower in direct victims as compared to indirect victims. Cortisol levels showed a strongly significant positive linear correlation with the frequency of somatization and of life-change events and a strong inverse correlation with s-IgA levels in both groups. High cortisol levels and suppressed s-IgA are associated with a higher prevalence of somatization among direct victims than among indirect victims. Further, these findings were supported by ethnographic findings concerning *"hwapyong"* which refers to a culturally constructed anger illness related to the Korean ethos of *"Han'"* a form of victimized-anger syndrome. These results suggest that those Korean Americans who were direct victims of the riot became physically, mentally, and socially ill as a result.

INTRODUCTION

Since 1903, the United States has been the primary focus of Korean immigration. The process of immigration from Korea to America is tedious and painstaking, but the symbols of America, such as the Statue of Liberty and the ideas of freedom, justice, equal opportunity, protection of human rights and labor, and economic and educational opportunity have persisted as elements of Koreans' version of the American Dream. The dream of immigration to America causes a psychological state among Koreans called *"iminpyong* (immigration illness)" that was especially infectious from 1970 to 1980 among urban Koreans. With this vital American Dream, Koreans have been one of the most rapidly successful immigrant groups in the United States, particularly in Los Angeles, California. According to the 1980 U.S. Census Report, there were 354,529 Korean Americans, but since then, the number has risen rapidly with approximately 30,000 Koreans being admitted annually. The percentage of increase over previous years from 1970 to

1980 was over 400 percent. If this trend continues, the number will reach over a million within the next decade (Gardener et al. 1985).

Los Angeles has been a launching area for new arrivals. The Korean American community of Southern California numbers over 400,000 or approximately 30 percent of the total number of Korean immigrants in the United States (Kim 1993). (According to the 1990 census, the total number of Korean Americans is 798,849.) They were composed almost entirely of middle-class urban Korean immigrants who have arrived in the last twenty years (Yu 1982; Kim 1993). Over 120,000 Korean Americans reside in Koreatown in Los Angeles (Kim 1993; Figure 1).

Figure 1.

South-Central Los Angeles County

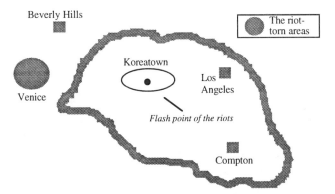

The economic achievement of Korean Americans is outstanding (Light and Bonacich 1988; Min 1990; Yu et al. 1982). According to Light and Bonacich, Korean Americans brought economic prosperity to the ghetto areas in south central Los Angeles. Through hard work Korean Americans built their economic success over a period of 30 years, by a work ethic that some segments of American society abandoned long ago. One recent study indicates that 53 percent of Korean male workers and 45 percent of all Korean workers in Los Angeles are self-employed. The 1980 census showed that Korean immigrants had the highest self-employment and educational rates among 17 recent immigrant groups.

Surprisingly, little research has been done on Korean Americans, particularly on their psychological health. Some of the research available has revealed that stressful life changes experienced by immigrants in spite of their success have contributed to problems such as juvenile delinquency, alcoholism, alienation of the elderly, spouse abuse, intergeneration conflict, and mental disorders (Yu 1983; Koh et al. 1986; Kuo 1984).

An examination of the prevalence of symptoms of depression among Asian Americans in Seattle revealed that Koreans exhibited the highest depression rates in comparison with Chinese, Japanese, and Filipino Americans (Kuo 1984). There are several factors that may explain the high prevalence of depression among Korean Americans: acculturation stress due to shorter length of residence in America and to the higher concentration of small businesses located in life-threatening districts (Min 1990). A study of Korean Americans in the Chicago area revealed that there was a significant correlation between mental health and economic success, especially among males (Hurh and Kim 1990). There is an extremely high rate of failure in Korean small businesses. Fifty percent of Korean-owned small businesses in Los Angeles fail within one year, and as many as 70 percent fail within three years (Kim 1993). According to the findings of a study done on the Belfast riot, the unemployed were more likely to develop symptoms under riot conditions (Lyons 1971).

The April 29 to May 2, 1992, Los Angeles riot resulted in 58 deaths, 2,382 injuries, and 5,200 buildings damaged; thus it was the most destructive civil disorder in contemporary U.S. history. Over $785 million in property damage and approximately 16,000 businesses were destroyed by nearly 8,000 arson fires in Los Angeles (*Los Angeles Times,* May 11, 1992).

Approximately 30 percent of the total property damage occurred among Korean American businesses in South Central Los Angeles. About 80 percent of the Korean American economy in the riot area was destroyed by 1,800 incidents of fires and looting. The total amount of damage reached about $200 million. About 2,250 Korean businesses were destroyed with an average individual damage of $50,000 to $60,000. Over 40 percent of Korean Americans who live in Los Angeles County had an economic dependence on businesses located in Koreatown. The majority were Korean American victims and experts agree that the damage to the Korean American economy is permanent and irreversible (Korean American Inter-Agency Council 1992; Edward Lee Memorial Scholarship Foundation 1993; Association of Korean-American Victims of the L.A. Riots 1993). Previous studies asserted that personal and property damages were highly correlated with mental health consequences (Young 1989; Shore et al. 1986). In this study the social, psychological, and physical consequences of the economic devastation of direct property-damaged Korean American victims were assessed. The need for empirical research on Korean American victims' mental health associated with the riot damage is thus evident.

Riots are a social disaster and are defined in this study as "a situation of massive collective socioeconomic disorganizational stress." There are three different approaches of mental health studies related to natural or human-made disasters. The first, a psychopathological approach, depends on pathological case findings using psychiatric clinical records or self-rating psychometrics. The second, a psychophysiological approach, focuses on chemical responses such as stress hormones related to self-rating psychological states using blood or urine samples in conjunction with psychometric scales. The third, a sociological approach, focuses on group-behavioral changes using surveys.

Psychopathological and psychophysiological studies have argued that human-made (technological and social) disasters, as well as natural disasters, create severe pathological mental health consequences. Tyhurst (1951) found that during the impact period of disasters, many victims are stunned or shocked. One recent analysis, the Buffalo Creek Disaster study, found that the post-disaster incidence of mental illness in the disaster-struck community increased enough to destroy the community (Church 1974; Erickson 1976; Lifton and Olson 1976). In another example, stress effects were found in residents of the area surrounding the Three Mile Island (TMI) nuclear power plant, site of a serious accident in 1979 (Schaeffer and Baum 1984; Baum et al. 1983, 1985). Cortisol (stress hormone) levels remained high over an 18 month period in this population because of the persistent threat of another incident and of potential long-term health consequences of exposure to radiation (Baum et al. 1985). MacKinnon et al. (1991) found suppressed immune components, including high levels of neurophils, and fewer B and Natural Killer cells were positively correlated with high cortisol levels among Three Mile Island residents compared with demographically-matched control groups living in another area.

While the incidence of negative psychophysiological effects of a natural disaster is undisputed, the findings of mental health studies documenting the psychopathological effects of disaster have remained controversial as a result of contradictory findings from sociological studies which focused on group behavioral change (Shore et al. 1986; Fishbain 1991). Sociological studies have claimed that the negative psychological impact of natural disasters has been overstated or misinterpreted by news media (Quarantelli and Dynes 1970). None of the studies of riots categorized as a social disasters in the United States support the existence of riot-induced psychopathological morbidity. Klee and Gorowitz (1970) found no increase in psychiatric admissions after the Baltimore, Maryland riot and a decrease in the number of African American admissions. Greenley et al. (1975) found fewer psychological symptoms in suburban men and women after the New Haven, Connecticut riot as compared with before the riot. Fishbain (1991) reported that there was no increase or decrease in psychiatric admissions after the Miami, Florida, riot.

One possible reason for the discrepancies among studies might be a lack of distinction between the personal or property-damaged innocent victims and rioters who may experience an elated cathartic effect and/or group cohesion. Most studies of urban riots have not clearly examined this point. A second reason for the discrepancy is that some studies focus on dominant phenomena of a population's behavior while others focus on the underlying facts of individual psychology. Some studies are insensitive to sociocultural differences in the riot-affected populations. Another factor contributing to different findings is the time at which the research is conducted. Many studies have been carried on long after the disaster when the expression of psychological states has been transformed into cultural norms and values. Also, most of these studies are cross sectional rather than longitudinal, lacking a control group or a pre-disaster baseline. Furthermore, studies from the 1960s and 1970s failed to recognize the signs and symptoms of post-traumatic stress disorder now widely recognized to occur under a variety of circumstances (Davidson and Baum 1986; Solomon and Flum 1988).

Many of the foregoing problems are avoided in the present study, which incorporates a clear distinction between rioters and victims, is longitudinal in design (six weeks, six months, one year after the riots), includes both psychological (mental) and immunophysiological (physical) measures of stress, and interprets these results in appropriate sociocultural and ethnopsychological contexts. The distinction between direct victims and indirect victims is very important to clarify psychological effects due to the riot compared to general depression, since Korean Americans were reported to have the highest depression rates among Asian Americans (Kuo 1984). The other reason is that under the stress of riot, those who had previous psychiatric history tended to be readmitted (Lyons 1971).

The purpose of this study is three fold. First, the effects of the riot, a social disaster on the mental and physical health of Korean American victims, were documented, and then psychophysiological profiles of salivary cortisol and salivary immunoglobulin to self-reported responses to questionnaires on life-change events, somatization, and loneliness were related. Second, chemical profiles of victims in social disaster studies to investigate physical and mental health were attempted for the first time. Third, this study sheds light on how ethnic differences activate the mechanisms by which stressful social events affect the human mind and body. In particular this study will provide a possible explanation of the mechanism by which social distress suppresses the immune system by activating the nervous system. Last, this study calls attention to the physical, mental, and social suffering of Korean Americans who lost their property and their belief in the American Dream as a result of the riot.

THEORETICAL CONSIDERATIONS

The theoretical model of this study is based on the biocultural paradigm of medical anthropology (Goodman et al. 1988; McElory 1990). Traditionally, medical anthropologists have focused on human behavior and beliefs related to human health and illness rather than on the social and institutional health care systems, especially among minority populations (Foster 1974).

According to the biocultural model, the environment is composed of abiotic, biotic, and cultural factors that act as stressors or constraints on the human host. The cultural environment (cultural ecology) consists of the sociopolitical organization, ideology, and subsistence technology. The biocultural paradigm in medical anthropology looks at how cultural stressors affect the human host at the population, individual, and sub-individual levels. Using this biocultural paradigm, this study examines the riot as a socioeconomic disorganizational stressor affecting the human hosts (direct Korean American victims) at the individual and the sub-individual levels. Measurable indicators of stress are composed of changes in life-change events, changes in health behavior, and changes in emotions at the individual level. A high profile of salivary cortisol and a low profile of s-IgA are also useful indicators of stress at the sub-individual level (Figure 2).

Figure 2.

Theoretical Study Model for
Psychosocial-Neuroimmunological Changes
in Korean American Victims of the Riots.

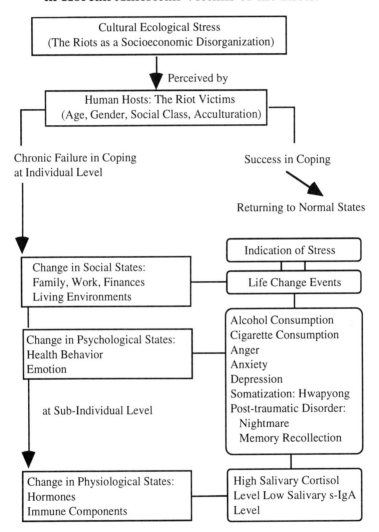

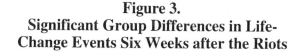

Figure 3.
Significant Group Differences in Life-
Change Events Six Weeks after the Riots

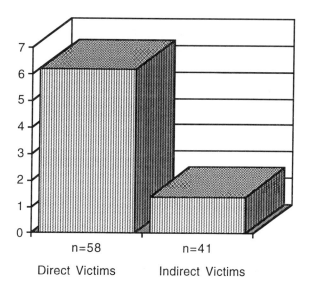

MATERIALS AND METHODS

An opportunistic sample was drawn of 194 adult Korean Americans living in Los Angeles from June 14 to June 24, 1992 (six weeks after the riots). Two groups were formed based on self-reported status as direct property-damaged (including inventory damaged) victims (n=126) or indirect property-damaged victims (n=68). Later, the direct victims were verified by name on the list of the Association of the Korean-American Victims of Riots in Los Angeles. All interviews were conducted in Korean and/or English, and questionnaires, consent forms and other written materials were translated from English to Korean. Saliva samples were collected at the time of the interview. While the present paper focuses on the six weeks after the riot, future reports will follow up the results of 6 and 12 months after the riot. (See Figure 3.)

1) Saliva Sample Collection

Unstimulated whole saliva was collected after a mouth rinse with cold water, at least 15 minutes after eating. To minimize time of day variations, all collections were done between noon and 3:00 p.m. Saliva (2-5ml) was collected in 50cc polyethylene collection tubes in the field. Samples were immediately treated with sodium azide as a bacteriostatic agent, frozen, air transported to Florida, and stored at -70C.

2) Laboratory Analysis

Secretory immunoglobulin A (s-IgA: antibody) in saliva levels were assayed blindly and replicated using the single radial immunodiffusion assay technique (Mancini et al. 1965). Cortisol levels were determined using a serum radioimmunoassay kit purchased from INCSTAR Corporation, MN, USA, and modified according to Aakal-ansari et al. (1982) for saliva.

3) Self-Rating Psychometric Questionnaires

The frequency of life-change events were determined by a scale modified from the Recent Life Changes Questionnaire (Holmes and Masuda 1974). The frequency of somatization was determined by a scale modified from the Symptom Checklist-90 (Derogatis 1977), and the degree of loneliness was assessed from the UCLA Loneliness Scale (Russell 1980).

4) Statistical Analysis

Using the Systat 5.1 program, t-test and multivariate analysis of variance (MANOVA) were used to determine group differences. Pearson's correlation and multiple regression were used to assess the relation between the salivary profiles and the psychometric scales. The significance level was set at $p < 0.05$. Deltagraph Professional and Fullpaint were used for graphics.

RESULTS

The results of the questionnaires and saliva profiles were analyzed in the following ways: (1) general characteristics; (2) group differences between Korean American direct victims and indirect victims in psychometric measurements, and in salivary psychoneuroimmunological profiles; (3) correlations between self-rated psychometrics and chemical profiles.

1. General Characteristics of Korean American Victims

General characteristics of the direct victims and indirect victims were similar except for their present occupational conditions. Ninety-one point one (91.1) percent of direct victims who were previously business owners were jobless (at the time of the survey) due to riot-related damage. The average length of time that businesses destroyed by rioting had been in business was 7.6 years.

Table 1.

General Characteristics of Victims.

Characteristics	Direct Victims (N=126)	Indirect Victims (N=68)
Age	47.2yr	47.8yr
Gender (Male)	56.8%	48.7%
Marital Status (Married)	76.8%	80.4%
No. of Children	2.0	1.9
Home-Shop Address	Riot Area: 30.1%	Riot Area: 31.2%
% Immigrated Since 1970	100%	100%
Length of Immigration	11.72yr	13.16yr
1st Generation Immigrant	100%	100%
Present Job	Jobless: 91.1%	Business Owner: 64.5%
Length of Previous Job	7.6yr	8.1yr
No. of Social Support: (Church+Family)	90.2%	94.3%
Religion (Christian)	84.6%	87.5%
Anglicization of First Name	13%	12.1%
American Citizenship	54.2%	59.2%

The mean age of the respondents was 47.2 years for direct victims and 47.8 years for indirect victims. The direct victim group had a slightly greater number of males and individuals who were business owners. All respondents immigrated to the United States of America after 1970. Mean years of residence in the United States was over ten years. All respondents are first generation immigrants, and over 50 percent are American citizens. Over 30 percent of respondents were home-shop (small business) owners who resided, as well as had their businesses, in the riot-torn areas of Koreatown. Over10 percent of them use Anglicized first names and over 80 percent of them are Christians (Table 1).

2. Group Differences Between Direct and Indirect Victims

1) Differences in Self-Rating Psychometric Measurements:

There were significant group differences in the frequency of life-change events (p>0.0001) and of somatization (p>0.0001). The frequency of life-change events of direct victims (6.45) was 4.65 times greater than that of indirect victims (1.39). The frequency of somatization in direct victims (4.39) was 2.20 times greater than that of indirect victims (1.98). However, there was no significant difference in loneliness scores (Table 2; Figures 3, 4).

Table 2.
Group Differences in the Frequency of Life-Change Events and the Frequency of Somatization.

Variables	Group	N	Mean	SEM.	T
Life Events	Dir. Vict.	58	6.45	0.38	
	Ind. Vict.	44	1.39	0.23	-11.37*
Somatization	Dir. Vict.	36	4.36	0.48	
	Ind. Vict.	41	1.98	0.29	-4.28*
Loneliness	Dir. Vict.	34	45.32	1.25	
	Ind. Vict.	36	48.06	1.17	1.60

*p<0.0001

Figure 4.
Significant Group Difference in
Somatization Six Weeks after the Riots.

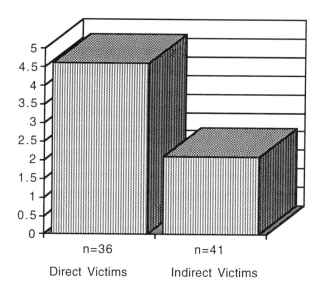

n=36   n=41

Direct Victims   Indirect Victims

2) Differences in Psychoneuroimmunological Profiles:

The average salivary cortisol level was higher and s-IgA level was lower in direct victims than in indirect victims. There were highly significant group differences in cortisol levels (ug/dl; $p<0.0001$) and in s-IgA levels (ug/ml; $p<0.0001$). The cortisol level was 2.08 times higher in direct victims (0.44ug/dl) and s-IgA levels were 2.18 times lower in direct victims (245.1ug/ml) than those of indirect victims (0.21ug/dl, 533.6ug/ml, respectively) (Table 3; Figures 5, 6).

Table 3.
Group Differences in
Psychoneuroimmunological Variables.

Variables	Group	N	Mean	SEM	T
Cotisol (ug/dl)	Dir. Vict.	72	0.44	0.03	
	Ind. Vict.	43	0.21	0.02	-5.91*
s-IgA (ug/ml)	Dir. Vict.	81	245.11	14.59	
	Ind. Vict.	45	533.64	32.13	8.16*

P<0.0001

Figure 5.
Significant Group Difference in Salivary
Cortisol Levels Six Weeks after the
Riots.

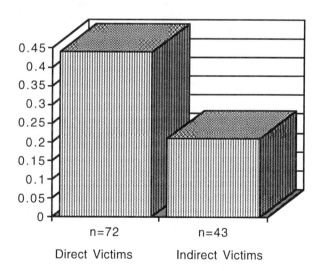

Figure 6.
Significant Group Difference in Salivary
s-IgA Levels Six Weeks after the Riots.

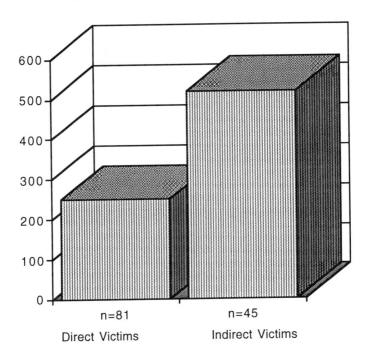

n=81   n=45
Direct Victims   Indirect Victims

3) Relationships Between Self-Rating Psychometrics, Psychoneurological, and Immunological Profiles

There was a strong, significant linear correlation between life changes and somatization ($r=0.51$; $p<0.0001$) and cortisol levels ($r=0.39$; $p<0.0001$) in both groups. There was a significant inverse relation between s-IgA and cortisol levels ($r=-0.33$; $p<0.05$) and s-IgA and the degree of somatization in both groups ($r=-0.30$; $p<0.05$). However, the correlation between somatization and cortisol levels was not significant (Table 4; Figure 7).

Table 4.
Pearson's Correlation Metrics between Psychometrics and Psychoneuroimmunological Variables (N=53).

	s-IgA	Life Changes	Somatization	Cortisol
s-IgA	1.00			
Life Changes	-0.58**	1.00		
Somatization	-0.30*	0.51**	1.000	
Cortisol	-0.33*	0.39**	0.118	1.000

* P<0.05

**P<0.0001

Figure 7.
Significant Inverse Relationship between Salivary Cortisol and Salivary s-IgA Levels Six Weeks after the Riots.

• (Cortisol (ug/dl)

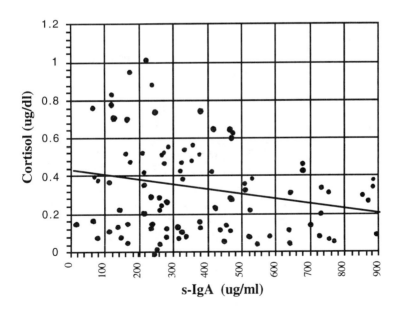

s-IgA (ug/ml)

DISCUSSION

Discussion of the results of this study focuses on three different areas; (1) demographic characteristics and stress; (2) psychoneuroimmunological changes and stress; (3) and ethnographic findings concerning *"hwapyong"* (culturally constructed psychosomatization).

1. Demographic Characteristics And Stress

The opportunistic sample was representative of Korean American victims in Los Angeles. The mean age, gender, number of family members and religion of respondents in this study were similar to a report about the economic damage of Korean American victims eight months or less after the riot (Korean American Inter-Agency Council 1992). Over 90 percent of direct victims in this study became jobless after the riot. However, in the report of the Korean American Inter-Agency Council, 55.6 percent of the victims had opened new businesses within 8 months of the riots. All of the respondents were first generation immigrants who moved to America after 1970. They were among the fourth wave of Korean immigrants originating from the well-educated middle class of urban Koreans (Hurh and Kim 1988; Kim 1993; Yu 1982, 1983). Studies showed that church participation has become a way of life among Korean immigrants in America, acting as a source of comfort and contributing to spiritual and psychological satisfaction (Hurh and Kim 1990; Kim 1993). There are over 300 Korean American ethnic churches in Los Angeles, and over 80 percent of the respondents to this study were church-goers.

It is generally accepted that the length of residence in the United States, use of Anglicized personal name, and naturalization are related to the degree of acculturation. Over 50 percent of the respondents in this study were naturalized citizens, but only about 12 percent used Anglicized first names.

Previous studies argued that stress could be seen as a process that is affected by demographic variables such as age and gender. Aging is negatively related to the stress response. Functional measures of lymphocyte activity have been noted to be negatively affected by normal aging (Clot et al. 1972). Studies relating stress to gender have demonstrated that men are more severely distressed than women (Verbrugge 1985; Froberg et al. 1986). This difference is related to coping styles of men and women. Women maintain stronger emotional ties with others, while males engage a social brooding or the use of alcohol, drugs or smoking. However, in this study, age and gender were not significant co-variables with the psychophysiological measurements.

Recent studies of acculturation and stress have argued that higher levels of acculturation create more, rather than less, stress on immigrants, especially so in a culturally plural society such as the U.S. (Dressler 1982, 1992; Dressler et al. 1982, 1987; Berry et al. 1988; Portes and Rumbaut 1990; Espino 1990). This may be either because acculturation itself is a stressful process or because they are acculturated into a more stressful society. However, this study found no difference between the level of acculturation and psychological variables as measured by the length of residence in the U.S., naturalization and Anglicization of first name. Some studies have shown that members of lower social classes experience more stress, not because of more stressful life events, but because of fewer resources for coping or social buffering (Kessler et al. 1986; Dressler 1992). However, in this study, there is no difference in stress related to occupational status.

To summarize, in this study, stress related to psychological measures were independent of age, gender, marital status, religion, type and length of occupation, amount of social support, and level of acculturation. Possibly, severe emotional distresses associated with the riot overshadowed demographic differences in stress responses. The follow-up data from six months (phase two) to one year (phase three) after the riot may show the effects of demographic differences.

2. Psychoneuroimmunological Changes and Stress

The relationship between emotional distress and disease have been studied as a field of psychoneuroimmunology. This field has rapidly progressed since Bartrop et al. (1977) studied the effects of depression from spousal death on mitogen-stimulated lymphocyte number and function. The effects of psychosocial stress on immune functions have been well documented (McClelland et al. 1985; Jemmott and Locke 1984; Jemmot and McClelland 1989; Jemmott et al. 1983; Jemmott and Magloire 1988; Glaser et al. 1987, 1991; Kiecolt-Galser et al. 1984; Ballieux 1991; O'Leary 1990).

Psychoneuroimmunological responses are associated with physiological changes, including the hypothalamo-pituitary-adrenocortical (HPAC) system, and other endocrine systems (Cannon and De la Paz 1991; Selye 1956). The HPAC system has been described as a distress system. Activation of the adrenocortical system results in the release of adrenocorticotropic hormones (ACTH) and corticosteroids (cortisol). Cortisol regulates, in part, interactions between the central nervous system and the immune system. When a person perceives stress, the hypothalamic corticotropin releasing hormone in the brain is activated and via ACTH stimulates secretion of corticosteroids (cortisol) from the adrenal glands into the blood stream. Thus, cortisol levels are high in stressful situations. High cortisol levels suppress immunity (antibodies) such as IgA. Cortisol and IgA levels in saliva parallel those in blood (Aakal-ansari et al. 1982). Therefore, cortisol and s-IgA in saliva were used in this study to indicate the stress level of an individual. Cortisol is the primary immune suppressive in both the cellular and humoral immune response (Cupps and Fauci 1982; Baum et al. 1987; Dorian et al. 1982; Gatti et al. 1987).

This study found a significant correlation between cortisol levels and the frequency and intensity of life-change events. Direct victims had higher cortisol levels, perceived the riot as being more stressful, and had more severe life-change events than indirect victims.

We found a significant inverse relationship between cortisol level and saliva immunoglobulin A level (s-IgA). This finding supports the mechanism of cortisol suppression of immunity. In addition, there was a significant group difference in s-IgA levels. Direct victims presented lower s-IgA levels than indirect victims, which indicates that higher cortisol levels suppressed s-IgA to a greater degree in the direct victims.

Suppressed immunity will increase the vulnerability of direct victims to infection, especially upper respiratory infections (MacKinnon et al. 1989; Glaser et al. 1987, 1991; Jemmott et al. 1989; Jemmott and Locker 1984; Kasi et al. 1979). In this study, the higher frequency of the upper respiratory infection, measured by an item from the somatization scale among direct victims, further supports other evidence for stress-related immune-system suppression.

There was no difference among the groups in the loneliness scores. This result might depend on three reasons: (1) the scale used to assess loneliness (the UCLA Loneliness Scale; Russell et al. 1980) was developed for loneliness caused not by social conflict such as riots but by individualistic isolation; (2) the scale was not developed for Asians who generally have strong family relations. Therefore, it was unsuccessful in assessing this dimension; (3) the multiple correlation between the scale and psychological states such as anxiety, depression, and isolation did not reflect specific psychological states of victimization. For these reasons, this study needs to employ specified and valid scales for Korean Americans. Another reason for the low report of loneliness might be that victims are in a psychological phase of apathy, are stunned, or are in shock. The victims may have been too stunned to realize their loneliness. The studies related to psychological stages of disaster found that during the impact period of the disasters, up to 75 percent of the victims may be stunned and bewildered (Tyhurst 1951). This psychologically stunned phase occurs immediately after the disaster event (Wolfenstein 1977). However, this field survey was done six weeks after the riot when psychological expression could have been transformed into cultural norms and values (Wolfenstein 1977).

3. Ethnographic Findings Concerning Psychosomatization

There were significant physiological changes associated with the riot distress; specifically, changes in hormone and in immune components which are related to the high prevalence of somatization among Korean American victims. During the survey we noticed that Korean American victims rarely complained of anxiety, depression or other psychological problems, except anger and somatic complaints. Psychosomatization is common in Koreans, especially females (Lin 1983; Kim 1993). Koreans view mental illness as a stigmatizing and threatening experience for themselves and their families. Thus, victims tend to express more bodily complaints than psychological complaints such as expressing emotional distress, anxiety, depression. In Korean families, physical complaints are readily accepted. However, psychological or mental complaints tend to be either ignored or taken as a luxurious complaint. Koreans do not express emotion openly. When emotions go beyond a certain threshold level they are manifested physically as a form of illness: "*hwapyong* (anger illness)" (Kim 1993; Lin 1983), "*iminpyong* (immigration illness)", "*sarangpyong* (love illness)", "*kasum ari* (broken heart illness)", or "*kyejolpyong* (seasonal illness)."

Among the victims, we found mostly *hwapyong* due to extreme anger and shame originating from the Korean ethos, *han,* which refer to unresolved precipitated anger related to victimization or to unfair treatment (Kim 1993). Feelings of scapegoating, of abandonment by main-stream society in the failure of equal protection, and of hopelessness and helplessness to rebuild businesses were predominant. Unexpectedly, most Korean American victims were not angry at African Americans but rather were sympathetic to the African American situation in the ghetto area. The major symptoms of *hwapyong* are hypertension, back pain, upper respiratory infection, dizziness, severe dry mouth, shortness of breath, and heart problems. Noticeably, many female victims complained of amenorrhea which might be due to suppressed reproductive hormones by a high secretion of cortisol and/or weight loss. The negative relation between stress and infertility has been empirically documented (Harrison et al. 1986; Giblin et al. 1988). However, this finding needs to be further investigated to prove a negative effect on reproductive competence due to riot distress.

Culturally influenced somatization is an important concept to understand in discussing Korean American riot victims because it allows us to deal with underlying problems that link together emotional and bodily distresses. *Hwapyong,* related to *han* as a psychosomatic illness, is constructed by culture. The suppression of anger, shame, hopelessness, and helplessness among Korean American riot victims is transformed into physical illnesses, *hwapyong,* which are socially accepted as such in Korean culture.

According to the classic theory of group conflict, social disturbances could have salutary effects on psychological status by strengthening the integration of society and increasing group cohesion (Simmel 1955; Coser 1956). Another possible positive effect of urban riots is "catharsis," which means the release of symptom-producing tensions and frustrations through scapegoating powerless groups (Fogelson 1970; Coser 1956). Studies of urban racial riots initiated by African Americans are reported to have reduced emotional distress and produced feelings of accomplishment. However, the riot distress among Korean American direct victims was considerable in psychophysiological changes, including hormonal and immunological components. Low immunity among victims may lead to a high frequency of infection, especially of the upper respiratory tract and delayed healing or prolonged infections. Both physiological and psychological stress impair social functioning.

These results are supported by a report by Dr. M. M. Cho, a psychiatrist who counseled Koran American victims at the Asian Pacific Counseling and Treatment Center in Los Angeles where about 700 victims consulted psychotherapists within the first year after the riot. Among them, 600 victims took medication for anxiety and depression. Several were admitted for pathological mental states, and 10 to 15 continued undergoing psychotherapy. Most victims had psychosomatization symptoms (*The Korea Times, Los Angeles*, July 14, 1993).

To summarize, this is the first empirical study that provides psychophysiological evidence for adverse effects of riot distress. This study indicates that riots create not only mental health problems but also physical and social problems. Psychological analysis of riot victims may be an important indication of the need for organizational intervention.

CONCLUSION

This study provides evidence of the negative psychological effects of riot distress on Korean American victims (as compared with a control group) based on their psychophysiological profiles and self-rated psychometrics. Ethnographic information was introduced for interpretation of the results. Questions remain concerning the persistence of deleterious psychoneuroimmunological changes and their consequence for health and well being beyond the twelve months after the riot.

We would like to suggest that future disaster studies should consider using random samples rather than clinical cases, comparisons of the control groups, direct property-damaged victims of riots and other victims. Cross-sectional as well as longitudinal laboratory and field studies are needed. Ethnographic information is needed to investigate underlying factors of psychological effects of disaster in multicultural societies.

In addition, the cultural components of mental illness and healing must be reflected in community disaster intervention. The utilization of an alternative medical system (ethno-medicine), such as a Korean-traditional medical system which mainly treats mental illness as a psychophysiological disorder, should be used along with Western psychotherapy.

ACKNOWLEDGEMENTS

This work was supported by grants from the Patricia Roberts Harris Fellowship and the Gatorade Fund of the University of Florida. The authors specially acknowledge the Korean American victims who voluntarily participated in this project. The authors acknowledge Dr. Y. Lee, Dr. B. Yoon, Mr. J. Lee (Chair of the Association of Korean American Victims of the L.A. Riots), Mr. B. Oh (Treasurer of the Association of the Korean American Victims of the L.A. Riots), Mr. H. Byun (Chief Editor of *The Korea Times, Los Angeles*), Reverend T.. Ba, and Reverend H. Yang, who helped collect data. We thank Dr. Thomas Brown, Dr. David Dusek, Dr. Mona Boules, and Mrs. Latha B. Pathangey for their help with the laboratory analysis. We also extend thanks to Dr. Steven Brandt for helping with computerizing research materials. This paper is a part of Juna Byun's doctoral dissertation.

BIBLIOGRAPHY

Aakal, A. A. K., L. A. Perry, D. S. Smith, and J. Landon (1982) "Salivary Cortisol Determination: Adaptation of a Commercial Serum Cortisol Kit." *Annals of Clinical Biochemistry.* 19:163-166.

Amaro, H. (1990) "Acculturation and Marijuana and Cocaine Use: Findings From the HHANES 1982-84." *American Journal of Public Health* 80(12):54-61.

Association of Korean-American Victims of the L.A. Riots (1993) "Korean-American Claims Statistics for a Suit Against the Government," n.p., n.d.

Ballieux, R. E. (1991) "Impact of Mental Stress on the Immune Response." *Journal of Clinical Periodicals* 18:427-430.

Bartrop, R.W., E. Luckhurst, L. Lazarus, and L. G. Kiloh (1977) "Depressed Lymphocyte Function After Bereavement." *The Lancet,* April 16:834-836.

Baum, A., L.M. Davidson, J. E. Singer, and S.W. Street (1987) "Stress As a Psychophysiological Process," In *Handbook of Psychology and Health V: Stress.* A. Baum, and J. E. Singe, eds. pp. 1-24. Hillsdale: Lawrence Erlbaum Associates.

————, R. Gatchel, and M. A. Schaeffer (1983) "Emotional, Behavioral and Physiological Effects of Chronic Stress at Three Mile Island." *Journal of Consulting and Clinical Psychology* 51(4):565-572.

————, M. A.Schaeffer, C. R.Lake, R. Fleming and D. L. Collins (1985) "Psychological and Endocrinological Correlates of Chronic Stress at Three Mile Island," In *Perspectives on Behavioral Medicine* Vol 2, R. Williams, ed. pp. 201-217. San Diego, CA: Academic Press.

Berry, J. and U. Kim (1988) "Comparative Studies of Acculturative Stress." *International Migration Review* 21(3):491-509.

Blalock, J. E. (1989) "A Molecular Basis For Bidirectional Communication Between the Immune and Neuroendocrine Systems." *The American Physiological Society* 69(1):1-32.

Cammara, E. G. and T. C. Nanao (1989) "The Brain and the Immune System: A Psychosomatic Network." *Psychosomatics* 30(2):140-146.

Cannon, W. B. and D. De La Paz (1991) "Emotional Stimulation of Adrenal Secretion." *American Journal of Physiology* 29:64-70.

Church, J. S. (1974) "The Buffalo Creek Disaster: Extent and Range of Emotional and/or Behavioral Problems." *Omega* 5(1):61-63.

Clot, J., E. Charmasson and J. Brochier (1972) "Age-Dependent Changes of Human Blood Lymphocyte Subpopulations." *Clinical Experimental Immunology* 32:346-351.

Coser, L. A. (1956) *The Functions of Social Conflict*. Chicago: The Free Press.

Cupps, T. R. and A. Fauci (1982) "Corticosteroid-Mediated Immunoregulation in Man." *Immunological Review* 65:133-155.

Davidson, L. M. and A. Baum (1986) "Chronic Stress and Post-Traumatic Stress Disorders." *Journal of Consulting and Clinical Psychology* 54(3):303-308.

Derogatis, L. R. (1977) *The SCL-90 Manual I: Scoring, Adminstration, and Procedures for the SCL-90*. Baltimore, MD: Johns Hopkins University School of Medicine, Clinical Psychometrics Unit.

Dorian, B., P.Garfinkel, G.Brown, A. Shore, D.Gladman and E. Keystone (1982) "Aberration in Lymphocyte Subpopulations and Function During Psychological Stress." *Clinical Experimental Immunology* 50:132-138.

Dressler, W. W. (1982) *Hypertension and Culture Change: Acculturation and Disease in the West Indies*. Redgrave Publishing Company.

———. (1987) "The Stress Process in a Southern Black Community: Implications for Prevention Research." *Human Organization* 46(3):211-220.

———. (1992) "Culture, Stress, and Depressive Symptoms: Building and Testing a Model in a Specific Setting." In *Anthropological Research Process and Application*. J. J. Poggie, B. R. Dewalt and W. W. Dressler, eds. New York: State University of New York Press.

——— and H. Bernal, (1982) "Acculturation and Stress in a Low-Income Puerto Rican Community." *Journal of Human Stress* 9:32-38.

Edward Lee Memorial Scholarship Foundation (1993) *Koreatown Before and After the Riot*.

Erickson, K. T. (1976) "Loss of Community at Buffalo Creek." *American Journal of Psychiatry* 133(3):302-305.

Espino, D. (1990) "Hypertension and Acculturation in Elderly Mexican Americans: Results from 1982-84 Hispanic HANES." *Journal of Gerontology* 45(6):209-14.

Fishbain, D. A. (1991) "Impact of a Human-Made Disaster on the Utilization Pattern of a Psychiatric Emergency Service." *Journal of Nervous and Mental Disease* 179(3): 162-166.

Fogelson, R. M. (1970) "Violence and Grievances: Reflections on the 1960's Riots." *Journal of Social Issues* 26:141-163.

Fraser, R. M. (1971) "The Cost of Commotion: An Analysis of the Psychiatric Sequel of the 1969 Belfast Riots." *British Journal of Psychiatry* 118:257-264.

Froberg, D., D. Gjerdingen, and E. Preston (1986) "Multiple Roles and Women's Mental and Physical Health: What Have We Learned?" *Women and Health* 11:79-96.

Foster, G. M. (1974) "Medical Anthropology: Some Contrasts with Medical Sociology." *Medical Anthropology Newsletter* 6(1): 21-26.

Gardner, R. W., B. Robett, and B. Smith (1985) "Asian-Americans: Growth, Change and Diversity." *Population Bulletin.* Washington, DC: Population Reference Bureau.

Gatchell, R. J., M. A. Schaeffer and A. Baum (1985) "A Psychophysiological Field Study of Stress at Three Mile Island." *Psychophysiology* 22(2):175-181.

Gatti, G., R. Cavallo, M. L. Sartori, D. D. Ponte, R. Masera, R. C. Salvadori and A. Angeli (1987) "Inhibition by Cortisol of Human Natural Killer (NK) Cell Activity." *Journal of Steroid Biochemistry* 26(1):49-58.

Giblin, P., J. W. Ager, M. L. Poland, J. M. Olson, and S. M. Kamren (1988) "Effects of Stress and Characteristic Adaptibility on Semen Quality in Healthy Men." *Fertility and Sterility* 49(1):127-132.

Giller, E. (1990) *Biological Assessment and Treatment of Post-traumatic Stress Disorder.* Washington, D.C.: American Psychiatric Press.

Glaser, R., G.R. Pearson, J. F. Jones, J. Hillhouse, S. Kennedy, H., Mao and J. K. Kiecolt-Glaser (1991) "Stress-Related Activation of Epstein-Barr Virus." *Brain, Behavior And Immunity* 5:219-232.

Glaser, R., J. Rice, J. Sheridan, R. Fertel, J. Stout, C. Speicher, D., Pinsky, M. Kotur, A., Post, M. Beck and J. Kiecolt-Glaser (1987) "Stress-Related Immune Suppression: Health Implications." *Brain, Behavior, and Immunity* 1:7-20.

Goodman, A. H., R. B., Thomas, A. C. Swedlund and G. J. Armelagos (1988) "Biocultural Perspectives on Stress in Prehistoric, Historic, and Contemporary Population Research." *Yearbook of Physical Anthropology* 31:169-202.

Graham, N. M. H., R. M. Douglas and P. Ryan (1986) "Stress and Acute Respiratory Infection." *American Journal of Epidemics* 124:389-401.

Green, B. L., J. D. Lindy and M. Grace (1985) "Post-traumatic Stress Disorder: Toward DSM-IV." *Journal of Nervous and Mental Disease* 173(7):406-411.

Greenley, J. R., D. P. Gillespie and J. J. Linfenthal (1975) "A Race Riot's Effect on Psychological Symptoms." *Archives of Genral Psychiatry* 32:1189-1195.

Harrison, R. F., R. R. O'Moore and A. M. O'Moore (1986) "Stress and Fertility: Some Modalities of Investigation and Treatment in Couples with Unexplained Infertility in Dublin." *International Journal of Fertility* 31(2):153-159.

Holmes, T. H. and M. Masuda (1974) "Life Change and Illness Susceptibility," In *Sressful Life Events: Their Nature and Effects.* B. S. Dohrenwend and B. Dohenwend, eds. pp. 45-72. NY: Wiley.

Hurh, W. M. and K. C. Kim (1980) "Social and Occupational Assimilation of Korean Immigrant Workers in the United States." *California Sociologist* 3:125-142.

————. (1988) "Uprooting and Adjustment: A Sociological Study of Korean Immigrants' Mental Health." *Final Report Submitted to National Institute of Mental Health*, U.S. Department of Health and Human Services, Washington, D.C.

————. (1990) "Adaptation Stages and Mental Health of Korean Male Immigrants in the United States." *International Migration Review* 24(3):456- 479.

———— (1992) "Religious Participation of Korean Immigrants in the United States." *Journal for the Scientific Study of Religion* 29(1):19- 34.

Jemmott, J. B. and K. Magloire (1988) "Academic Stress, Social Support, and Secretary Immunoglobulin." *American Journal of Personality and Social Psychology* 55(5):803-810.

Jemmott, J. B., J. Z. Borysenko, M. Borysenko, D. C. McClelland, R. Chapman and D. Meyer (1983) "Academic Stress, Power Motivation, and Decrease in Secretion Rate of Salivary Secretory Immunoglobulin A." *The Lancet*, June 25:1400-1402.

Jemmott, J. B. and D. C. McClelland (1989) "Secretory IgA as a Measure of Resistence to Infectious Disease: Comments on Stone, Cox, Valdimarsdottir, and Neale (1987)." *Behavioral Medicine* 15:63-70.

Jemmott J. B. and S. E. Locke (1984) "Psychosocial Factors, Immunologic Mediation, and Human Susceptibility to Infectious Disease: How Much Do We Know?" *Psychological Bulletin* 95(1):78-108.

Kasi, S. V., A. S. Evans and J. C. Niederman (1979) "Psychosocial Risk Factors in the Development of Infectious Mononucleosis." *Psychosomatic Medicine* 41(6): 445-466.

Kessler, R. C., R. H. Price and C. B. Wortman (1986) "Social Factors in Psychopathology." *American Review of Psychology* 36:531- 572.

Kiecolt-Galser, J. K., W. Garner, C. Speicher, P. H. Holliday and R. Galser (1984) "Psychosocial Modifiers of Immunocompetence in Medical Students." *Psychosomatic Medicine* 46(1):7-14.

Kim, L. I. C. (1993) "Psychiatric Care of Korean-Americans," In *Culture, Ethnicity and Mental Ilness.* A. C. Gaw, ed. pp.437-376. Washington, DC: American Psychiatric Press.

Kim, Y. M. (1993) "A History of the Korean-American Community in Southern California," Paper Presented at the Conference on "New Directions for the Korean American Community: After the Civil Unrest of April 1992" in Los Angeles at the University of Southern California.

Kinston, W. and R. Rosser (1974) "Disaster: Effects on Mental and Physical State." *Journal of Psychosomatic Research* 18:437-456.

Kinzie, J. D. (1990) "The Prevalence of Posttraumatic Stress Disorder and Its Clinical Significance among Southeast Asian Refugees." *American Journal of Psychiatry* 147(7):913.

Klee, G. D. and K. Gorwitz (1970) "Effects of the Baltimore Riots on Psychiatric Hospital Admissions." *Mental Hygiene* 54:447-449.

Kobasa, S. (1979) "Stressful Life Events, Personality, and Health: An Inquiry into Hardness." *Personality and Social Psychology* 37(1):1-11.

Kronfol, Z., J. D. House, J. Silva, Jr., J. Greden, and B. J. Carrol (1986) "Depression, Urinary Free Cortisol Excretion and Lymphocyte Function." *Journal of Human Stress* 148:70-73.

Korean-American Inter-Agency Council (1992) *Executive Summary Highlights: Needs Assessment Interim Report.*

Koh, S. D., R. Sakauye and T. Koh (1986) *Mental Health and Stresses in Asian-American Elderly.* P/AAMHRC Research Report. Chicago: Pacific/Asian American Mental Health Research Center.

Kuo, W. (1984) "Prevalence of Depression Among Asian-Americans." *Journal of Nervous and Mental Disorders* 172:449-457.

Lifton, R. J. and E. Olson (1976) "The Human Meaning of Total Disaster: The Buffalo Creek Experience." *Psychiatry* 39:1-18.

Light, I. and E. Bonacich (1988) *Immigrant Entrepreneurs: Koreans in Los Angeles, 1965-1982.* Berkeley: University of California Press.

Lin, K.M. (1983) "*Hwa-byung:* A Korean Culture-Bound Syndrome?" *American Journal of Psychiatry* 140(1): 105-107.

Lin, N., R. S. Simeon, N. M Ensle and W. Kuo (1979) "Social Support, Stressful Life Events and Illness: A Model and Empirical Test." *Journal of Health and Social Behavior* 20:108- 119.

Loughrey, G. C., P. Bell, M. Kee, R. J. Roddy and P. S. Curran (1988) "Post-Traumatic Stress Disorder and Civil Violence in Northern Ireland." *British Journal of Psychiatry* 153:554-560.

Lyons, H. A. (1971) "Psychiatric Sequel of the Belfast Riots." *British Journal of Psychiatry* 118:265-273.

Mackinnon, L. T., F. S. Hooper, R. Gordon and T. Tunny (1988) "Immune Parameters and Stress Hormones in Overtrained Swimmers." *Sports Medicine* 7:141-149.

Mancini, G., A. O. Carbonara and J. F. Heremans (1965) "Immunochemical Quantitation of Antigens by Single Radial Immunodiffusion." *Immunochemistry* 2:235-254.

Mason, J. W., E. I. Giller, T. R. Kosten and R. Yehuda (1990) "Psychoendocrine Approaches to the Diagnosis and Pathogenesis of Posttraumatic Stress Disorder," In *Biological Assessment and Treatment of Posttraumatic Stress Disorder*, E. I. Giller, ed. Washington, DC: American Psychiatric Press.

McClelland, D. C., G. Ross and V. Patel (1985) "The Effect of an Academic Examination on Salivary Norepinephine and Immunoglobulin Levels." *Journal of Human Stress,* Summer:52-59.

McClelland, D. C., C. Alexander and E. Marks (1982) "The Need for Power, Stress, Immune Function, and Illness Among Male Prisoners." *Journal of Abnormal Psychologist* 91:61-70.

McElory, A. (1990) "Biocultual Models in Studies of Human Health and Adaptation." *Medical Anthropology Quarterly* 4(3): 243-265.

McFarlane, A. C. (1985) "The Effects of Stressful Life Events and Disasters: Research and Theoretical Issues." *Australian and New Zealand Journal of Psychiatry* 19:409-421.

McKinnon, W., C. Weisse, C. P. Reynolds, C. A. Bowles and A. Baum (1989) "Chronic Stress, Leukocyte Subpopulations, and Humoral Response to Latent Viruses." *Human Stress* 8(4):389-402.

McKinnon, W., C. S. Weise, C.P. Reynolds, C.A. Bowles and A. Baum (1991) "Chronic Stress, Leukocyte Subpopulations, and Humoral Response to Latent Viruses." *Health Psychology* 2(3): 46-58.

Min, P. G. (1986) "Filipino and Korean Immigrants in Small Business: A Comparative Analysis." *Amerasia Journal* 13(1):53-71.

——— (1990) "Problems of Korean Immigrant Entrepreneurs." *International Migration Review* 24(3):436-451.

O'Leary, A. (1990) "Stress, Emotion, and Human Immune Function." *Psychological Bulletin* 108(3):363-382.

Portes, A. and R. Rumbaut (1990) "A Foreign World: Immigration, Mental Health, and Acculturation," In *Immigrant America: A Portrait*. pp. 143-175. Berkeley: University of California Press.

Quarantelli, E. L. and R. R. Dynes (1970) "Property Norms and Looting: Their Patterns in Community Crises." *Phylon* 31(2):168-182.

Rangell, L. (1976) "Discussion of the Buffalo Creek Disaster: The Course of Psychic Trauma." *American Journal of Psychiatry* 133(3):313-316.

Russell, D., L. A. Peplau, and C. E. Cutrona (1980) "The Revised UCLA Loneliness Scale: Concurrent and Discriminant Validity Evidence." *Journal of Personal and Social Psychology* 39(3):472-480.

Schaeffer, M. A. and A. Baum (1984) "Adrenal Cortical Response to Stress at Three Mile Island." *Psychosomatic Medicine* 46(3): 227-237.

Schleifer, S., J. Keller, S. E. M. Camerino, J. C. Thornton and M. Stein (1983) "Suppression of Lymphocyte Stimulation Following Bereavement." *Journal of Human Medical Association* 250:364-377.

Seyle, H. (1956) *The Stress of Life*. New York: Mcgraw-Hill.

Shore, J. H., E. L. Tatum and W. M. Vollmer (1986) "Psychiatric Reactions to Disaster: The Mount St. Helens Experience." *American Journal of Psychiatry* 143(5):590-595.

Simmel, G. (1955) *Conflict and the Web of Group-Affiliations*. Chicago: The Free Press.

Solomon, Z. and H. Flum (1988) "Life Events, Combat Stress Reaction and Post-Traumatic Stress Disorder." *Social Science Medicine* 26(3):319-325.

Tan E. S. and R. C. Simons (1973) "Psychiatric Sequelae to a Civil Disturbance." *British Journal of Psychiatry* 122:57-63.

Totman, R., J. Kiff, S. E. Reed and J. W. Craig (1980) "Predicting Experimental Colds in Volunteers From Different Measures of Recent Life Stress." *Journal of Psychosomatic Research* 24:155-163.

Tyhurst, J. S. (1951) "Individual Reactions to Community Disaster." *American Journal of Psychiatry* 107:764-771.

Vega, W., R. Kolody, B. Valle and R. Hough (1986) "Depressive Symptoms and Their Correlates Among Immigrant Mexican Women in the United States." *Social Science Medicine* 22(6):645-652.

Verbrugge, L. M. (1985) "Gender and Health: An Update of Hypotheses and Evidence." *Journal of Health and Social Behavior* 56:156-182.

Williams, C. and J. Berry (1991) "Primary Prevention of Acculturative Stress Among Refugees." *American Psychologist* 46(6):632-641.

Wolfenstein, M. (1977) *Disaster: A Psychological Essay.* New York: Arno Press.

Young, M. A. (1989) "Crime, Violence, and Terrorism." In *Psychosocial Aspects of Disasters.* R. Gist and B. Lubin, eds. pp. 140-159. NY: Wiley.

Yu, E. Y. (1983) "Korean Communities in America: Past, Present, Future." *Amerasia Journal* 10(2):23-51.

———, E. Phillips and E. Yang, eds. (1982) *Koreans in Los Angeles: Prospects and Promises.* Los Angeles: Center for Korean American and Korean Studies. Los Angeles: California State University, Los Angeles.

Zusman, J. and J. Simon (1983) "Differences in Repeated Psychiatric Examinations of Litigans to a Lawsuit." *American Journal of Psychiatry* 140:1300- 1304.

IV

USC AND THE

KOREAN AMERICAN COMMUNITY

Radio Shack at 1714 S. Western Ave.

USC AND LOS ANGELES

Steven Sample
President
University of Southern California

USC and Los Angeles grew up together. In fact, at USC's opening in 1880, one tenth of the entire population of the city of Los Angeles turned out for the event. Admittedly that was but one thousand Angelinos in 1880, but those one thousand turned out with a vigor and extended USC a magnificent welcome. Now, more than one hundred and thirty years later as Los Angeles faces the long task of reinventing itself, the University of Southern California plans to return that support by playing an integral role in the city's rediscovery and redevelopment process. The University intends to accomplish its objective through teaching, research and public service; by cultivating its ties throughout the community as a bridge-building institution; and by serving as a catalyst for positive change, especially for economic and cultural development.

A primary philosophy of the University of Southern California is the belief that true scholarship is rooted in ethnic, religious and racial pluralism. USC's academic and extracurricular programs promote understanding, respect and acceptance for Korean Americans and for all peoples. Diversity is not something to be shunned; rather its something to be prized.

Korean Americans, their institutions, their values are an important part of USC. Asian cultures and Asian issues have been the focus of the University's teaching and research for more than sixty years. Today, USC's faculty represents one of the largest and most diverse concentrations of Asian expertise in the United States. The University's Asian Pacific American Student Service organization provides a wide range of academic, personal development and community service programs designed to give students a multifaceted educational experience. This organization is unique also because in its daily operations it utilizes the resources of USC's many Asian American alumni and friends. These alumni come onto the campus and serve as counselors, advisors and mentors for Asian American students.

While many Americans still confuse Koreans with Chinese and Japanese, USC students, by contrast, quickly learn that Asia is as diverse as Europe. To facilitate that learning experience, USC has designed and implemented a wide variety of programs that compare and contrast Korea with other cultures in the Asian Pacific region. Teaching programs, for example, encompass the Korean language, literature, politics, international relations, Korean society, religion, music, painting, and both ancient and modern Korean history. A first-hand learning experience is effected through the exchange of faculty and students between Korean colleges and universities and USC. And outside the University, USC's community outreach programs teach Los Angeles school children of all races about Korea and Korean culture.

USC believes that it is through the efforts of multiethnic conferences such as this "New Directions for the Korean American Community" conference—and the new proposals and policies that will spring from it—that southern California will be able to meet the challenges it faces. The University of Southern California is proud to be a partner in this effort, in educating students, in helping to meet the needs of the Korean American community, as it continues to grow in size and influence, and in improving the quality of life for everyone in Los Angeles and the surrounding region.

Problems notwithstanding, Los Angeles is truly one of the great cities of the world. The diversity of its many cultures gives it a special dynamism and creativity. Many scholars believe that Los Angeles is the most culturally and racially diverse city in the history of the world. But in many ways—perhaps in part because of that diversity—Los Angeles has lost its sense of community. Tensions are just as evident as they were a year ago; anxiety, anger and frustration are out in the open. People everywhere are watching to see how these tensions will be resolved. The eyes of the world are upon Los Angeles as it prepares to address the multicultural issues that will face every city at some point in the future. To be successful, everyone must put their shoulders to the wheel, the job can't be and shouldn't be left to the devices of government alone. This "New Directions for the Korean American Community" conference is a good example of people—scholars, business leaders, government representatives and community activists—working together to marshal their experience and expertise. The people of Los Angeles have before them an opportunity to build the city anew; not as it was, but perhaps as it should be. The time to begin is now.

Amazon Aquarium at Western and Venice

Korea Times, L.A.

THE KOREAN HERITAGE LIBRARY AT USC

Kenneth D. Klein,
East Asian Librarian
University of Southern California

The Korean Heritage Library constitutes the University of Southern California's longest sustained outreach to the Southern California Korean community, as well as the central feature of its commitment to the permanent establishment of Korean studies in its academic program.

The Korean Heritage Library was formally established on April 1, 1986. The preparations for the Library, however, predate this by a number of years. Most significantly could be noted the USC Korean Colloquium, held on September 15, 1985, at which USC librarians and the USC Korean studies faculty met with representatives of many of the most prominent Korean libraries across the country. This meeting, in effect, constituted a planning session for the Korean Heritage Library and served as a notice of USC's serious intentions in the field.

The rationale for making the Korean collection a particular emphasis of the University Library derives from several factors. The most important reason was the need to support the research and teaching needs of the faculty and students of USC. Korean studies have been growing steadily at the University for more than two decades and have built upon the solid base of consistent faculty research and class enrollment. Second, as a major research university, USC assumes the responsibility for building the library resources necessary to support advanced research in a select number of specialized fields, and for providing generalized access to those materials for scholars from across the nation. One such field of particular importance to the University is East Asian studies, the least well-served area of which had long been Korean studies. This reflected the national situation. USC, thus, saw a chance to make a contribution on the national level. Third, a broad agreement was reached between the two dominant universities in the Southern California region that UCLA would be the primary site for the collection of Japanese and Chinese library materials, while USC would take responsibility for collecting Korean materials. Finally, the University of Southern California has a close and long-standing relationship with the Korean community in Los Angeles, dating back almost ninety years, when the first Korean immigrants to Southern California settled in an area adjacent to the University.

The Library has assumed a mission to build a research collection which will serve all areas of Korean studies, with particular emphasis on Korean society since the late nineteenth century. Due to its close relationship to the local Korean community, the Korean Heritage Library has felt a natural mandate to gather a special collection of materials relating to Korean communities outside the Korean peninsula: the Korean diaspora. Another focus centers on the Korean Independence Movement, much of which was centered in the Los Angeles Korean community. Much effort has been put towards collecting unpublished, archival materials in these areas, as well as the published records.

From the very beginning, the Library has enjoyed the active and enthusiastic support of the Friends of the Korean Heritage Library, a committee of prominent members of the Korean community (most of whom are USC alumni) dedicated to advancing the Library's program. The Friends have been a central element in the development strategy of the Library, offering both intellectual and material assistance. The Friends of the Korean Heritage Library deserve much of the credit for the fact that the Library's endowment for the purchase of Korean materials now stands at approximately three quarters of a million dollars.

Over the years, the Library has received the generous support of the Korean Research Foundation and the Korea Foundation in building its collection. Alumni and other private supporters in Korea have also played important roles.

The Library has established exchange relationships with several academic and other research libraries in Korea. These include the libraries of Seoul National University, Yonsei University, the National Central Library, and the National Assembly Library. The USC Korean Heritage Library is also a "depository" for North Korean materials.

May 8th, 1992 11 AM at S. Central Ave.

The Korea Central Daily

THE EAST ASIAN STUDIES CENTER AT USC AND ITS OUTREACH

John E. Wills
Director, East Asian Studies Center
University of Southern California

The East Asian Studies Center is the interdisciplinary organization of the faculty and staff of the University of Southern California who engage in teaching and researching information relevant to China, Japan and Korea. The Center has members in ten departments of the College of Letters, Arts and Sciences and in more than six professional schools. With the support of general University funds, grants from the United States government, and contributions from private donors, the Center supports the work of graduate students concentrating on East Asia, shares in the administration of region-wide seminars on Chinese Studies, Japanese Studies and Korean Studies, and disseminates information learned from these studies to primary and secondary school teachers in Los Angeles. In addition, the Center has participated in fund-raising efforts for the Korean Heritage Library and for other East Asian collections.

The East Asian Studies Center organized and continues to administer an interdisciplinary program for undergraduate students and is presently organizing an interdisciplinary masters program. Already in place is a program which sends USC students abroad for a semester or a year of study in Japan, and plans are being made to have a similar arrangement with the Korean Language Institute at Yonsei University in Korea.

The Center also arranges for visiting scholars from various countries in Asia to come to USC. The outstanding contributions these people make is felt not only during their tenure here, but in the friendships which develop and remain strong, long after their return to their native countries. Visiting scholars provide information and materials which can be used in the Center's Korean Studies program, and many are able to provide hard-to-obtain data such as government publications which, while not secret, are not readily available in bookstores. These valuable connections allow the East Asian Studies Center in general, and the Korean Heritage Library in particular, to compile a diverse collection, strong in both depth and scope.

Up until the early 1970s, East Asian studies at USC, as at most universities in the United States, focused on China and Japan, with Korea mentioned only in passing. With the establishment of the USC Center for East Asian Studies as an independent body, headed by Dr. George Totten, great strides were made in expanding the teaching of East Asian cultures; specifically in illustrating the differences among those cultures while encouraging the uniqueness of each to surface for closer examination. East Asia was no longer talked about as though it were one large group with a common mind-set, rather, each culture was taught as a separate entity, thereby allowing for more concentrated, in-depth focus.

Early in the development of the Center, the Department of East Asian Languages and Cultures began to teach the Korean language. Soon after, the Department of History offered a class in Korean history. Much of this was done with the support of funds raised in Korea, through the auspice of the USC Center. In the 1970s, Professor Nam Kil Kim joined the USC faculty to teach the Korean language and generally guide the fledgling development of the Korean Studies program. In 1980, a full tenure appointment was extended to a scholar in Korean history, Dr. Michael Robinson, the first such appointment to the USC Department of History. Later in the 1980s, a brilliant young sociologist, Professor Eun Mee Kim came on board—and the program continues to grow. Through deliberate and carefully made appointments the University safeguards the scholastic integrity of the program, yet its intent is always to provide as many intellectually challenging opportunities for the students as possible.

So far, the expansion plan has succeeded brilliantly. Those faculty members who have had the honor of serving as director of the East Asian Studies Center, including Dr. Gordon Berger, concur that they have expanded their own horizons as a direct result of their increased consciousness of the Korean facet of East Asian civilization. Moreover, the many friends they have made enabled them to see and understand the pride Korean scholars take in their own accomplishments and in their culture. The tremendous willingness of the Korean scholars and of members of the Los Angeles Korean community to give their time, share their materials and, in some cases, part with their own hard-earned funds, all to facilitate the development of the Korean Studies Program and the Korean Heritage Library, have not gone unnoticed.

THE USC CENTER FOR MULTIETHNIC AND TRANSNATIONAL STUDIES (CMTS) AND THE URBAN ENVIRONMENT

Alvin Rudisill
Vice President for External Affairs
University of Southern California

The earliest Korean immigrants to Los Angeles lived in the neighborhood surrounding the University of Southern California; indeed, settling in areas which have since become part of the campus. The Old Presbyterian Church on Jefferson Boulevard is one such landmark. Others include the Syngman Rhee House and the Dongsan House, situated across the street from the School of Engineering quad. Eventually, Koreatown established itself north and west of the campus, but this neighborhood was the Koreans' first home when they came to Los Angeles so many years ago.

The Center for Multiethnic and Transnational Studies was created to facilitate an understanding of and appreciation for the cultural differences between other nations and the United States, specifically with regard to the numerous multiethnic communities which comprise the Los Angeles area. Indeed, the multiethnic dimension of the entire world becomes more obvious every day, thereby suggesting that the nation state, as we have traditionally known it, is no longer sufficient to deal with rapidly changing issues. But these changes cannot and should not be denied. Rather, the whole issue of transnationalism i.e., those issues which transcend the traditional nation state, deserves to be studied and discussed, in hopes, of course, of finding a positive means of facilitating transnationalism.

To that end, the USC Center for Multiethnic and Transnational Studies aspires to develop programs which will ensure that scholars from many backgrounds and disciplines share information. In other words, that they get out of the books once in a while and actually "talk" to each other. Universities love to specialize and that's part of their strength, especially in regards to research. Yet, the price that we sometimes pay for that specialization is that we don't talk to one another enough. To correct that deficiency one of the Center's goals is to encourage interactive discussion among scholars.

A second goal is to expand these discussions to include people from all walks of life throughout the world. While scholars worldwide are studying and teaching politics, culture, social events, religion, history, literature, economics and other topics, they are also interacting with the people who live in those countries. What better opportunity to exchange information. The faculty of the USC Multiethnic and Transnational Study Center is committed to the idea that we all have to learn from one another.

The Korean American community, along with other newer communities in Los Angeles, is challenging each of us to learn from each other, respect each other, and ultimately to create a world where we all can live side by side in peace and harmony to everyone's benefit.

A third goal of the Center is to facilitate the creation of a successful multiethnic community within the diversity that is Los Angeles that will serve as a model for the rest of the world. Considering that Los Angeles is one of the most culturally diverse cities in the world, if success can be achieved here, it will signal hope for cities throughout the globe facing multiethnic and interracial challenges.

V

WHERE DO WE GO FROM HERE?

New Directions For the
Korean American Community

The Korea Central Daily

People participating in the peace march on May 2nd.

POLITICAL MOBILIZATION OF THE KOREAN AMERICAN COMMUNITY

Winnie Park
Woodrow Wilson School of International Affairs
Princeton University

Certainly we [Korean Americans] understand that coming and making the decision to be in this country, and to make our lives, and to raise our children and see our future in this country means making that adjustment. I think it's very unfair, and I thinks it's very unrealistic, for demands to be made upon an immigrant population—and I'm talking about an 85 percent first-generation, that means immigrant population to be able to instantaneously pick up the language, instantaneously participate in the political process, instantaneously establish an economic base, and instantaneously deal with human relations. The issue of race relations is something this country has struggled with from its inception, and I think that at this point in time it is extremely unfair and extremely unrealistic to expect this new wave or most recent first-generation Korean Americans to suddenly make that shift. [1]

Angela Oh's response to Ted Koppel, after he posed the commonly expressed African American opinion that Korean Americans should bridge the cultural gap, is significant not only for its content, but for its symbolic value. Oh points out that Korean Americans are very recent immigrants and that Americanization, assimilation into the larger society, requires both time and experience. Oh's commentary is significant for its symbolic value because she emerged as the spokesperson for

---

1 Angela Oh, interview by Ted Koppel, ABC News, "Nightline: Two Facts of the Los Angeles Riots," May 6, 1992.

the Korean American community by virtue of her ability to articulate the Korean American experience to mainstream society on national television. Since her appearance on "Nightline," Oh, a criminal lawyer and the president of the Korean American Bar Association, has become the voice for Korean Americans after the riot.

Controversy, however, surrounds Oh's prominence in the riot's aftermath, as first generation Korean Americans are quick to point out that she, as a 1.5 generation professional, is not attuned to the needs of the immigrant merchants. Oh is the first to admit that she neither expected nor claimed to be a spokesperson or representative of the community. Oh remarked in a recent interview, "I spoke my mind, but I did not claim to speak for Koreatown. There is an urgent need for a voice in the community."[2] Oh's position as the undeclared spokesperson for Koreatown demonstrates the challenges of filling the leadership vacuum in the Korean American community, especially in the face of intergenerational rifts and the lack of a unified voice and agenda.

Despite these obstacles, Oh and other 1.5 and second generation Korean Americans promptly responded to victims' cries for leadership, counsel and guidance in the riot's aftermath. Ryan Song, also a 1.5 generation attorney, put his own career at a downtown law firm on hold in order to serve as the Director of the Korean American Grocers Association (KAGRO). Song commented on the emerging leadership in the Korean American community: "After the riots, there was a need to have a voice, and since many first-generation Koreans have language limitations, the 1.5 and second-generation were charged with bigger roles."[3]

The urgent need for political action and group mobilization in the riot's aftermath elicited a response from all sectors of the Korean American community, not just from 1.5 and second generation professionals. The riots ignited a veritable explosion

---

[2] Oh, President, Korean American Bar Association, interviewed by Winnie Park, February 1, 1993.

[3] Diane Seco, "Fire and Pain," *Los Angeles Times*, January 31, 1993, quoting Ryan Song.

of Korean American political activity, ranging from the protest and demand strategy of Korean riot victims to the collective actions of community groups. Moreover, the riots alerted Korean Americans to the importance of mainstream politics to their own interests in Los Angeles and in the American system. Korean Americans also recognized the lack of political coherence in their own community which was divided along generational and socio-economic lines.

The riot catalyzed a political mobilization in Koreatown. This political mobilization took several forms: protest and demand, the collectivization of community groups, and the articulation of a political agenda.

PROTEST AND DEMAND ACTIVITY

Thirty thousand Korean Americans marched along Olympic Boulevard, Western Avenue, Third Street, and Vermont Avenue—the heart of Koreatown—in an unprecedented show of unity on May 11, 1992.[4] Korean Americans demonstrated their grief and mourned the death of Edward Lee, an 18-year-old Koreatown resident, was shot on April 30 when he was caught in the crossfire of a gun battle involving police and two groups of Korean Americans who mistook the others for looters. The demonstrators concluded their march in Ardmore Park, where members of the community publicly criticized political officials and the Los Angeles Police Department for their ineffectiveness in preventing and quelling the riots. This demonstration not only unified the Korean American community, it allowed the community to articulate their grievances and their opinion of local government. The Korean American community had never before engaged in such a mass showing of public sentiment.

This demonstration marked the first in a series of Korean American protests that Los Angeles witnessed during the summer of 1992. More than 250 Korean American riot victims

---

[4] Brenda Paik Sunoo, "Out of Ashes, Solidarity," *Korea Times Los Angeles: Weekly English Edition*, May 11, 1992.

marched in front of city hall from June 17 to July 2, 1992.[5] Organized by the Association of Korean American Victims of the Riots, the rally sought to protest the bureaucratic delays in the approval of intergovernmental aid and grants to rebuild businesses. Protesters beat drums, chanted "We can't wait," and carried placards that read "We demand reparations" and "Our American dream went up in flames."

The political significance of this protest manifested itself on several levels. First, the act of organizing and staging a protest, in and of itself, consolidates individual interests for a common cause. The fact that riot victims who represented businesses as different as liquor stores and swap meets, both of which are represented by separate trade associations in Koreatown, united to demand a response from city hall, is a crucial political maneuver for a community noted for its political apathy.[6] This protest activity demonstrates the "Structural Theory of Ethnic Collective Action," proposed by Michael Hechter, Debra Friedman and Malka Applebaum.

This theory assumes that when members of ethnic groups occupy distinct positions in the class or occupational structure, or in the labor market (especially disadvantaged positions), and when they become aware of a common plight, it will only be a matter of time before collective action ensues.[7]

The collective action which ensued from the "common plight" of having lost businesses in the riot was to protest and demand activity at the local level. This protest is also significant because it indicates a consciousness in the Korean American community of the importance of local government and the acknowledgment that local government must be just as responsive to their needs as it is to those of any other group in

---

5 Richard Reyes Fruto, "Riot Victims: We Can't Wait," *Korea Times Los Angeles: Weekly English Edition,* June 22, 1992.

6 Swap meets are indoor "flea markets," where groups of merchants band together to sell their goods.

7 Michael Hechter, Debra Friedman and Malka Applebaum, "A Theory of Ethnic Collective Action," George E. Pozzetta, ed. *Politics and the Immigrant* (New York: Garland Publishing, 1991), p. 104.

Los Angeles society. In other words, this demonstration was a public affirmation of the Korean American community's awareness that they too deserve local governmental attention, and that they too can affect the local officials. This consciousness of their own political viability is central to the political mobilization of an immigrant group, which has been accused not only of political apathy but also of the "sojourner mentality" of middleman minorities.

The protest-and-demand strategy of Korean American riot victims, the majority of whom are first generation immigrants, resulted in meetings with Mayor Bradley, Councilman Nate Holden and with City Council. When the protesters threatened civil disobedience on July 2, 1992, Bradley and Holden finally agreed to hear protester's demands.[8] Both officials promised to intervene in cases of disaster relief applications that the Small Business Association (SBA) and the Federal Emergency Management Agency (FEMA) rejected.

The City Council also responded to protesters' demands by forming an *ad hoc* committee on Recovery and Revitalization. The committee's goals were defined as follows: provide financial assistance for victims whose loans from the SBA and FEMA were denied; compensate riot victims; lobby the federal government and FEMA for grants to make payments on second and third mortgages; provide redevelopment funds for Koreatown; and create a single police precinct for Koreatown which is currently split between Wilshire and Rampart precincts.

Protest-and-demand proved to be a successful strategy for eliciting governmental responsiveness. Korean American riot victims not only won conferences with top elected officials, but elicited a pro-active, post-riot recovery assistance policy from local government, as well. Through their protest at City Hall, the victims' associations exhibited political mobilization which had been uncharacteristic of the Korean American community. The normative perception of Korean Americans, as well as

---

8 Richard Fruto and Gloria Chung, "Bradley and Holden Pledge Support for KA Merchants," *Korea Times Los Angeles*, July 6, 1992.

other Asian Americans, paints these groups as the "silent minority." Social scientists claim that, as an ethnic group, Korean Americans are singled out for their marginality in mainstream American society. Hwa Soo Lee asserts that Korean Americans "seem to be regarded as having little social prestige by the average American." Lee argues this point by citing the fact that studies on social distance reveal that "American people tend to associate less with Koreans than with other Asian groups."[9] Lee also contends that "various forces and social elements in the Korean community discourage solidarity and initial political organization."[10] He ranks these debilitating forces in the following manner:

(1) lack of access to information about the effects of political decisions; (2) lack of politically experienced and skilled leadership; (3) culture of subordination; (4) lack of financial resources; (5) pursuit of personal rather than group interests; (6) lack of personal trust among group members; and (7) opiates which divert energies from political paths.[11]

Though Los Angeles Korean Americans have faced these obstacles to a political involvement, the riot forced Koreatown to overcome these barriers and engage in the political process, as witnessed by the protest-and-demand activity of riot victims. In fact, to mobilize victims for the protest at City Hall, Korean Americans overcame several of these obstacles, including the tendency to pursue personal rather than group interests and the lack of trust among group members.

Each of these obstacles has been overcome in the various political strategies the Korean American community pursued after the riot. For instance, the leadership vacuum has recently been filled with the rise of Korean American spokespersons and community organizers such as Oh and Song, mentioned earlier. Moreover, the collectivization of community groups for the

9 Hwa Soo Lee, "Toward Korean American Participation and Representation in American Politics: The Case of Los Angeles," in Yung-Hwan Jo, ed. *Political Participation of Asian Americans: Problems and Strategies* (Los Angeles: University of California Press, 1983), p. 76.

10 Ibid., p. 85.

11 Ibid.

common goal of dispensing relief to riot victims disproves the status quo view that Korean Americans are self-serving and unable to work as a group. Finally, both the "culture of subordination" and the dearth of information about political participation is being combated by community groups such as the Korean American Coalition (KAC). Each of these venues of political participation have come about in response to the cry from Koreatown for post-riot help.

COLLECTIVIZATION OF GROUP INTEREST

The collectivization of community groups first occurred during the rioting itself when seven community organizations banded together to form a defense force of 220 people in order to protect businesses in South Central from looters and arsonists.[12] In this instance, the Korean American community responded swiftly to crisis, especially in the face of police abandonment of South Central and Koreatown. This collective activity lasted only a few days, but the riot's aftermath witnessed unparalleled mobilization, organization and collectivization among community groups in Koreatown.

KAIAC

Most notably, the formation of the Korean American Inter-Agency Council (KAIAC) signaled a new era of cooperation and ethnic mobilization in Koreatown. KAIAC is the product of coordinating the resources and services of nine Korean American voluntary associations: Coastal Asian Pacific Mental Health, Korean American Coalition, Korean American Food and Shelter Services, Korean American United Students for Education and Services, Korean Family Counseling and Legal Advice Center, Korean Health Education and Information Referral Center, Korean Immigrant Workers' Advocates, and Koryo Health Foundation.[13]

---

12 Fruto, "Cry Koreatown," *Korea Times Los Angeles: Weekly English Edition*, May 4, 1992.

13 Korean American Inter-Agency Council, "Press Packet," Los Angeles, CA, December 23, 1992.

Prior to the riot, each of these organizations played a distinct role in social service delivery to the Korean American community. For instance, the Korean Immigrant Workers' Advocates (KIWA) outlines its goals in its mission statement:

> Korean Immigrant Workers' Advocates (KIWA) is a non-profit, community service organization that provides bilingual job-related legal assistance and services to Korean immigrant workers. KIWA's mission is to empower Korean immigrant workers and to promote political awareness and social responsibility throughout the entire Korean community. Our motto is "Working with Dignity."[14]

KIWA's programs include job-related legal assistance, such as claims for back wages and overtime, counseling and referral for sexual harassment, as well as educational programs such as computer training and English as a Second Language (ESL) instruction. Immediately after the riot, KIWA and other community groups pursued their individual victims' assistance programs in keeping with their distinct organizational goals and purposes. For instance, KIWA's response to the needs of riot victims took several forms:

> KIWA has directly serviced 150 compensation appeals as well as providing support and organizing strategies for the Korean Victims' Association. KIWA opened a volunteer service center where KIWA staff and concerned youth volunteered to prepare documents and follow through the complicated application process with the relief applicants. KIWA organized several public meetings and demonstrations attended by hundreds of supporters and riot victims to protest against police inactivity and legal injustice.[15]

These post-riot activities are listed in an application for funding that KIWA sought in June of 1992 to produce a multilingual resource booklet "bringing together the voices of grassroots leaders in the Asian, Latino and African American communities to learn each others' experiences and perspectives and strive for common goals."[16] KIWA's initiatives to provide assistance for riot victims and to generate preventive,

---

14 Korean Immigrant Workers of Southern California, "Application for Funding," Los Angeles, CA, June 1992.

15 Ibid.

16 Ibid.

educational measures against future rioting exemplify the individuality of organizational response to riot victims. At the same time that KIWA's staff and volunteers were assisting victims with applications for compensation, the Korean Family Counseling and Legal Advice Center was also providing some of the same services. Moreover, these two organizations were competing for funds from the same intergovernmental agencies and private sponsors. The overlap not only proved to be inefficient, but ineffective, as the application for funding KIWA's booklet was competing with the educational programs of other agencies. In the end, all these organizations lost both money and time, as Roy Hong director of KIWA attests, "Prior to that [KAIAC], agencies were not working together. But we felt individual agencies could not effectively help the victims. This effort [KAIAC] symbolizes the coming together in the community."[17]

KAIAC developed a case management model in coordinating service delivery among the various agencies. KAIAC describes its case management model as follows:

> In an effort to coordinate victim assistance, the Inter-Agency Council seeks to implement a family-focused case management service delivery model which will provide the following for each individual family: (1) assess the needs specific to both health and welfare economic recovery; (2) monitor the recovery process along a continuum; (3) intervene at points where specific needs are identified; and (4) maintain aggregate data on outstanding needs for use in advocating policy or systemic changes. The proposed family-focused case management approach has three components: Needs Assessment, Case Management, and Resource Development.[18]

These three components outline the sequence in which service delivery will take place. First, Needs Assessment identifies the number of victims in need of service and also determines exactly what services these individuals need. This task is carried out through phone surveys and the systematic

---

17 Seco, "Fire and Pain," *Los Angeles Times*, January 31, 1993, quoting Roy Hong.

18 Korean American Inter-Agency Council, "Overview of Proposed Model", Los Angeles, CA, December 1992.

collection of data on victims' situations. After this information is compiled, the Case Management coordinators are assigned to victim families in order to deliver the actual services— counseling and guidance. Finally the third component or Resource Development acts as "springboards from the needs assessment analysis." This committee has two responsibilities. First, this group keeps abreast of the assistance available to victims from various intergovernmental and private sources. Second, this group acts as "the advocacy arm of the Inter-Agency Council and pressures government to meet the immediate needs of victims as well as proposing public policy initiatives."

KAIAC's comprehensive approach to service delivery not only mobilizes and consolidates the efforts of Koreatown's voluntary sector, it also actively engages itself in the political process by monitoring government and formulating public policy. Hechter, Friedman and Applebaum also point out a latent function that KAIAC can perform in the mobilization of the Korean American community:

> To the degree that members value the private benefits provided by ethnic organizations and to the degree that these benefits are not available to them elsewhere, they will be dependent on the organization. The greater their dependence, the more willing they will be to engage in collective action.... These organizations have an important effect on the stability and solidarity of ethnic communities since they become the focus around which extensive interaction on a regular basis takes place. [19]

As the only provider of long-term assistance for Korean American riot victims, KAIAC is a bastion of stability for a community which has not only undergone traumatic losses, but has also encountered tremendous obstacles in attaining the meager assistance that it has received. KAIAC has also been instrumental in maintaining networks in Koreatown. For instance, KAIAC features a biweekly column in Korean language papers in order to keep the community aware of the organization's progress and to keep the community aware of the

---

19 Hechter, Friedman, and Applebaum, p. 116.

situation among riot victims. The victims' community's dependence on KAIAC is growing. The organization possesses tremendous potential for mobilizing riot victims in their advocacy projects.

KAGRO AND OTHER COMMUNITY INITIATIVES

Besides KAIAC and the voluntary sector's response to the needs of the victims, other organizations have answered the post-riot cry for help. Most notably, the National Korean American Grocers Association (KAGRO) launched a "three-prong campaign to help their embattled members."[20] The project seeks to fulfill three tasks: (1) provide relief to riot victims; (2) set up an interethnic dialogue; and (3) create a distribution system to make prices in small mom-and-pop businesses competitive with bigger stores. By establishing a national cooperative, merchants can save up to 40 percent on merchandise by eliminating middleman profits. KAGRO hopes that such measures will help relations between Korean merchants and Black customers, who often complain that Korean small businesses exploit them by raising the prices of goods. KAGRO announced this plan while issuing a statement on the riots to the mainstream media:

> ...the real issue [in South Central Los Angeles] is pervasive racism and poverty. Korean Americans have been wrongly and unjustly scapegoated for America's societal problems. We believe the U.S. government is responsible for restoring our community's confidence and faith in our own system.[21]

This statement epitomizes the pro-active stance that community groups have taken in charging the government with responsibility for the riot and in protecting their own group's interest. KAGRO's position that Korean Americans are not to be blamed certainly goes against the "culture of subordination" view of Korean Americans proposed by Lee. Furthermore, the

---

20 Sophia Kyung Kim, "KAGRO Launches Relief for Embattled Merchants," *Korea Times Los Angeles: English Edition,* May 26, 1992.

21 Kim, quoting KAGRO.

concept of a national cooperative for Korean grocers represents a collective action of great significance for Korean small businesses which, though informally networked through trade associations, have yet to engage in business partnerships.

Cooperative efforts have also been witnessed among Korean American professionals, as five Los Angeles law firms banded together in order to gather riot-related claims to be filed against local government for damage and injuries.[22] The Korean American Bar Association, Asian Pacific Legal Center, the ACLU, the law firms of Ko and Adest, and Alfred, Maroko, Goldberg and Robokoff have collectively offered their services to aid riot victims. This union of both non-profit and private firms seeks to make local government accountable for the losses of riot victims. Koreatown has, therefore, initiated legal, protest-and-demand, and collective action strategies to make local government responsive to their needs. Such political mobilization addresses the immediate needs of the victims, but does not ensure long-term political voice and representation, which are achieved most effectively through multiracial coalition building and electoral strategy.

KOREAN AMERICAN COALITION

Like other voluntary associations in Koreatown, the KAC reacted to the riot by coordinating their own efforts with those of other groups which possessed similar goals. On November 22, 1992, forty Korean American civil rights leaders from four cities met in Koreatown in order to forge a national Korean American civil rights group.[23] The Korean American Voters in New York, the Korean American Alliance in Washington, D.C., the Korean American Professional Society, and the Korean Center in San Francisco, along with the Korean American Coalition (KAC), decided to initiate the national group at a

---

22 Fruto, "Asian Pacific Law Coalition Formed to Collect Riot Claims," *Korea Times Los Angeles: English Edition,* September 14, 1992.

23 Fruto, "Plans for National Civil Rights Group Under Way," *Korea Times Los Angeles: Weekly English Edition*, December 9, 1992.

convention in May 1993. In the interim, these four groups engaged in an organizing committee, the Korean American National Organizing Committee (KANOC). KANOC has defined the national organization's goals as follows:

Bilingual voting ballots, bridging generations, electoral politics, information resources including census data about the Korean American community, leadership development, legislative lobbying, media monitoring (English language), media relations with English and Korean language media, political education for Korean Americans, public information about the Korean American community, race relations, racist violence, racism, racially motivated hate crimes, voter education, and voter registration.[24]

The goals of the national group seek to remedy the apathy notoriously connected with the Korean American community. According to KAC President Gary Kim, "The Korean American Coalition has been tossing around the idea for years, but the 1992 riots painfully showed the need for a national voice in government and mainstream society and media."[25]

This effort to forge a nationwide alliance among Korean American advocacy groups is in keeping with KAC's mission statement:

KAC's mission is to promote and advance the civic, legislative, and political interests of the Korean American community so that it can become a full participant within the broader society. KAC's goal is to educate, organize, and empower the Korean American community through social, cultural, educational and political activities.[26]

Executive Director Jerry Yu states that KAC was established ten years ago "in response to the changing needs of a growing Korean American community."[27] Yu claims that in the last three years KAC has made a conscious effort to expand and to establish itself in Los Angeles: "My position as Executive Director just came about in the past few years

---

24 Yu, "KAC and Four K.A. Groups Form National Organizing Committee," *KoreAm Journal* (December 1992), p. 31.

25 Fruto, "Plans for National Civil Rights Group Under Way," quoting Gary Kim.

26 Korean American Coalition, *Yearbook: 1983-1991* (Los Angeles, California, 1991), p. 14.

27 Yu, Executive Director of the Korean American Coalition, interviewed by Winnie Park, February 2, 1993.

because our projects could no longer be manned by volunteers. We needed full-time advocates and a staff."[28]

According to Yu, KAC is the only political advocacy group for Korean Americans in Los Angeles. Since the riot, the organization has fielded calls from media representatives world-wide, including Great Britain, Australia, France, and even Rumania.

KAC is actually the only existing venue for advocating civic participation in the Korean American community. Their activities represent a whole spectrum of community needs. An analysis of KAC's activities from 1983 to 1991, as listed in the organization's *Yearbook*,[29] reveals that the organization has focused its attention on several broad categories: (1) addressing education and leadership among Korean American youth; (2) serving the needs of recent immigrants by offering legal advice and other counsel; and (3) promoting membership and fundraising for KAC itself. Secondary activities for this organization were: (a) teaching the Korean American community about American civic society; (b) promoting electoral involvement; and (c) building coalitions with other groups. The most significant contributions that KAC has made in engaging the Korean American community in electoral politics were voter registration drives every presidential year since 1984 and community forums for local elections. KAC has held four such forums in the seven-year span since its inception in 1984, until 1991. There is not a single mention of coalition-building listed in the *Yearbook* for these same seven years. Despite the lack of coalition-building activities, the *Yearbook* features a section entitled "KAC—Striving to Build Coalitions." This article, written in 1991, is rather ironic, for it highlights the very issues which KAC and Koreatown faced in the 1992 riot. For instance, the article emphasizes the Black/Korean conflict:

---

28 Ibid.

29 *The Korean American Coalition Yearbook, 1983-1991* (Los Angeles: 1991) has served as the primary record of the group's activities and history, according to Executive Director Jerry Yu.

Asians and other minorities are beginning to make up a greater percentage of the population than ever before. As this percentage continues to grow, more interactions between Asians and other minorities and whites will occur. Many times the interactions will be positive. But sometimes, the difficulties of learning to coexist together can also result in violence. Hence the heart wrenching aftermath of the Latasha Harlins and other Black/Korean incidents beckons us to take notice and start taking concrete steps to prevent them from occurring in the future.[30]

This article was originally printed in the KAC *Newsletter* in May 1991, along with an article condemning the police brutality witnessed in the King beating. Both articles stress the importance of making public officials accountable for the needs and protection of minority interests:

We [Korean Americans] must keep up with issues and politicians. We must vote. We must write letters to elected officials to remind them of their campaign promises. We cannot do it alone. If we do not join hands with other people of color in recognition of our own common struggle for equality, the inevitable increase in minority tensions will fall on our children.[31]

This plea for coalition-building and the foreshadowing of increased racial tensions indicate that the Korean American community was well aware of the potential for increased conflict between African Americans and Korean Americans in Los Angeles.

Irony not only riddles KAC's warning about increased ethnic tension, but also marks KAC's activities on the first day of rioting. Jerry Yu, the executive director, explains that KAC had announced a cooperative effort between the NAACP and the Urban League to support the passage of a police reform measure, Charter F, the day the rioting broke out.[32] In fact, Jerry Yu and nine other members of KAC attempted to attend the meeting at the First AME Church at 6:30 p.m. on April 29. The historical church meeting was followed by an eruption of violent activity as rioters took to the streets. Yu and his

---

30 Ibid., p. 54
31 Ibid.
32 Yu, "1992 Year in Review," *KoreAm Journal* (December 1992), p. 31.

colleagues could not gain entrance to the church and decided to return to KAC headquarters at 8:00 p.m. In the midst of the rioting, KAC was instrumental in dispensing information to Koreatown. KAC not only informed the primary Koreatown communications networks, Radio Korea and KCB, of the verdicts, but they also organized press conferences to express the Korean American community's horror and disbelief over the not-guilty verdicts. The immediacy of their response to the rioting was invaluable to the Korean American community, especially in the face of police abandonment and isolation.

KAC's activities after the riot closed the promise/performance gap between the organization's promotion of coalition-building and mobilization of Koreatown in electoral politics and the actualization of such rhetoric. KAC not only launched its national civil rights group, but it also engaged in a full-scale voter registration drive in conjunction with two newly-formed groups, the Korean American Republican Association (KARA) and the Korean Democratic Coalition (KDC). These three groups sponsored a mayoral candidates forum on March 18, 1993, in an effort to engage Korean Americans in local politics.

THE KOREAN AMERICAN REPUBLICAN ASSOCIATION AND THE KOREAN DEMOCRATIC COALITION

It is appropriate that KAC, KARA and KDC work in conjunction with one another to promote electoral politics in Koreatown. Gary Kim, who acts as both the president of the KAC and the vice president of KARA, embodies the fact that the membership of these organizations are by no means mutually exclusive. Kim explains, "The membership of these three groups overlap. KARA does not seek to compete with KDC or KAC, which is non-partisan. We split up because the [Korean American community's] chances of being represented are that much greater if we support both Democratic and Republican candidates."[33] Gary Kim claimed that the

---

33 Gary Kim, President of Korean American Coalition and V. P. of Korean American Republican Association, interviewed by Winnie Park, Oct. 18, 1992.

membership of KAC is inclusive of both KARA and KDC, but the split along partisan lines occurred after the riot. KARA's press statement explains the riot's influence on the formation of partisan political groups:

> One bitter dose of reality that became all too apparent during and after the Los Angeles riots was that Korean Americans were politically nonexistent as far as the politicians were concerned. Our so-called elected representatives did very little in coming to aid our community. During this presidential election year, more Korean Americans have turned their attention to what it is we can do to ensure that such an injustice will never take place again. We must mobilize and organize the KA community to make our elected officials be accountable for their actions or lack thereof. Korean Americans must start playing a more active role in mainstream politics whether it be at the local, state or federal level.... The Association will serve to support those candidates who best support the interests of the KA community. The Association will also serve to educate our community of Republican philosophy and beliefs which we firmly believe is very much in line with the Korean culture and values that our Parents have instilled in us.[34]

This statement of KARA's formation and mission again acknowledges the importance of mainstream politics in the riot's aftermath as Korean Americans were left defenseless before hordes of rioters without proper governmental protection. KARA's first initiative to engage Korean Americans in the electoral process was a voter registration drive, which solicited voters at churches, supermarkets and office buildings as KAC had done since 1984. KARA boasted 700 new registered voters after its effort. KARA's other activities include sponsoring a public service announcement stressing the importance of voting and an absentee ballot drive. KARA assumed the traditional role of partisan political groups by hosting luncheons with candidates and fund-raisers for the Bush/Quayle 1992 campaign. KARA also pursued innovative measures to increase public awareness of political opportunities, such as a workshop on the application process for the White House Fellowship.

KARA's spontaneous formation in the wake of the riot gives testimony to the Korean American community's ability to

---

34 Korean American Republican Association, Press Statement, 1992.

mobilize quickly and effectively in response to crisis. KARA
was formed the first of October and by October 12 hosted a
luncheon for U.S. Senate candidate Bruce Herschensohn. In
fact, by October 28 the agenda for KARA's weekly meeting
included media appearances, the formation of a KARA election
hotline and plans for getting chartered by the Republican
National Committee. Within a month KARA had mastered a
complex organizational structure, complete with officers and
membership fees, and had initiated measures to increase voter
turnout. KARA's ability to mobilize so quickly demonstrates the
fact that the Korean American community possessed the
infrastructure for political mobilization prior to the riot; and yet
it required a crisis to catalyze Korean American involvement in
the political process.

The catalysis of political responsiveness from the Korean
American community after the riot was not only witnessed
through the collective efforts of community groups, but also
through individual activity. According to Robert Park, the
program director of KAC, "of the 167,000 Korean Americans
living in Los Angeles County, about 21 percent are registered
voters. About 2,000 Korean American voters registered after the
riots."[35] Park goes on to say, "Right before the June primary, we
received 1,000 calls in one week from people wanting to
register to vote. Many people were frustrated and they realized
what kind of effect the lack of political power had on them.
They now want to be part of the process."

KOREAN AMERICAN ISSUES IN LOCAL POLITICS

After the riot, the forced recognition of the importance of
mainstream political involvement compelled Korean Americans
to respond in several ways other than simply registering to vote.
For instance, Korean Americans formed partisan organizations
to provide more venues for political participation. The riot also
engendered the political mobilization of Korean American
secondary associations which banded together to confront
government in the name of victims' needs. The riot opened up

---

35 Seco, "Fire and Pain," quoting Robert Park.

channels of communication between groups of Korean Americans who had previously shared no dialogue. This political mobilization proved to be both necessary and timely as the riot's aftermath witnessed many new problems for Koreatown.

Besides the difficulty that victims have faced in attaining SBA loans and FEMA grants, they also faced obstacles in rebuilding their businesses, be it bureaucratic delays in granting building permits or licenses, or outright denial of the rights to rebuild, as in the case of liquor stores. On May 14, Assemblywoman Marguerite Archie-Hudson proposed ABX40, a measure to void licenses for destroyed liquor stores if authorities determined that too many alcohol-related crimes existed within a 500 square foot area of a liquor store.[36] African American leaders have advocated the reduction of liquor stores in South Central for years. Supporters of ABX40 point out that there is a disproportionate number of liquor stores in South Central, as 760 stores serve the population of 500,000.[37] Advocates of ABX40 claim that the high concentration of liquor stores increases the incidence of violent crime in South Central.

In spite of such claims, KAGRO President Ryan Song insists that ABX40 violates the rights of Korean American merchants to reestablish the businesses they once operated. Song and a coalition of attorneys spoke in defense of Korean American liquor store owners, who had the right to rebuild what they had received permission to build prior to the riot.[38] Song and his colleagues were successful in fighting on behalf of Korean American liquor store owners against ABX40, which was defeated in a 0 to 8 vote in the State Assembly Committee on Governmental Organization on June 29, 1992.[39]

---

36 Fruto, "Liquor Bill Dies: Bradley Forms Special Task Force," *Korea Times Los Angeles: Weekly English Edition*, July 6, 1992.

37 Ibid.

38 Ryan Song, presentation to University of Southern California Conference on New Directions for the Korean American Community, Los Angeles, CA, March 19, 1992.

39 Fruto, "Liquor Bill Dies . . . "

Liquor store owners face other obstacles in addition to ABX40. The Los Angeles City Council passed a law requiring liquor store owners to undergo a public hearing process before rebuilding their businesses.[40] Under the ordinance city officials can impose regulations on liquor store owners, including the restriction of store hours and the mandatory hiring of security guards. As of January 31, 1993 only 16 liquor stores had undergone the public hearing. Although all 16 stores were allowed to rebuild, the feeling among Korean American small business owners is that city hall has been dragging its feet, purposely postponing some of the hearings.

The ordeals which the Korean American liquor store owners face alerted the community to the salience of local politics to their own livelihood. Political officials exercise considerable power over the riot victims, as they possess the power to issue (or withhold) building permits and the political influence to elicit federal governmental response such as FEMA grants. The importance of local politics compelled Korean American community groups to increase their political leverage in the city council by seeking to create a single district to represent Koreatown. KAC instigated a redistricting plan which would gather all of Koreatown, presently divided into three districts, into one district. Councilman Nate Holden has represented the bulk of Koreatown, but as Jerry Yu asserted:

> We like Nate Holden. It's [redistricting] not a referendum on his performance as Koreatown's representative. The issue is trying to reunify Koreatown. If that is resolved... Koreatown will be able to have a much greater voice, not only in determining who that representative will be, but also who will become a larger part of that person's district and influence that person more.[41]

KAC's proposal for a single Koreatown district was supported by the Filipino American Public Affairs Council as well as the Chinese American Citizens Alliance, both of which sought to coalesce with Korean Americans in order to gain

---

40 Seco, "Fire and Pain."

41 Kay Hwangbo, "Holden, Groups Differ on One-District Plan for K-Town," *Korea Times Los Angeles: Weekly English Edition*, May 4, 1992.

greater representation on the city council. In fact, the KAC proposal advocated that Filipino Americans in the Temple-Beauchy/Westlake-Echo Park area be lumped together with Koreatown's district. KAC's primary backers for redistricting in Koreatown included the Korean Garment Industry Association, Koreatown Crime Task Force, Korean Business and Professional Association, and the Women's Association.

KAC's efforts to unite Koreatown in one district and the initial attempts at coalition-building with the Filipino American community were defeated on May 29, 1992, when the city council voted nine to four to divide Koreatown between three districts.[42] The council's decision divides Koreatown between the Tenth, Fourth and First Districts. In each of these three districts, Asian Americans represent 15 to 16 percent of the population. Latinos comprise the majority in both the Tenth and First Districts, while Anglos constitute the majority of the Fourth District. This plan portends either very well or very badly for Korean American influence on city council. In the worst case scenario, Korean American needs will be ignored or overlooked for those of the majority. In the best case scenario, Korean Americans will win the ears of three rather than just one council member. What is clear is that Korean Americans must forge alliances with the other ethnic groups in their district in order to achieve political leverage in the city council.

Although the plan to contain all of Koreatown in one district was overruled, KAC's efforts to increase Korean American representation initiated coalition-building between Korean Americans and Filipino Americans. This initial step in forming bi- or multiracial coalitions promises to be the key to Korean Americans' future in mainstream Los Angeles politics.

CONCLUSION

The riot marked a political watershed for the Korean American community. Koreatown mobilized through both individual and collective efforts. Angela Oh and other members

---

42 Hwangbo, "Council Remapping Plan Keeps Koreatown Divided," Ibid., July 20, 1992.

of the 1.5 and second generations did not abandon Koreatown, instead they volunteered their time and their professional counsel to riot victims, most of whom were recent immigrants. Even first generation immigrant entrepreneurs challenged the stereotypical "culture of subordination" view of Asian Americans, by organizing and protesting outside City Hall. These victims were aided by various voluntary associations throughout Koreatown. Several of these organizations collectivized their services and consolidated their fundraising efforts, as in the case of the Korean American Inter-Agency Council (KAIAC). Overall, Koreatown's aggregate response to the riot can be categorized as mass political mobilization.

The immediacy of Koreatown's response to riot victims demonstrates the fact that Koreatown already possessed the infrastructure for effective political mobilization. The Korean American community has exhibited effective leadership and tremendous organization. If Koreatown can mobilize its voters and coalesce with other groups as effectively as it has mobilized its community advocates and consolidated interests within Koreatown after the riot, the future for Korean Americans in mainstream politics is truly promising.

CREATING MULTICULTURAL HARMONY?
A CRITICAL PERSPECTIVE ON COALITION-
BUILDING EFFORTS IN LOS ANGELES

James A. Regalado, Ph.D.
Executive Director
Edmund G. "Pat" Brown Institute of Public Affairs
California State University, Los Angeles

RIOTS, STRAINED RELATIONS, AND ASKING THE WRONG QUESTION: AN OVERVIEW

In the wake of the inter-racial and inter-ethnic conflict and violence which have been significantly growing in Los Angeles County over the past several years, and ultimately culminated in the riots and civil disorder of Spring '92, numerous calls have been made to "join together" in the efforts being made to heal the wounds which badly separate racial and ethnic groups in the City and its environs. Much of the call has been aimed at bridging "dialogue gaps" between Korean and African Americans. Fewer calls have been made to bridge dialogue and other gaps separating Latino and African Americans while still fewer have been made to bring Latino, Korean and other Asian Americans together. The commonality of the calls, whether many or few, has been to begin the process of dialogue, finding and building on common ground, good faith negotiation, and the healing that would inevitably result in building towards the multi-cultural plurality the city had—symbolically—become before last year's telling events.

These calls have, for the most part, been shortsighted. Based on simplistic analyses of fundamental problems responsible for much of the segregation and polarization found in both the city and county of Los Angeles, the calls for more and more dialogue without accompanying structural remedies are similar, in a sense, to the bland messages of the L.A. mayoral candidates in the election campaign of 1993. During the mayoral primary campaign, candidates ranging from front-runners Michael Woo, Richard Riordan and Richard Katz to the less formidable candidacies of Nate Holden, Linda Griego, Tom Houston and Julian Nava, provided simplistic law-and-order responses both to the cause of last year's "bread riots" (see Pastor 1993) and to the likelihood of a similar event following the federal civil rights trial involving the LAPD and Rodney King. Most of their "recipes" for city healing focused on hiring and allocating more LAPD officers, targeting undocumented immigrants in one form or another, and promoting simplistic rhetoric devoted to building inter-ethnic group dialogue. In the mayoral runoff election pitting Councilman Michael Woo against businessman Richard Riordan, class, ideological, and policy choices abounded but were drowned out in a sea of ad hominem attacks and simplistic calls for "healing."

In this paper, which is part of a larger historical study of multi-racial coalition-building in Los Angeles, I briefly explore selected theories of multi-racial coalition-building and apply tenets of those theories to five coalition formations created since the mid-1980s, ostensibly to confront increasing racial polarization and inter-racial hostility in the City of Angels. I argue that coalition failures in this period were due to (1) improperly defining and assessing the problem, (2) relying on building a middle class membership and constituency, (3) being unclear on goals, objectives, strategies and precise actions, and (4) being unable to overcome provincialism.

METHODOLOGY

Methods employed in this paper, as well as in the larger research undertaking, comprised traditional means. Literature on race relations, coalition theory and political incorporation, was selectively surveyed as were press reports on coalition activity in both the mainstream and independent written press. In addition, I acted in participant-observer roles in three of the five coalitions addressed in this work. Conversations were held with members of the five coalitions as well as with scholars involved in related forms of research. Interviews were conducted with selected coalition members as well. Finally, information was also gleaned from a year-and-a-half long forum and conference series on race relations in Los Angeles sponsored by the Edmund G. "Pat" Brown Institute of Public Affairs on the campus of California State University, Los Angeles.

COALITION BUILDING AMIDST AND AGAINST "L.A. REALITIES": A THESIS STATEMENT

Although there are many well-intended and well-founded efforts (ranging from conflict resolution/moderation programs, public forums, and fledgling attempts to coalesce) to prevent further disruption in relations among the city's predominant cultural groups, any discussion of broad "healing" is entirely premature. It is my contention that in order to more fully confront the major issues which divide Los Angeles around race and class, and which prevent broader and more pervasive multicultural understanding and more consistent and sustainable coalition-building, broad and diverse streams of citizens and residents need to more honestly and thoroughly confront a series of fundamental questions.

First, the meaning of representative democracy in a rapidly changing city, particularly in communities of color, must be critically examined and honestly rethought. This is especially meaningful in the context of the increasing reach and influence of global economies amidst diminishing local resources, continuing struggles over voting rights and political representation, historical class and race biases of local political systems and structures, and political incorporation/coalition necessities and strategies (see Regalado, 1991; Sonenshein, 1989).

Second, the nature of economic "rebuilding" and development/redevelopment must be examined, especially with reference to a more inclusive (and democratic) role for residents in communities of color and to models of development which make such inclusion possible. Historically, local and regional policy makers have strongly endorsed corporate center economic development models and strategies that minimized or totally ignored roles for and input from working, poor and middle-class communities while denying economic development projects to the city's most needy communities (see Mann, 1993; Dymski, 1992; Regalado, 1991; Pastor and Hayling, 1989).

Third, key issues of race and class, which act both as personal and collective community barriers and divides, must be concretely defined, articulated and examined, including how they are interlinked. Examining one without the other begets only partial and incomplete analysis. This becomes especially crucial given the historical class and racial biases structured into local political systems. Recent bi-racial or multi-racial coalition-building activities discussed in this paper have failed to be effective in large part due to the ignoring of this dimension of the city's past and present reality.

Fourth and last, the very meaning of multicultural pluralism, beyond "L.A. symbolism," must be rethought, especially in this urban context so beset by fear, segregation and polarity. This sub-topic begs a series of sub-questions on co-existence and governance. Is L.A., as it presently exists, governable? Is segregation and division, much less pluralism, governable? How do we make the city more inclusive, interactive and governable? Responding to the first three question areas on this and the previous page, of necessity, leads to making decisions on these following questions.

It is my contention that tackling such questions, especially in beginning coalition formation, can be used as a guiding framework for the establishment of more sustainable coalition formations and, through such efforts, beginning policy and action guides. In large part, the future of the city has always resided with a coalition of players who often controlled major economic decisions and the body politic as well. In the wake of the demise of the "Bradley coalition" (see Sonenshein 1993), on the one hand, and the riots and disorder of last Spring, on the other, the time for fashioning a newly dominant coalition is ripe. However, the "calls" must be made on the basis of focusing on an agenda of relevant questions and concerns.

EXPLORATION OF COALITION AND INCORPORATION THEORY

It is widely acknowledged (Calderon, 1993; Regalado 1992; Munoz and Henry 1991, Sonenshein, 1991) that few theoretical works exist on the creation of bi-racial, much less multi-racial, coalitions beyond the African American and liberal White models. Eisinger (1976), Browning, et. al. (1984, 1990), Mollenkoph (1989), Sonenshein (1989, 1993) and others have used such models largely to explain an African American political incorporation thesis. However, for coalition-building more broadly among communities and groups of color, few scholarly works exist.

Perhaps for this reason, in part, earlier works by Martin Luther King (1967) and Carmichael and Hamilton (1967), and, more recently Browning, Marshall and Tabb (1984, 1989) and Henry and Munoz (1991), still resonate. For King, political alliances (coalitions) among people of color must be honestly and openly based on some self-interest of each participant and group as well as on a common interest into which they merge as a larger group. His vision, created in and through the civil rights movements of the 1950s and 1960s, was that of a coming together of people of color, liberal and progressive Whites, organized labor, and selected clergy for the larger purpose of advancing civil rights agendas.

Carmichael and Hamilton became more specific. They contended that four issues must be understood and resolved in building multi-cultural coalitions. First, all parties involved must recognize the self-interest of each party/participant. Second, there must be an accompanying mutual belief that each party to the coalition stands to benefit from allying with others. Third, there must be broad acceptance that each party has its own independent base of power and external decision-making. Fourth and finally, there must be widespread agreement that the coalition must deal with specific and identifiable goals and issues, as opposed to theoretical abstractions. I believe that this remains a valid test of more recent attempts to build multi/bi-racial coalitions of color. That application will be mentioned below.

However, Uhlaner (1991) provides notes of caution to inter-racial coalition-building in her recent study of inter-racial/ethnic attitudes in Los Angeles. She contends that although "clearly, a coalition of minorities must rest on some common ground" (340), discrimination which most groups of color feel does not necessarily lead to cooperation, much less coalition-building. Discriminating experiences, she writes, "might produce antagonisms instead of coalitions" (341). Whether or not this is a defining variable for inter-racial antagonisms, clearly inter-racial antagonisms continue to abound in Los Angeles.

Rufus Browning, Dale Rogers Marshal, and David Tabb (1984, 1986, 1990, respectively) developed a theory of minority political incorporation that has been applied to a variety of cities in the United States and abroad. Their dominant thesis is that in order for a community of color to become incorporated into a local political system (i.e., sustained coalition policy influence over a city council), it must coalesce and mobilize as a community before it seeks coalition partnership with at least one other group. In other words, it is difficult in urban America to find an example of a community of color that can "make it" politically on its own. Most of the Browning model applications, including those in the city of Los Angeles by Sonenshein, found a White liberal community, often Jewish, had become the favorite coalition partner begetting African American political incorporation.

If the models of both coalition building and political incorporation among communities of color in Los Angeles are applicable to the "City of Angels" in the aftermath of both the riots and the bi-racial electoral coalition which was largely responsible for the City Hall successes of African American politicians including Tom Bradley, recent history might be telling. In the next section, five selected case examples of multi/bi-racial coalition-building over the last seven years will test various tenets of theories referenced above.

THEORY APPLIED: CASE STUDIES OF MULTI/BI-RACIAL COALITION-BUILDING IN LOS ANGELES

Contrary to reports of the news media and city and county officials before Spring '92, Los Angeles had long been a segregated and polarized society. This is not to deny that the city has a progressive and coalition-building history. However, within the "balkanized" metaphor that Los Angeles is, the society known as "L.A." has also changed substantially. Old models, old explanations, and old analyses need to be either discarded or seriously updated. However, old messages and old "calls" for the city to "regenerate" still dominate most "rebuilding" designs. Witness the title of Professor Raphael Sonenshein's impressive new book—*Politics in Black and White*—itself a throw-back to a more simplistic view of the city's social troubles which never truly fit with the reality of the city's historical multicultural harmonies and disharmonies.

Recent history is illustrative here. Among a number of well-intentioned but shortsighted and failed bi-racial coalition calls and ventures, the Black-Korean Alliance and the Black-Latino Roundtable come immediately to mind. Both were created with assistance from, and guidance by, the Los Angeles County Commission on Human Relations in the 1980s, with the participation of approximately thirty "community groups" (but without the community).

Black-Korean Alliance: As reported by Doherty (1992), the "Alliance," as it came to be known, was the city's oldest organization (created in 1986) "dedicated to easing tensions between these two ethnic groups." The reason for the breakup? It became painfully obvious, especially after the Soon Ja Du-Latasha Harlins issue and the spring riots, that talk and dialogue were simply not enough. The Alliance could never get beyond an "elite" dialogue stage. Understated were the Alliance's remove from class issues and, relatedly, from other than professional and public sector elite constituencies. The serious class differences and issues to confront, and the grassroots community constituencies to be led, were nowhere to be found. Korean merchants and residents from south central Los Angeles were never involved in the Alliance. Other problems included the lack of permanent staff, sparse meeting attendance, and an inability to forge a consensus on a number of issues. Also, the Alliance could never get beyond the provincialism of individual member group and racial-group loyalties. Therefore, the common interest needs, rising above the tide of provincialism, which were called for in both the King and Carmichael-Hamilton models, were not met.

The Black-Latino Roundtable: Similar conditions afflict the Black-Latino Roundtable, which was also created in 1986. This coalition among bi-racial elites has all but formally failed for many of the same reasons. Tensions and conflicts among the area's burgeoning Latino populations and its declining African American populations have long existed in the southland. However, they have been increasing at alarming rates, whether measured by housing project intimidation or gang violence, public school brawls, competition over few employment opportunities, immigration, and/or redistricting and political representation issues. Most of these issues affect grassroots communities. However, the composition of the Roundtable has been heavily membered and dominated by professional African and Latino Americans, although some, such as recent former co-chairs Mark Ridley-Thomas (then representing the Los Angeles Chapter of the Southern Christian Leadership Conference [SCLC]) and Antonio Villaregoisa (then representing a number of community organizations and United Teachers of Los Angeles), were sensitive to community groups and issues. The sometimes well attended symposia and conferences of the past, sponsored by the Roundtable, could not hide their failure to overcome provincial racial-group loyalties and suspicions of others on the Roundtable, its primarily elite membership, and its inability to mobilize the grassroots community. In both coalition examples, members frequently could not get beyond the narrow nationalism and racial-group loyalties necessary to bridge gaping community wounds and divides. As a result, broad consensus on important and timely issues was seldom reached. This formation failed to clearly and, for the most part, honestly articulate points of member, self, and mutual interests. In the process, it also failed to meet the criterion of rising above provincial agendas and suspicions.

Two additional organizations, The Ethnic Coalition and the New Majority Task Force, are, unlike the examples of the Alliance and the Roundtable, not tied to a public sector sponsor and continue to pursue multiracial/ethnic goals from different ideological perspectives and political approaches.

The Ethnic Coalition is, however, traveling a more familiar route than the New Majority Task Force, in attempting to reach multiracial consensus goals. Created in the hope of becoming a powerful forum for multicultural issues and membered by a professional "who's who" of local Asian, Latino and African Americans, the Coalition reflects a mainstream approach by essentially well-meaning professionals of color. Ideologically moderate, most of its energies seem to be incorporated into holding an annual conference, providing public policy perspectives, and lobbying policy makers at both state and local levels on an array of public policy issues. To its credit, it has recently become involved in pushing, at an elementary stage, single-member district inclusion models of representation on regional governmental and planning bodies. The Coalition should not be dismissed but its membership does not presently reflect a capability of rising above its intellectual and professional middle class membership roster and origins. Again, the assumption may be made that it does not connect with grassroots class and community diversity where much, if not most, of the inter-racial/ethnic tensions exist. This coalition does not link well with the type of progressive coalition King called for and its agenda and style of work appear to be much broader and diffuse that the focus on specific agendas and issues within that agenda stressed by Carmichael and Hamilton.

The New Majority Task Force is the most politically progressive of the bi-racial or multi-racial "coalitions" yet referenced. Created in a founding conference in 1989, its multi-cultural membership is also largely professional and intellectual but with two significant differences. First, the membership makeup of the Task Force is decidedly more politically left-of-center, that is, more obviously progressive. Second, and relatedly, the membership of the Task Force more clearly represents an inclusive economic development agenda for the city and region and a direction for the coalition. Thus, it has a more tightly focused agenda concentration than the groups referenced above. It has been effective in getting one of its founding members (Mark Ridley-Thomas) elected to the L.A. City Council, where it considers him to be its policy "lightning rod" on that important legislative body. In this regard, the Task Force might be considered to be incorporating itself politically into the politics of the city, including City Hall. In order for true political incorporation to occur however, the coalition must remained organized, mobilized, and in influential contact and interaction with the dominant coalition on the City Council. Until recently the Task Force had not been meeting these criteria. It met irregularly and although its academic and professional members have conducted important policy-related studies concerning housing, practices of inner city lending agencies, and enterprise zones, the organization has been also beset by lack of sustained links to grassroots community residents. To its credit, differing class perspectives are noted and discussed and guide much of its work. More recently, the Task Force has begun meeting regularly, created staff positions through member organization internships, linked up with a grassroots activist coalition, and begun preparing for a policy-driven community economic development summit.

The Multicultural Collaborative is the most recent coalition formation, born only in 1992, mentioned in this paper. The Collaborative is seeking to get beyond the failures of the Alliance and Roundtable as well as the limitations of the Ethnic Coalition, in part by focusing on key issues involving race and class, in part by assessing needs in a variety of communities of color, in part by developing a grassroots organizing component, and in part by having full-time staff members and organizers. The Collaborative is made up of a number of multi-racial organizations which have histories of seeking solutions to inter-ethnic conflicts in Los Angeles. Funded at significant levels for its first two years, the Collaborative has begun participating in joint ventures with the New Majority Task Force and other organizations.

With the exception of the New Majority Task Force and the Multi-Cultural Collaborative, social class is largely absent from the perspectives and analyses of most of the "coalition" efforts responding to increasing calls to unite the city. This absence factored heavily into the failures of two of the coalitions mentioned earlier. Additionally, limited constituency bases, narrow foci on dialogue, and unclear generalized goals, also helped to preempt their efficacy and longevity. As such, they became part of the failed elite vision that had prematurely labeled Los Angeles as already being a model of multi-cultural pluralist inclusion and democracy. The events of Spring 1992 thoroughly exposed this as merely symbolism and charade. Also exposed was the notion that dialogue opportunities alone, especially in the absence of class and racial analyses, mixtures, and directed efforts, on the one hand, and sustainable agendas for structural changes in the city and county, on the other, cannot close the severe "racial" divides.

SUMMARY

It has become obvious that the public sector lacks the will and resources to commit to bridging serious divides in "human relations" in the city. This is revealed by the extremely limited staffing (of two full time employees) of the city's Department of

Human Relations and in the City's turning over economic
development responsibilities and obligations to the private-
sector-driven, and secretive, Rebuild L.A. (RLA).

With this particularly in mind, I contended in this paper that
the shape and substance of the future of Los Angeles resides, in
large part, on the extent to which influential multi-cultural,
class-based coalitions are created and sustained. The building of
such coalitions, in my view, must begin by asking and assessing
key questions and critical concerns, such as those relating to the
(1) practical meaning of representative democracy and political
incorporation particulary among communities of color, (2)
degree to which working class and poor communities can
become incorporated into economic development planning and
outcome scenarios in the city, (3) interlinked issues of race and
class which act as communication barriers and socio-economic
divides, and (4) practical meaning of multi-cultural pluralism as
a goal for the city.

Of the five coalitions referenced in this paper, only the New
Majority Task Force and the Multi-Cultural Collaborative
appear to meet most of the concerns and questions raised in this
paper. However, their future is anything but certain.

REPRESENTATIVE DEMOCRACY
IN CONTEMPORARY LOS ANGELES

The City of Los Angeles has changed enormously over the
past twenty years. However, most of the profound change has
come in the form of (1) demographic makeup, (2) downtown
and westside economic development and (3) the political
dominance of a viable governing coalition. What has not
significantly changed is a more democratic inclusion keeping up
with the city's rapidly changed demographic landscape. This is
less true for the city's African American population, which, if
taken as a whole with no attention to class differences and
deviations, has controlled 20% of the city's council seats and the
office of the mayor since 1973. This is also not the case with the
city's Jewish population which, since the 1950s, has had better
than proportional representation on the city council. However,

neither Latinos nor Asian Americans, unlike African Americans and Jews, have been proportionally represented on the council in this century.

The Latino population of Los Angeles has grown enormously since 1970. Officially, Latinos have grown from representing 19.7% of the city's population in 1970 to 27.6% in 1980 and 39.9% in 1990. By the year 2000, half of the city's population will be Latinos. However, in 1990 only approximately 12% of the city's registered voters were Latinos. When it comes to being represented on the city's policy making body, the city council, in a strong-council and weak-mayor format, in this century Latinos were represented by a lone council member (Edward Roybal) from 1949 to 1962. The second Latino council member (Richard Alatorre) was elected as the council's lone Latino in 1986 and still serves. For the first time in this century, two Latinos served at the same time when in 1987 Gloria Molina was elected to a reconfigured 1st District created as the settlement of a voting rights lawsuit against the city. Mike Hernandez, who was elected to Molina's 1st District seat when she moved on to the County Board of Supervisors in 1991, currently serves along with Alatorre. Combined, the two, who represent overwhelmingly Latino majority districts, represent but 13.3% of all council seats/districts. Often bitter infighting among Latino and African Americans over the city's 1992 redistricting overshadowed coalition-building attempts in both communities. In general, African Americans fear the prospect of losing political ground in the wake of less and less impressive demographic ground. On the other hand, Latinos have been pressing hard to obtain two additional and more substantial Latino majority districts, one in the downtown area and the other in the San Fernando Valley.

The first, and only, Asian American council member was elected to the City Council in 1985. Asian growth in the City was even more vociferous than the formidable growth of Latinos. In 1970, Asian Americans represented 2% of the city's population. By 1980 Asians represented 5% and by 1990 10% of that population. If Michael Woo had been elected mayor,

Asian Americans would have been without an Asian council member—a potentially formidable consideration since in L.A.'s weak mayor format the mayor has little to no control over the making of public policy. Additionally, if he had been elected it is not a given that an Asian would have replaced Woo in his 13th councilmanic district, which does not have an Asian majority.* The riots of Spring '92 have brought even more to the forefront the issue of Asian American, particularly Korean American, representation in the city's politics. Even with Woo on board, he alone could not prevent the council's targeting of Koreatown and other heavily Asian populated areas of the city being either artificially or culturally split apart in mooting out the 1985 voting rights lawsuit against the city.

REFERENCES

Browning, Rufus P., Dale Rogers Marshall and David Tabb (1986) "Minority Power in City Politics," *PS* 19:3 (Summer): 573-640.

———— (1984) *Protest Is Not Enough: The Struggle of Blacks and Hispanics for Equality in Urban Politics.* Berkeley: University of California Press.

———— (1990), eds. *Racial Politics in American Cities.* New York: Longman.

Carmichael, Stokely and Charles V. Hamilton (1967) *Black Power.* New York: Vintage Press.

Calderon, Jose (1993) "Latinos and Asian Pacific Americans: The Role of Leadership and Strategy in Multi-Ethnic Coalition-Building." An unpublished paper.

Doherty, Jake (1992) "Black-Korean Alliance Says Talk Not Enough, Disbands." *Los Angeles Times* (December 24): A-1.

Dymski, Gary A. and John M. Veitch (1992) "Race and the Financial Dynamics of Urban Growth: L.A. as Fay Wray." In Gerry Riposa and Carolyn Dersch, eds. *City of Angels.* Dubuque: Kendall/Hunt, pp 131-57.

Eisinger, Peter K. (1976) *Patterns of Interracial Politics.* New York: Academic Press.

———— (1983) "The Politics of Racial Economic Advancement." In William C. McCready, ed. *Culture, Ethnicity, and Identity:*

---

* Michael Woo was not reelected in 1993 to the City Council.

Current Issues in Research. New York: Academic Press, pp. 95-109.

Henry, Charles and Carlos Munoz, Jr. (1991) "Ideological and Interest Linkages in California Rainbow Politics." In Byran O. Jackson and Michael B. Preston, eds. *Racial and Ethnic Politics in California.* Berkeley: IGS Press, pp. 323-38.

King, Martin Luther, Jr. (1967) *Where Do We Go From Here?* New York: Harper and Row.

Mann, Eric, ed. (1993) *Reconstructing Los Angeles From the Bottom Up.* Los Angeles: Labor/Community Strategy Center.

Mollenkoph, John (1989) "New York: The Great Anomaly." In Rufus Browning, et. al., eds. *Racial Politics in American Cities.* New York: Longman Press, pp. 75-87.

Munoz, Carlos, Jr. and Charles P. Henry (1990) "Coalition Politics in San Antonio and Denver: The Cisneros and Pena Mayoral Campaigns," In Rufus P. Browning et al., eds. *Racial Politics in American Cities.* New York: Longman, pp. 179-90.

Pastor, Manuel (1993) *Latinos and the Los Angeles Uprising: The Economic Context.* Claremont, CA: The Tomas Rivera Center.

———— and C. Hayling, eds. (1990) *Economic Development: The New Majority in Los Angeles.* Los Angeles: Occidental College.

Regalado, James A. (1991) "Organized Labor in Los Angeles City Politics: The Bradley Years." *Urban Affairs Quarterly* 27 (September): pp. 87-108.

———— (1992) "Political Representation, Economic Development Policymaking, and Social Crisis in Los Angeles, 1973-1992." In Gerry Riposa and Carolyn Dersch, *City of Angels.* Dubuque: Kendall/Hunt Publishing Company, pp. 159-79.

———— (1991) "Reapportionment and Coalition-Building: A Case Study of Informal Barriers to Latino Empowerment in Los Angeles County." In Roberto Villarreal and Norma Hernandez, eds. *Latinos and Political Coalitions.* New York: Greenwood Press, pp. 126-43.

Sonenshein, Raphael J. (1993) *Politics in Black and White: Race and Power in Los Angeles.* Princeton: Princeton University Press.

———— (1989) "The Dynamics of Bi-racial Coalitions: Crossover Politics in Los Angeles." *Western Political Quarterly* 42 (June): 333-53.

Uhlaner, Carole J. (1991) "Perceived Discrimination and Prejudice and the Coalition Prospects of Blacks, Latinos, and Asian Americans." In Byran O. Jackson and Michael B. Preston, eds. *Racial and Ethnic Politics in California.* Berkeley: IGS Press, pp. 339-71.

Korea Times, L.A.

Peace Rally at Olympic Blvd.

THE IMAGES OF MINORITIES
IN THE MASS MEDIA

Jung S. Ryu
Publisher, *KoreAm Journal*

Because of the popular perception of the mass media as a powerful force in shaping social reality, it is often blamed for having a bad influence on society and for distorting reality, especially with regard to ethnic minorities. Evidence shows no clear-cut formula or mediating factors through which the media exerts force. Thus, it is argued that it is not media, but a socio-cultural hierarchy in the U.S. that engenders discrimination against ethnic minorities. In order for Korean Americans to have positive images in the mass media, Korean Americans should become a part of the institution, and should eventually change it.

MASS MEDIA EFFECTS

The emergence of a mass society laid the foundations for various forms of mass communication, such as newspapers, magazines, radio, film, and television. Members of a mass society are preoccupied with their own individual pursuits and development, and eventually lose their ability to identify with and feel in community with others. They are psychologically isolated individuals. Although interacting with one another, they are inwardly oriented and bound together primarily through contractual ties. The mass media readily satiated these isolated individuals with all kinds of information, entertainment, advertisement, etc., and in the process, the mass media became a social system.

At first, the functions of the mass media seemed to be very simple. Newspapers supplied readers with news or information and radio supplied listeners with news or entertainment. It wasn't long, however, until profit started to play a major factor in the media business, generating various complaints from both producers and receivers. Producers wanted freedom to produce higher quality programs. Parents, who sensed damaging effects from some of the media's content, demanded, for the sake of their children, more pro-social norms and less depiction of sex and violence. Legislative bodies were enlisted to streamline industries, protect consumers/voters rights, and regulate the financial backers of production. When it appeared obvious that the effects of the mass media seemed enormous, many social science scholars engaged in the study of the social effects of the mass media.

During and after World War I, propagandists produced outrageous lies against others through the mass media. This raised many serious questions on the effectiveness, along with the morality, of propaganda. Lasswell (1927) wrote:

> But when all allowances have been made, and all extravagant estimates pared to the bone, the fact remains that propaganda is one of the most powerful instrumentalities in the modern world. It has arisen to its present eminence in response to a complex of changed circumstances which have altered the nature of society. Small primitive tribes can weld their heterogeneous members into a fighting whole by the beat of the tom-tom and the impetuous rhythm of the dance. It is in orgies of physical exuberance that young men are brought to the boiling point of war, and that old and young, men and women, are caught in the suction of tribal purpose.

This innocent observation was the basis for a relatively straightforward instinctive stimulus-response (S-R) theory (often called "hypodermic needle theory" or "transmission belt theory"). Then came the radio dramatization of H. G. Wells' "War of the Worlds" on Halloween Eve, 1938. Although carefully announced in advance that the radio play was fictitious, the broadcast struck the audience with such terror that many of them fled their homes to avoid the "invasion." After this incident, people became increasingly aware of the media's influence on themselves and society.

By the end of World War II, a new medium, television, started gaining popularity much faster and more widely than people had imagined. The advancement of television opened a new age for audiences in the mass society. In 1949, Cantwell and Ruttinger found that television was rapidly displacing other popular leisure-time activities such as radio-listening, movie-going, and reading. In 1956, Bogart wrote that "television had achieved indisputable ascendancy over the other mass media." The average school child in grades 1-8 was watching television over three hours a day. Educators believing in the "learning" theory, which explains how we learn by observation, argued that the visual media, especially television, is the major source of social learning. Since the content of television is often far more violent than reality, public attention focused on the effects of television violence on audiences, especially children. DeFleur and Ball-Rokeach best described the situation:

Attempts to understand and identify how television audiences are affected by violent television programming were intensified in the 1960s and early 1970s by a national sense of urgency concerning the causes of real-world violence. The 1960s will probably be remembered by social historians as a decade of violence—a time of urban riots, increasing rates of violent crime, and collective protests against such matters as the Vietnam War, institutionalized racism and pollution. It was also a decade of assassinations of such major political figures as Martin Luther King, Jr., John Kennedy, and Robert Kennedy.

The American Family Association put a full-page ad in *The Los Angeles Times* (March 2, 1993) blaming the mass media for its bad influence on children, families, and society. Part of it reads:

We Are Outraged: We're dismayed that today 1.1 million girls between the ages of 15 and 19 get pregnant each year. We're shocked when we learn that two-thirds of all births to 15- and 19-year-old girls are out of wedlock. We're frightened at the way violence and crime are spreading everywhere and threatening our children, our families and our homes. We say it's time to put the blame where we think it belongs: Shame on the music industry for letting singers who are the idols of our children put out records and music videos which blatantly encourage sex and "say" to our children that sex is proper at any age ... that everyone is "doing it" and abstinence is old fashioned. Shame on Hollywood .... NBC TV ... TV programmers ... the film industry .... TV Soap Opera producers ....

While there is evidence and research findings that the mass media is a powerful social force, there is also solid research findings which indicate that the media's effect is negligible. As early as 1940, a study of voter behavior conducted by Lazarsfeld and his associates at Columbia University, in Erie County, New York, during the election of 1940, reported that the media had relatively few direct effects with regard to changes in voting during the election campaign. McQuail (1969) after reviewing many studies on media effects wrote:

> For those who want a simple answer about the power of the mass media, it would have to be in the negative. Such an answer, although in many respects misleading, would fit most of the available evidence. The most careful experiments and surveys have failed to substantiate the wide claims on behalf of mass media or the fears of critics of mass communications.

In 1960, Klapper in *The Social Effects of Mass Communications* contended that television violence usually does not produce significant increases or decreases in the probability of audience aggression, and concluded that "persuasive mass communication functions far more frequently as an agent of reinforcement than as an agent of change." When the report from the Surgeon General's Scientific Advisory Committee on Television and Social Behavior (1972) was released, many critics of television violence were disappointed to read that it found no direct cause-effect relationship between television and children's aggressive behavior. A study by Vidmar and Rokeach (1974) clearly supports Klapper's notion. They have found that the viewers, whether prejudiced or not, regarded Archie Bunker in "All in the Family" as enjoyable or funny. Significantly, high-prejudiced persons were more likely than low-prejudiced persons to admire Archie over Mike, and to perceive Archie as a victor in the end. More interesting was the finding that high-prejudiced adolescents were more likely than low-prejudiced adolescents to perceive Archie as making "better sense" than Mike. The findings tend to prove that watching a TV program is influenced by an existing attitude or value, including prejudice in viewers, not vice versa.

MEDIATING FACTORS

With these seemingly conflicting evidences emerging out of tireless research, some social scholars introduced different theories. Difficulty to change any opinion or behavior through communication is explained by the principles of selective exposure, selective retention, and selective perception. Thus, the main effect of communication becomes reinforcement. Given these dimensions of research findings and theories, Berelson's following observation in 1948 still holds true: "Some kinds of communication, on some kinds of issues, brought to the attention of some kinds of people under some kinds of conditions, have some kinds of effects." Researchers try to find those "some kinds of people under some kinds of conditions with some kinds of effects." And research on "mediating factors," rather than direct linkage between media and people's behavior, received a great deal of attention. Conditions, personalities, social factors, sociological and psychological variables are some examples of "mediating factors" found.

1. Theories of Persuasion

The development of research on message reception and audience personalities was influenced by three theories of persuasion. They are: the learning theory, the dissonance (or consistency) theory, and the functional theory. Tan (1981) summarized the research findings on audiences in seven general principles. They are stated with various conditions:

1) People do not necessarily avoid information that contradicts their opinions, choices, or behaviors. There are many qualities of messages which are important determinants of audience attention, other than whether they are supportive or not. If there are rewards in a message which can cancel out possible discomfort from contradictory information, it will not be avoided;

2) Perception is often subjective. We often perceive objects to serve an immediate purpose (e.g., to satisfy a need or reinforce a mood, mental set, or cultural value);

3) Accurate and favorable perceptions of the message can be facilitated by (a) using objects and categories familiar to the audience; (b) establishing a positive bond with the audience early in the communication interaction; and (c) using message cues that the audience will readily recognize and evaluate favorably;

4) Although early research indicated that we learn information which supports our attitudes and behaviors to a greater extent than material which opposes or contradicts them, recent research has shown no evidence of selective retention;

5) In an ongoing communication situation, receivers will selectively attend to the message;

6) The most common relationship between personality variables and persuasibility is non-monotonic—an inverted U-curve, with intermediate levels of the personality variable being associated with the most persuasibility. Most personality traits have opposite effects on message reception and yielding. The net effect on persuasion, then, is non-monotonic;

7) Communicators adjust their messages to minimize differences with extreme audiences and to emphasize similarities. These strategies facilitate acceptance by the audience.

2. Selective Perception

In a summary of selective perception study, Dennis (1978) listed the three factors, all of which work together to restrict selective perception, as follows:

1) The ubiquity of the media. The ability to be everywhere, to dominate the information environment. The media are so ubiquitous at times that it is difficult for a person to escape a message;

2) The accumulation of messages. One should look beyond the individual, fragmented messages to the cumulative effect over time. Periodic repetitions of the message tend to reinforce its impact;

3) The consonance of journalists. There is an amazing and unrealistic agreement and harmony among journalists and others involved in the message. There tends to be a sameness to newspapers and newscasts. This limits the options the public has for selective perception.

Whereas "effect studies" consider socio-demographic variables and crude classifications of media content as independent variables, "uses-and-gratifications studies" attempt to find independent sociological and psychological variables. Audience needs are more important than media content in gratifications research. Individuals' various needs are served by both the mass media and the contents of each medium. Katz, et al. (1973) defined three mass media-use variables which could lead to media gratifications: (a) media content—news, soap operas, television crime drama, etc.; (b) media attributes—print vs. broadcasting, reading vs. audio or audio-visual modes of reception; and (c) typical exposure situations—at home vs. out-of-home, alone vs. with others. Elliott et al. (1976) found that there is some cross-cultural consistency between media utilization by an Israeli sample and by a sample of American university students. Ryu (1980) found that Korean Americans in the Los Angeles area used the mass media for their various needs in the neo-socialization process. Roberts and Schramm (1973) distinguished two kinds of content in television programs—reality content and entertainment content—and argued that each type of content has its own functions.

This short review of the related literature suggests the mediating factors in responding to the media's contents are numerous and complex. There is no clear-cut media formula or mediating factors through which the media exert force. With this in mind, we turn our attention to the main theme of this paper: How images of ethnic minorities are formulated among members of the mass society.

CONSTRUCTION OF SOCIAL REALITY THROUGH THE MEDIA

Actual social reality and a person's perception of social reality do not usually coincide. Besides, a human being has the capability to perceive reality with abstract concepts that leads to a constant clash of ideas among people. In this sense, what really counts in a person's social life seems to be the person's social reality. Roberts (1971a) explains how a person's social reality is created throughout his/her life:

> Regardless of how we subdivide and label its various aspects, it is clear that man creates a reality which extends well beyond the objective environment. His world contains abstract concepts such as justice, morality, and love. It spans continents, oceans, cultures; it recognizes roles, norms, and expectations; it extends backward into history and forward into the future; it touches on gods and angels, devils and furies. In short, human reality contains many features which an individual never directly experiences, many dimensions for which no tangible referents exist. Such a reality cannot possibly be structured completely out of the information contained in natural sign. Indeed, one of the more remarkable characteristics of human reality is the large portion of information concerning it that can be passed on *only* by other persons, whether in a face-to-face exchange or through the pages of a book or the channels of a television set. In other words, much of human reality is structured not from interpretation of informational signs which occur naturally in the environment, but from interpretation of informational signs which men create and through which they exchange information - from human communication.

In this age of mass communication, people rely on the mass media for much of their information. Thus, it becomes very critical to know how mass media constructs a social reality for the members of a society. Garbner et al., (1978) referred to the construction of social reality as an effect of mass communication as media "cultivation" or "enculturation." The basic assumption was that the media is able to determine people's perceptions about the facts, norms and values of society through selective presentations and by emphasizing certain themes. Because of this assumption, people started complaining that the media's portrayal of reality is untrue or distorted.

This argument is ever-increasing when it relates to the depiction of minorities. The battle rages as each minority—racial, religious, occupational, or sexual—tries to get the mass media to portray its members the way they would like to be depicted.

When Warner Brothers released the movie *Falling Down* in February 1993, the reaction from two minority groups, the Korean American community and aerospace workers, was outrage. There was a scene where the main character, Foster, referred to as D-FENS, physically destroys a Korean American grocer's property, assaulting Lee, the store owner. D-FENS insults him for his ignorance, heavy accent, high prices of the item sold, etc. Laura Park wrote in *KoreAm*'s March 1993 issue:

> The negative, stereotypical portrayal of Lee are the images that Korean Americans have been combating before, and especially after the Latasha Harlins incident. Many Korean American store owners have and still continue to suffer abuse from other communities because of the spread of these types of misrepresentation. This movie's insensitivity toward victimized Korean American store owners will only serve to encourage cruel stereotypes.... Influential companies such as Warner Brothers should not contribute to society's downfall by distributing and promoting movies like *Falling Down*.

Michael K. Woo, a Los Angeles City councilman, wrote an open letter to Robert Daly, chairman of Warner Brothers, claiming that "*Falling Down* offers up the most objectionable racial stereotypes imaginable of Asian Americans and Latinos. I believe Korean Americans in particular will be—and have a justifiable right to be—incensed over the one-sided stereotype presented."

The *Los Angeles Times*' business section of March 1, 1993, printed a headline "Fed Up With 'Down' Some Aerospace

Workers are Outraged at Film" with a story of angry aerospace workers in the Los Angeles area. "But some workers interviewed by the *Times* expressed outrage at what they considered the movie's unfair and damaging portrayal of their profession." In the article, Jacqueline Jones, who was laid off in recent months from the McDonnell Douglas plant in Long Beach, was quoted as saying that, "some people believe what they saw in movies, and it could make them think aerospace workers were kind of loony and that it could be really misleading to the public."

All the complaints against the mass media, if recorded, would be too voluminous to comprehend. The portrayal of various minorities in mass media cannot be the whole picture of any group. It is partial and fragmental by the nature of the media. Media and minorities are on a collision course. O'Connor (1979) observed:

> There are Jews who come out fighting at the slightest criticism of Israel, justified or not. There are Irish who don't like to be reminded of their humble beginnings in this country. NBC's recent dramatization of *Studs Lonigan* drew strong protest from some Irish-Americans, because they found insulting the use of crude language or the scenes of sexual promiscuity, or a hundred other details. The fact that these things may have been portrayed accurately is totally beside the point for these "Defenders of the Image." For consumption by outsiders, they are content to limit perceptions of the Irish to the lovable slyness of a Barry Fitzgerald in *Going My Way*.

One of the reasons why the media's depiction of minorities is partial and distorted may be found in cheap commercialism or sensationalism. For several centuries, racism against colored ethnic groups was institutionalized in the United States. The irrational ideas that perpetrated racism in America were imported from Europe, although by no means were they confined to that continent. One must realize that, in a long-range, historical perspective, racism was a common element in every major culture. The unique element in America was racism's gradual disappearance or diminution. Yet, because of the racial, cultural and ethnic diversity of America, racial stereotypes have not disappeared. The mass media only too frequently exploits these stereotypes for sensationalist purposes. These pursuits of the media then play into the hands of those who, for whatever reason, wish to convince the common consciousness that racism is still a vital force in American culture.

RACISM AS INSTITUTIONALIZED IN AMERICA

Robert Blauner (1972) of the University of California, Berkely, argues that racism is institutionalized in American society:

> The United States was founded on the principle that it was and would be a white man's country. Nowhere was this insistence expressed more clearly than in the hegemony of Western European values in the national consciousness and in the symbolic forms that have expressed this cultural hegemony-institutionalized rituals (such as the ceremonies of patriotism and holidays), written history, the curriculum of the schools and today, the mass media.

He further argues about Asian immigrants that, although they came to this country by their free will and are thus different from African Americans who entered as slaves, the status and size of these ethnic groups have been rigidly controlled, contrary to those of European immigrant people.

The same trend is well illustrated by a cover story from *Time* magazine's November 18, 1991, issue when it reported California's status as endangered. The story was written and edited with the implication that the legal and illegal immigrants in California are to blame for that state's problems. Three stories in the issue were pure fabrication. First, in its preface, it said in large print: "Ethnicity comes in mindboggling variety: Los Angeles has . . . more Koreans than any other city outside Seoul. . . ." The facts are that Pusan, Taegu, Inchon, Kwangju and Taejon, all cities outside Seoul, each has over one million Koreans, while the number of Koreans in the U.S. (according to the 1990 Census) total less than one million. Los Angeles is reported to have less than 80,000 Korean-origin Americans.

Second, in a story of the same issue "Immigrants ... don't quite fit together," it was implied that every year new immigrants come to California endangering the American dream, when, actually, the majority, or 78.4 percent of one year's new arrivals of 836,700 people, were from other U.S. states. Third, Frank McCulloch, a veteran newsman of 50 years, expressed his viewpoint on "Why the smiles are gone," from the dominating stand of the White conqueror, ignoring the Native American's experiences of why smiles were gone when McCulloch's forefathers first came to the States. Thus, the editors of the stories consciously or subconsciously weaved the Klansman's theme—immigrants are to blame.

Because of these factually and philosophically false statements, those non-Whites who take the mass media's message seriously become rapidly alienated from the White population—or at least from what they perceive as such. Even "law and order" were viewed by African Americans during the Watts revolt as "the White man's law and order." About this Blauner (1972) wrote:

> The processes that maintain domination-control of whites over nonwhites - are built into the major social institutions. These institutions either exclude or restrict the participation of racial groups by procedures that have become conventional, part of the bureaucratic system of rules and regulations. Thus, there is little need for prejudice as a motivating force. Because this is true, the distinction between racism as an objective phenomenon, located in the actual existence of domination and hierarchy, and racism's subjective concomitants of prejudice and other motivations and feelings is a basic one.

When Martin Luther King, Jr. was assassinated, most of the newscasts, analysis, commentary and perspectives were done by White men. If ever there was an assignment appropriate for a Black reporter, this was it. Blauner continues:

> Although many local stations have hired blacks, and many more must be looking for that qualified Negro, the reportage of the King assassination underlined how systematically black men and women have been excluded, on the national level, from profitable careers with the mass media. Exclusion from the desirable values of the society—the best jobs, the best homes and neighborhoods, the best schools—is a basic mechanism of racial domination.

In order to correct the media's distortion of Asian Americans, it is necessary to change the whole institution, or cultural hierarchy, in America. The institution and cultural hierarchy can be changed only when the constituents or proportion of the constituents are changed. Korean Americans should become constituents of the institution. This process is different from assimilation which asks the immigrants to change their socio-cultural value system. More writers, reporters, editors, film producers, TV programmers, along with more policemen, city councilmen, state representatives, governors, senators, attorneys and judges of Korean and Asian American descent are needed for this change in the institution. It may take time, more than a few decades. And yet, it is possible. Rather, it is imperative. And only with this can we claim the right to have real images of Korean Americans and other minorities in the mass media. I believe that a Korean American with Korean American socio-cultural values is the one who can truly depict the images of the Korean American in the mass media. In order for African Americans to rise above the distorted minority level, they need to be part of the institution. In order for non-White ethnic minorities to enjoy the freedom and pursuit of a happy life in this land of opportunity, their goals should be to obtain careers where they can contribute to the reformation of the basic institutions in the United States.

REFERENCES

Berelson, B. (1948) "What Missing the Newspaper Means." In P.F. Lazarfeld and F.N. Stanton, eds. *Communications Research, 1948-1949.* New York: Harper and Bros.

Blauner, R. (1972) *Racial Oppression in America.* New York: Harper & Row.

Bogart, L. (1956) *The Age of Television.* New York: Fredrick Ungar.

Cantwell, F. V. and K. F. Ruttinger (1949) "Some Observations on the Social Effects of Television," *Public Opinion Quarterly.* (Summer).

Dennis, E. E. (1978) *The Media Society.* Dubuque, IA: W. C. Brown Co.

DeFleur, M. L. and S. Ball-Rokeach. (1975) *Theories of Mass Communication.* 3rd ed. New York: David McKay Co.

Elliott, W. R., et al. (1976) "Functional Similarity Between Media: A Cluster Analysis Based on Media Gratification." Paper presented to the Western Speech Communication Association at San Francisco.

Garbner. G. et al. (1978)"Cultural Indicators: Violence Profile No. 9," *Journal of Communication* 28.: 176-207

Katz, E., et al. (1973) "On the Use of the Mass Media for Important Things," *American Sociological Review* 38.: 164-181

Klapper, J. (1960)*The Effects of Mass Communication*. New York: Free Press.

Lasswell, H. D. (1927)*Propaganda Technique in the World War*. New York: Alfred A. Knopf.

Los Angeles Times, March 2, 1993, H6.

McQuail, D. (1969)*Towards a Sociology of Mass Communication*. London: Collier-Macmillan.

O'Connor, J. J. (1979) "Toward Balancing the Black Image" *The New York Times*. (March 25): B33

Roberts, D. F. (1971a) "The Nature of Communication Effects," *The Process and Effects of Mass Communication*. In W. Schramm and D. F. Roberts, eds. Urbana: University of Illinois Press.

———— and W. Schramm (1971b) "Children's Learning From the Mass Media." In W. Schramm and D.F. Roberts, eds. *The Process and Effects of Mass Communication*. Urbana: University of Illinois Press.

Ryu, J. S. (1980) "Media Functions Among Minorities: A Comparative Analysis of Media Uses." Paper presented at the Annual Convention of the Association for Education in Journalism, Boston, MA.

Tan, A. (1981) *Mass Communication Theories and Research*. Columbus, OH: Grid Publishing.

The Surgeon General's Scientific Advisory Committee on Television and Social Behavior. (1972) *Television and Growing Up: The Impact of Television Violence*. Washington, DC: U.S. Government Printing Office.

Vidmar, N. and M. Rokeach (1974) "Archie Bunker's Bigotry: A Study in Selective Perception and Exposure." *Journal of Communication* 24: 36-47

PORTRAYAL OF KOREAN AMERICANS IN THE MASS MEDIA

Kapson Yim Lee
Editor, *Korea Times*, English Edition

I came to the United States from Seoul, Korea, as an immigrant 20 years ago, and have lived in Los Angeles ever since. I have worked for the *Korea Times Los Angeles* since 1973, literally growing up with the newspaper and the Korean American community. In 1981, I established the English edition of this newspaper, and have been reporting and editing stories about the lives of Korean immigrants ever since.

For four years my husband owned a grocery market in South Central Los Angeles. While he was operating the store, seven days a week, not a single day passed without my worrying about his safety. Every evening, I would open the drapes of our living room window and watch for him to arrive. I breathed with relief only after he stepped into the house. My son, now a college student, was born and raised in Los Angeles. His life-long exposure to L.A.'s pluralistic society is manifested in the decorations which adorn his dorm room: a picture of Martin Luther King, Jr., a wall-size collage of 100 faces of African American leaders, and a Mexican national flag. His hero is Malcolm X.

For years now our family has considered Los Angeles "home," and we have tried diligently to be contributing members of this community. That feeling was undermined forever with the outbreak of the 1992 riot.

On the morning after the Rodney King verdicts, I saw a building burning just two blocks from our newspaper's office on Vermont Avenue. Along with other reporters and editors, I went outside to watch helplessly as black smoke billowed over a rooftop. As I watched, I saw a young Black male motorist—my son's age—slow his car alongside the curb. Shaking his fist, he yelled at us, "We gonna kill ya!"—then he drove off. The young man's outburst was terrifying. I hurried back to my office; my whole body was trembling, I was scared to death. I hadn't felt such terror and fear since the outbreak of the Korean War 43 years before. I can still see the anger in that young man's eyes.

I believe the anger of the Black motorist and his hostility toward me—and all other Koreans—was a creation of the mainstream media, which, for many years, had inflamed the rage and passion of Black people toward Koreans through superficial, insensitive and unbalanced coverage.

Long before the riots erupted, before Koreans and African Americans had an opportunity to get to know each other, the media pitted the two groups against each other. They inflamed the relations between Koreans and Blacks by covering these two communities only after unfortunate incidents. Until recently, none of the major news outlets, including the mighty *Los Angeles Times,* had even one experienced reporter, well-versed in Korean culture and language. What that effectively meant was that, for the most part, only the Black point-of-view got transmitted.

Koreans come from an ancient culture with a long history of oppression from within and without. If one does not know the historical and cultural heritage of Koreans, it is impossible to explain who they are and why they are in Los Angeles. Since 85 percent of Korean immigrants are Korean-speaking, it would have been absolutely essential for mainstream outlets to cover stories with qualified journalists. This was not the case, and the Korean American community suffered because of the media managers' ignorance and indifference.

What millions of Americans heard about the Black/Korean relationship was the case of Latasha Harlins, who, in 1991, was shot to death by Soon-ja Du. I believe that the targeted destruction of Korean businesses during the riot can be traced directly to the media coverage of the Soon-ja Du/Latasha Harlins case. The media's handling clearly engendered ill feelings in both communities.

The mainstream media unfailingly reported about "Korean-born grocer Soon-ja Du who killed a 15-year-old Black girl (Latasha Harlins) in a dispute over a bottle of orange juice." Of course, that was not an untrue statement, but there was more to the case than what the store's security camera recorded. The important background was that Mrs. Du's store had been the target of Black gangs for months before the shooting. The gangs had burglarized the store. Mrs. Du's family had even hired Black employees, but had had to let them go because they were stealing and working unsatisfactorily. Unfortunately, that side of the story never got full treatment. The mainstream media didn't try to present a balanced picture of this incident, thereby contributing to the ill feelings between African Americans and Korean Americans.

From the start, mainstream media outlets identified the races of the case's participants. That is, a Korean grocer killed a Black girl. This led certain Black community elements to organize against the store owner. Such racial descriptions sharply contradict the long-accepted practice in journalism which says that you don't mention the race of the persons involved unless it is critical for the reader to comprehend the story.

In early March 1993, a Black man was convicted of kidnapping, raping and killing an elderly Korean lady who was on her way to church in Koreatown early one morning. In another case, a 12-year-old Black boy fatally shot a Korean American bicycle shop owner in Monrovia, California. The victim was shot in the back of the head. Quite agreeably, none of the media reports identified the race of either victim or assailant. By contrast, the *Los Angeles Times,* in its special edition published on May 11, 1992, with the title "Understanding the Riots" juxtaposed a photo of Mrs. Du with that of Latasha Harlins, and compared Mrs. Du's light sentence to a relatively heavy sentence that had recently been handed out to a Glendale man for beating a dog. The man, a Mr. Brendan Sheen, happened to be Korean, but this fact the *Los Angeles Times* reporter either did not know or failed to mention.

During the riot, one of the most devastating blows the media struck Koreans with was ABC-TV's "Nightline" show of May 1, 1992. While reporting live from riot-stricken South Central Los Angeles, the program's host, Ted Koppel, went to an African American church to report on the "overt hostility that we have seen over the past couple of days between members of the Black community and members of the Korean community." Then he went on to solicit opinions about Koreans from Blacks, making no attempt to solicit views from Koreans. Admittedly, a week later, pressure from the Korean community in Los Angeles persuaded Mr. Koppel to interview a handful of Korean Americans, but it was too late. The damage had already been done. Thus, one could hardly refuse recognizing the emergence of a pattern: when a Korean killed a Black person, the media reported that the defendant was Korean, but in those cases where Korean store owners had been killed and robbed by Blacks, no mention of race was made. I do not believe that the mainstream media, as such, is prejudiced against Koreans. A more accurate explanation for the apparent bias is that the media is trying to be "politically correct" for fear of organized efforts by African Americans.

The effects of such a bias are clear. The Soon-ja Du case, for instance, was, at first, one of the countless homicides that took place in Los Angeles in 1991; court records show that there was no evidence of racism. Yet, when the judge sentenced Mrs. Du to a mere five-year probation following the manslaughter verdict, instead of sending her to prison, Black people implied that Mrs. Du had received favoritism from the justice system because she was Korean. Thus, the media's constant portrayal of Mrs. Du as a Korean had created an image in which the emphasis was shifted from "Mrs. Du" to "Korean," and in the public's imagination, it was quickly transformed into "Koreans." Now the conflict between Latasha Harlins and Soon-ja Du came to mean conflict between Blacks and Koreans. That court records indicate no racial conflict in the case is of no interest any longer. For what we have here is an image, a mixture of truth and fancy. And in such a blend, truth is the first, but not the only, victim.

In reporting on Korean Americans, we have seen at least two major steps by which, gradually, the truth was abandoned. First, the media unduly emphasized the Korean ancestry of Soon-ja Du, thus, indirectly, and perhaps inadvertently, contributing toward a negative image of Korean Americans in the eyes of Black people. Second, it played into the hands of those whose vested interest it was, and is, to exploit such fallacious images. The unbalanced reporting contributed to what became, as we have seen, a complete perversion of the type of democratic government one assumes exists in America. By fearing pressure groups in the from of observing the "sacred cow of political correctness," the media defaulted on its obligation to uphold honesty, and to report honestly.

When Soon-ja Du shot and killed Latasha Harlins, Black groups, led by opportunistic Denny Blackwell, decried the fact that a 15-year-old Black girl was killed. If their aim was to condemn murder and violence, perhaps the same groups should have said something about the killing of Korean American bicycle shop owner Sam Woo by a 12-year-old Black boy. But condemning violence was not, and never has been, their purpose.

Is there any real reason to fear these groups? Politically, there is none: one shall not be persecuted by police for uttering words that fail to please this or that bureaucrat. But they are right to fear the boycotts, the loud uproar they might receive from those whose political goals are endangered by uncovering their vested interest in maintaining tension, conflict, and myth. The most important argument against those myths is the truth. But is this the direction in which the media are currently going?

Today, the Soon-ja Du case seems to have been permanently etched in the libraries of the mainstream media as a classic prototype of race relations. Almost every article of newspapers, radio, and television broadcast refers to the case regardless whether their stories are relevant, or not. While reporting about the federal trial of the four police officers who beat Rodney King, radio station KFWB-Los Angeles repeated the same familiar line: "Korean grocer Soon-ja Du killed a 15-year-old Black girl over a bottle of orange juice." For the reporters and editors, the managers and publishers of the mainstream media, the short sentence may have become a handy, dramatic line. To me, this refrain sounds like an invitation to hurt Koreans, the kind of threat I received from the enraged young thug who threatened to kill all Koreans.

That these groups—or those who claim to be their spokesmen—use different standards, depending on what group the victims and the assailants belong to, is being abysmally ignored by the mainstream media. If, in giving way to the rules of political correctness, the media continues on its course, the thug and his fellows—and there are many of them—will have their way. But by reporting on the true nature of things, by uncovering that, for instance, some loud political figures decried the murder of a Black girl, but remained silent when Koreans were killed by Blacks, the fragile myth these figures have built to cover their true aim would be shattered. For it will be clear to anyone whose aim is to pit races against each other, to create conflict where there should be none, has the most contemptible goal in mind: political power. And the worst branch of the politically hungry is the one that hopes to become visible through what is called "ethnic" or "racial" politics. The media, by uncovering the truth behind their claims, have a good chance of eliminating them from the American political scene, thus contributing to the restoration of government from group-interest warfare to what it should be: the guarantor of individual rights. All that is needed to achieve that is an unfailing loyalty to the truth. That, and nothing else, is the mark of great journalism as well.

EMPOWERMENT WITHIN THE ASIAN AMERICAN COMMUNITY

Angelo Ancheta
Staff Attorney, Asian Pacific American Legal Center

When I speak of empowerment I am not talking just about getting people into political office: I mean empowerment in the sense of people being able to exercise more control over their own lives. This goal can be realized within the Korean American community, within the larger Asian Pacific American community, and within the broader community in our city.

It is important to think in terms of the broader Asian Pacific American community, because the problems evident in the Korean community are often shared by other Asian Pacific groups. Looking at the damage caused by the April 1992 riot, it was not only the Korean American community, and certainly not only the Asian American community, that was victimized. There were several Asian, non-Korean businesses damaged in that period. For example, over 200 small businesses owned by Cambodians and Vietnamese were destroyed in Long Beach alone. In addition, dozens of Chinese, Thai, Filipino and Japanese American-owned businesses were destroyed in other areas of Los Angeles County as well.

It is also important to consider what happened right after the riots, not just to the Korean American community, but to the Asian Pacific community in general in terms of visibility, involvement in policy decision making, and in the exercise of power. What happened right after those riots? The sad answer is, not much.

It is, indeed, symptomatic of earlier problems dealing with our portrayal in the media, with our lack of political and economic power. When people are in visible positions, they serve as role models, they serve as examples of their communities. We do not have those kinds of role models in the halls of power. We do have a few, we have had people like former Los Angeles Councilman Mike Woo, now we have Jay Kim in Congress; those are important people. Their presence in the halls of power, however, does not seem to be making a lot of difference.

We suffer, unfortunately, from the so-called model minority stereotype. Asians are perceived as the ideal minority that, centuries of racial prejudice notwithstanding, has somehow been able to "make it." This image persists in spite of the fact that large sectors of our population live in poverty, that there are many social welfare problems, that there are problems of substance abuse, there are problems of teenage pregnancies, problems that we don't want to think about too much. These problems are not portrayed in the media and, therefore, people do not understand that we have a full-bodied community here.

Mary Matsuda, who was a professor at UCLA's School of Law, characterized Asians, borrowing a term from Karl Marx— which is a bit out of date today—as a "racial bourgeoisie," placing Asians in a particular position relative to other groups. Although it is a simplified model, I think it is somewhat correct in terms of how the larger society views Asians. If you see Asians and Pacific Islanders somewhere in the middle, and Whites on the top, Blacks and Browns somewhere at the bottom, you get a simplified model. Where does it leave Asians in terms of political power, economic power, and in terms of relations to groups both on the top and on the bottom?

It is a hard problem. We do not have access to true power, the power on the top, and yet we have often been portrayed as a minority group that has been able to make its way to the top. There is a "glass ceiling," we can look at it, we can touch it, but we can't hold it in our hands, we can't have it. How does it affect our relationship to other minority groups? If we are portrayed as the group that can make it, is it going to create great resentment? Is that going to cause friction with those stuck at the bottom, unfortunately, because of those in the middle?

In spite of these tensions, we have to realize that there are commonalities among all these different groups. First, each community has to work outward to the broader Asian community and perhaps other communities of color. The Korean community in particular, after the riots, has become increasingly insular: it turned inward, it has been reluctant to look outward for help. Even the Asian Pacific American community—that has been friends through many different struggles—has become distanced from us. It has been difficult trying to turn the community outward so that it would look for help from other groups. For Korean Americans, the first group from where help should be expected is the Asian Pacific American community. Because of common problems, because of perceptions of race, of common class issues, that is a natural way to look outward; you have to start there.

There are common issues that affect all Asians: anti-Asian violence, dealing with immigration, lack of political empowerment. Those commonalities are things on which people can get together. These commonalities are often shared by non-Asian groups as well. Look at the Jewish community, the African American community, the Latino communities. There are common issues everywhere. Not only problems are shared, of course. Look at the common values: family, education, even religion. While it is very difficult to look outward for help, to trust other people, while the looting and burning in the 1992 riots are still vivid memories, one cannot ignore the fact that to gain political power, economic power, and social power without friends, without allies, is impossible.

In trying to empower the Korean American community, and the Asian community in general, we have to look at making those connections. This is the kind of work that has to be done. Already, there are coalitions forming: the Multi-cultural Collaborative, for instance. One organization dealing with Asian Pacific Islanders is the Asian Pacific Americans for a

New Los Angeles, looking at common strategies for economic and political development. I think those are the kinds of coalitions, those are the kinds of ties, that we have to look at. There are a lot of problems facing every community here. And I think, if we are willing to educate ourselves, educate each other, we will find common solutions and can make things happen.

THE KOREAN AMERICAN COALITION (KAC)

Steven Yang
Program Coordinator, Korean American Coalition

Since 1983, the Korean American Coalition (KAC) has been on a mission to advance and promote the civic, legislative and political interest of the Korean American community. And although the Korean American community has changed drastically since that time, many conditions remain the same.

The Korean American Coalition is still the only organization whose sole mission and purpose is to empower the community. In 1983, when few Korean American organizations existed, KAC played a vital role as liaison between the community and various government organizations. Today there are more than 150 Korean American community organizations in Los Angeles; and many groups contribute, either directly or indirectly, to the overall empowerment of the Korean American community. For example, the Korean American Grocers Association, the Korean American churches, and the Korean Youth and Community Center have all endeavored to advance political and other issues while expanding the work being done in their respective fields, as well. However, just as with every other community, the Korean American community is not a homogeneous group. As we have seen through the proliferation of activities, not all Korean Americans share the same political perspectives or values. Each sector of the community has a distinct set of interests. The community can be divided not only socially and economically; but also among church associations, business associations, labor associations, and the media. Groups representing these various sectors have worked hard to advance their respective interests, and have even combined with similar groups in other ethnic communities to promote their interests, as well. On a basic level, however, Korean Americans share a common heritage and have united around such non-partisan and non-controversial issues as immigrant services, racial discrimination and voting.

We at KAC, along with many other Korean Americans, believe that the community lacks political empowerment. Empowerment is needed to influence those forces that impact us, whether as individuals or as a community. That the Korean American community lacks the political strength to impact its own environment became clearly evident during the riots of April 1992. While the Korean American community makes up less than two percent of Los Angeles County's total population, it suffered over 50 percent of all property damage—more than any other single group. In the days, weeks, and months after the riots, the community could not find, and still has not found, the support that it needs for recovery. Lack of empowerment has resulted in a sluggish response from law enforcement agencies, public and private relief agencies, and elected officials; and those of us involved in the Korean American Coalition clearly recognize its effect. Indeed, the Korean American Coalition was formed in 1983 specifically to address these and other types of issues affecting our community. KAC and other organizations have worked, and continue to work, to unite and build strength within the community. However, because it is a very recent immigrant group and because it is a distinctly identifiable racial minority, the Korean American community has yet to realize its full potential.

Like other immigrant groups arriving in the United States, Korean Americans experience great difficulties. The first generation faces most of the challenges that need to be overcome, for instance language barriers, cultural differences and fitting into the social system of the society. This takes time, and the average length of residence here in the United States is only about 12 years. Furthermore, Korean Americans often have been victims of racism, as have other Asian Americans, African Americans and Latinos. Overall, the Korean American community is still at a very basic level in terms of development and sophistication.

KAC has the role of educating and organizing the community; and because many immigrants are unaware of the issues and policies that affect them, KAC endeavors to supply that information. The members of KAC organize people around particular issues which they think are important. KAC's goals and practices have been to formulate tactics that could be successfully used to empower people in those issues. Some examples include voter registration and education, electoral policies, social services, media monitoring, and legislative lobbying. In the past 10 years the Korean American Coalition has registered over 12,500 Korean Americans. This is a relatively modest number compared to the total population of Los Angeles County; however, it represents about 25 percent or more of all Korean Americans registered to vote in the United States. So, when we evaluate any program for its success or failure, it is vital that we use a historical context to measure relative progress.

KAC also tries to disseminate accurate information about Korean American activities to the larger, mainstream community. This effort was especially evident in the aftermath of the riots. KAC received numerous calls from all over the world, including Rumanian, Swiss, French, and British news agencies. The eyes of the world really are turned toward Los Angeles. No one person or one group alone can establish directions, policies, and agendas that will be applicable to all our various communities. If we are to achieve success, we must cooperate with, learn from, and appreciate each other.

Korea Times, L.A.

May 2nd, 1992   Peace demonstration at Wilshire and Western.

KOREAN SOCIAL AND POLITICAL STRATEGIES
FOR THE 1990S

Craig Shearer Coleman, Ph.D.
Executive Director, Korea Society, Los Angeles

Most of the visual evidence of the 1992 Los Angeles Riot has long since been cleared; the ashes of burned stores have been shoveled into trash bins. Koreatown and the Korean American community are still with us, although somewhat economically and emotionally damaged. The general social and political perception of the Korean American community has been largely unmanaged by the Korean communities themselves. Korean American participation in social and political activities outside of Koreatown has been limited. At the same the time, mainstream news and entertainment media have paid scant attention to this growing and dynamic immigrant community.

The combination of "unmanaged" social and political networking with the larger society, and the general lack of knowledge by the larger society of the Korean American community have resulted in poor communication, misunderstanding, and some notable tragedies. What we do know of the over the 350,000-member Korean American community in Southern California has been largely shaped by the fleeting news media coverage provided during the 1992 Los Angeles Riots known to the Korean community as 4.29 (April 29th or "*sa-yi-gu*"). What are the better social and political strategies needed to present the growing Korean American community's interests and needs to the larger society?

During and immediately after the riot, the Korean American community had difficultly in projecting through the mainstream media to the larger American society a clear, comprehensive and balanced image of itself. News coverage focused on the devastation suffered by Korean merchants in the riot zones, their tense relations with African Americans, and their attempts to recover economically and emotionally. A sympathetic and tragic *"kimchee"* angle was implanted on a national scale; reminiscent of the images of devastation and suffering of the Korean War which has long-been reinforced by reruns of M*A*S*H.

The damage to the over 2,000 Korean American businesses concentrated in South Central and across the vast reaches of L.A.'s Koreatown accounted perhaps for almost fifteen percent of businesses operated by Korean Americans in Southern California.

Many Korean victims must have asked, "What did we have to do with the Rodney King verdict?" But there are many layers of economic, social, cultural, and political factors which led to the suffering experienced by thousands of Korean American merchants and their families.

Years of poor communication in English among many recent first-generation Korean immigrants, ill-preparation for the demands of living and working in a culturally diverse society, occasionally resulted in cultural clashes. Colliding attitudes, worsening economic times for many, the Latasha Harlins case and the general deterioration of law and order, the numerous assaults and murders experienced over the years by Korean merchants all have taken their toll on the recent Korean immigrants' perceptions of American society.

A BRIEF REVIEW OF RECENT
KOREAN IMMIGRATION, 1965-PRESENT

Growing up and attending public schools in the Wilshire district of Los Angeles during the 1960s and 1970s, I began to take particular notice of new Asian kids arriving at my schools. They were different from my third and fourth generation

Chinese and Japanese American school friends. I did not get to know many Korean immigrant students because, for the most part, they were primarily enrolled in ESL classes in my junior and senior high schools and only a few were present in the regular math and science classes. Over the last twenty years, I have been learning about and working with both Korea and the Korean American community.

The Korean American community as we know it now began to take shape in the late 1960s and early 1970s. Over the last twenty-five years, Korean immigrants have established a significant presence particularly in the small service-oriented retail businesses in many areas of Southern California and elsewhere in most metropolitan areas of the United States. For most mainstream Americans, this is how we know of the Korean community. If you should be in the Los Angeles or Orange County Koreatowns in September and October, you probably find yourself in a middle of elaborate Korean festivals coinciding with the annual Harvest Moon Festival or Chusok celebrations.

We, meaning all of us living in Southern California, have almost no prior school-learned or media-introduced knowledge of Korea, the Korean people, their history or culture. We were not prepared or required to understand the backgrounds of what seemed to be yet another new ethnic enclave in Los Angeles. According to established American custom, new immigrants found or carved out economic and cultural niches in the social fabric which accommodated the larger needs of society. In this manner, so too did the new Korean immigrants in Los Angeles.

As a result of the 1965 U.S. immigration-law reform and various other types of legal and illegal immigration, about a million Koreans now have arrived and settled in the United States. In Los Angeles prior to 1965, only a few thousand Korean immigrants had settled. However, this core group laid the foundation for the later steady annual waves of new immigrants. At that time in Los Angeles, the Olympic Boulevard corridor had become a somewhat run-down commercial strip consisting of old storefronts. Small retail spaces were available and rents were bargain cheap. Prior to the late sixties, very few Korean language store signs were present anywhere in Los Angeles. The core group had begun to establish small shops, fish markets and book stores along Olympic Boulevard between Vermont and Western Avenues. Today, we can see the mixture of old storefronts and new Korean-built minimalls throughout this area.

THE FABRIC OF KOREAN SOCIETY

Korean society is tied firmly together by familial and voluntary associations. The dominating social framework is based upon Confucian precepts which dictate one's social status as defined by one's place in the hierarchy of family, business and class. In contemporary Korean terms, your family background, area of origin, your school affiliations, profession or business affiliations and, particularly in the United States, your church affiliation, dictate your circle of friends and influence within Korean society within the Korean American community.

In the United States, social and business networks are a microcosm of modern Korean society. These relationships intensified within the Korean American community due to language and cultural insularity. A substantial majority of the new Korean immigrant community members emigrated from Korea to seek upwardly mobile economic and social opportunities. South Korea has demonstrated remarkable economic growth over the last thirty years, dramatically increasing the development of the nation and the living standards of most of its people. However, despite the almost consistent double digit growth in GDP and intermittent export surpluses, the economy could accommodate only limited opportunities for the people.

The first half of the recent wave of immigrants had a high percentage of college-educated professionals in its ranks. The second half has more of an average cross-section of Korean society. Some of the earlier arrivals found mastering English and breaking into mainstream American professions difficult.

They opted to establish small businesses as a means to support themselves and their families through determined hard work. They raised capital from within the extended family and through a system of private money lending circles known as *kye*.

These *kye* provide a source of business capital and monies for major living expenses such as cars, college tuition and down-payments on homes, in addition to personal income and loans from Korean American banks. A *kye* is typically formed by a group of ten or more individuals who pool a set amount of money usually $1,000 or more. They are brought together by the *kye* manager, usually an entrepreneurial Korean American woman. The fund is loaned on a need-basis, with the first borrower paying the highest interest, well above bank rates. Capital is returned to the fund. The last user pays the least or no interest and treats it as interest-bearing investment. The manager typically gets five percent for her services. The first borrower is expected to buy dinner for the fund members. Sometimes, the first borrower skips with the money. But the system generally works well outside of the establish credit and finance system.

AN ETHNIC SOCIAL, CULTURAL, AND POLITICAL ENCLAVE OR COLONY?

The Korean American community in Southern California has evolved into an almost self-sustaining society, a contemporary version of a social and economic colony. Koreans traditionally were not global explorers, imperialists or voluntary migrants until this century. Most foreigners who came to Korea throughout its history came as invaders. Social and political interaction with other peoples is not ingrained in the Korean historical experience.

The growing Korean American communities throughout the United States represent the first historical experience for Koreans to voluntarily migrate and reside in a foreign country. Naturally, the new immigrants brought with them their own familiar social, cultural and economic institutions, and in essence, set up a parallel society in Koreatowns across the U.S. These parallel institutions include professional services, restaurants, markets, retail businesses of all types, broadcast television (KTE, ch. 18) and cable TV stations (KATV and KTAN), two daily newspapers (*The Korea Times, Los Angeles*, *The Korea Central Daily*) along with numerous weekly and monthly publications, three radio stations (Radio Korea, KCB, and Radio Hankuk), all in the Korean language. *The Korea Times* publishes an English section and the monthly *KoreAm Journal* targets 1.5 and second generation English speaking Korean Americans. Almost all the of the community can be reached through these publications, and they are in turn supported by extensive advertising.

The first generation typically remains in the small retail business sector throughout Southern California's communities. The 1.5 (the young children of the first generation) and the second generation are plying their way through American schools and are breaking into mainstream professions and businesses, ever encouraged/pushed by their hard-working, struggling parents. Many of the children are also enrolled in afternoon and weekend Korean language institutes, Korean dance, music and art groups, and Korean Christian church groups to maintain their ethnic and cultural identity.

THE KOREAN AMERICAN BUSINESS COMMUNITY

The social threads that weave through the Korean American business community are reinforced by the interconnecting group affiliations that a small businessman or professional may maintain. Larger business and professional associations include the Korean Chamber of Commerce of Los Angeles, the Korean American Grocers Association, the Korean American Bar Association, the Koreatown Association, the Koreatown Rotary Club and hundreds of other Korean high school and college alumni associations, service clubs, and professional associations, covering everything from swap meet operators to accountants.

These organizations have been and continue to promote better understanding of the requirements for living and working in a multicultural society within its memberships. Long before the spring 1992 L.A. Riot, a number of viable programs had been initiated and maintained to build inter-community relations and to participate more in mainstream civics and social activities. The above-mentioned organizations are accessible through direct contact or through introduction by a Korean American member.

KOREAN AMERICAN SOCIAL AND POLITICAL STRATEGIES FOR THE FUTURE

Hard and bitter lessons were learned as a result of the riot. Some of the old time first generation's leadership inadequacies in dealing with the larger society in an emergency surfaced during the riot. Their influence and power over segments of the Korean American community in Southern California dissipated with the extinguishing of the last burning Korean store. In the vacuum, a number of more acculturated, bicultural, politically and media-attuned Korean Americans stepped in representing both the first and 1.5 generations. One post-riot development has been the initiation and enlarging of American citizenship programs and voter registration programs in the Korean American community. The intention is to acquire more political clout within the mainstream society's leadership and institutions.

Perhaps more than most other ethnic community leaders in Los Angeles, Korean Americans have realized that the leadership of the mainstream society and other communities had failed miserably to manage events and conflicts in our city. These conflicts were further fueled by mass media exploitation of the visual images of these conflicts. The Korean American community found itself without a voice that could be heard across ethnic lines. The Korean American community especially found itself at a loss when the city was out of control for two days and it could not utilize any political muscle to mobilize mainstream institutions to protect its personal and economic well-being. We saw the results on TV.

The Korean American community is in the process of reorganizing itself to better deal with problems both within and without. Greater participation in the political process is just one avenue being explored. Korean American residential communities are spread throughout the Los Angeles area and among the suburban communities. Due to the lack of American citizenship and low voter registration, the Korean American community cannot as yet put someone in local office, but it can develop a voice that will be heard on local and regional levels.

There will probably never be one unified Korean American voice. The Korean American community is as diverse in its social, economic and political interests as is the larger society. Korean Americans have a number of options as to how to present their community's interests and demands. Certainly, the old model of donating cash and offering endorsements to political candidates while receiving little to no political payback is a procedure which no longer serves the Korean American community's needs or expectations.

The Korean American community cannot socially, economically or now politically afford to remain too isolated or alienated from the larger society much longer. What course will Korean American leaders and organizations take in guiding their segment of the Korean community in relating to the larger society is an important question. What tack or combination of approaches will best serve the immediate and future needs of the Korean American community? Liberal activism, along the lines of established ethnic and minority-rights movements, will pressure politicians to pay more attention to the needs and demands of the Korean American community. At the same time, movement towards presenting the Korean American community as interested in the same issues and demanding the same rights and benefits as many segments of the mainstream community could lead towards long-term social and political coalition building. As it is improbable that Korean Americans will ever live in one concentrated political district, coalition building is probably the most effective long-term measure.

Persons from other communities, wishing to build bridges between the Korean American communities in Los Angeles and Orange Counties and their businesses or communities, will have to be selective in their choice of alliances and build from the ground up because of the diversity and limited scope of most Korean American associations.

A key point for the future of L.A. is the building of social, economic and political coalitions. We must deal with what we realistically can. It is a diverse city, in all respects. It has never pretended to be otherwise. The Korean American community is a significant presence in Southern California and will remain so in the foreseeable future.

Southern California is not the only place where new Korean immigrants can establish themselves, and many have settled elsewhere in the country. But, Los Angeles is still the main port of entry for most new arrivals, and as our already settled Korean American community grows and deepens its roots, their contributions and voices will grow more compelling.

Korea Times, L.A.

Former Councilman Michael K. Woo surveying damage with community leaders.

KOREAN AMERICANS
SEEKING ELECTIVE OFFICE

Marn J. Cha
Professor of Political Science
California State University, Fresno

Korean Americans immigration to the United States approaches the century mark. Much of this history is a story of survival; a survival eked out against language barriers, discrimination, and poverty. When survival alone was such an arduous and difficult task, seeking political office was the least of the immigrants' concerns.

In 1962, Alfred Song, who practiced law and served as mayor of Monterey Park, a medium-sized, southern California city, was the first Korean American elected to the California State Assembly. For almost twenty years after Alfred Song left California politics in 1973, there was not a single Korean American running for political office in California or anywhere else. It is only within the last five years or so that we have begun to see a number of Korean Americans running for public office—and some winning. The record is startling: between 1987 and 1992, a total of fifteen Korean Americans have been on various ballots. A Chinese-born person, because he was raised and educated in Korea, is included in this number.

Seven of the fifteen Korean American candidates were elected to the offices they ran for. The year 1992 alone produced six winners, including one who was reelected. The nearly fifty percent success ratio should be considered extraordinary. The present study looks at the candidates' profiles: where they ran, for what offices, their party affiliations, generation, and political experience.

Table 1
A Profile of Korean American Candidates Seeking
Political Office Between 1987 and 1992

Office	State	Party	Gener-ation	Experience
US Cong (W)	CA	R	1	Mayor, KC act.
St. Sen (W)	OR	R	1	Bus, KC leader
St. Ass. (W)	WA	R	1	Ed./bus; KC leader
St. Ass. (W)	HI	D	3	Inc., reelected
C. C. (W)	CA	NP	1	Bus., KC leader
C.C. (W)	CA	NP	1	Bus, KC act.
C.C. (W)	WA	NP	1.5	Unknown
US Cong (L)	CA	R	1	Bus, no KC act.
St. Ass. (L)	CA	D	1.5	Atty/KC act.
St. Ass. (L)	WA	D	2	No KC act.
St. Ass. (L)	MD	R	1	Ed./no KC act.
C.C. (L)	CA	NP	2	No KC act.
C.C. (L)	CA	NP	1.5	No ties w/KC
C.C. (L)	CA	NP	1.5	Law Enf./no KC ties
Sch. Dist (L)	CA	NP	1	Ed./some KC ties

Cong.=Congress; C.C.=City Council; St.=State; Ass.=Assembly; Sen.=Senate; W=Winner; L=Loser; NP=Non-Partisan; act.=activist; R=Republican; D=Democrat; KC=Korean Community; Ed.=Education; Bus.=Business; Enf.=Enforcement; Atty.=Attorney

Almost all Korean American candidates ran in western states, with California dominating: nine in California, three in Washington, one each in Oregon and Hawaii. There is only one exception: one candidate who ran in Maryland. Of the seven elected, three were in California, two in Washington, and one each in Oregon and Hawaii. This may represent the West's being less tradition-bound, more diversity, and innovative. Washington's and Oregon's liberalism may also be validated, and so may Hawaii's Asian domination and California's pluralism. Three electoral successes in California are from conservative Orange County, perhaps an indication that California's conservatism is an open one.

The types of offices the candidates ran for yield another interesting point. Six of the fifteen (40%) ran for local council seats, five (33%) for state assembly, one for state senate, and one for Congress. Local offices are the most popular objectives, perhaps because they are most visible and easily accessible. Consequently, most successes are in local elections. Some political novices made it, however, beyond local elections: one in Oregon's state senate, and one in Washington's state assembly. In Hawaii, a state assembly person won a second term. The one who made it to Congress had served in city politics before he was elected to national office.

Novices are not exactly without any political training. Politics in the Korean American communities apparently serve a good training ground from which to launch a political career. Observe the candidates' pattern of experience. Four of the seven elected were active in local Korean community affairs, with three having served as presidents of their respective local Korean Resident Associations. One elected to Congress was active in city politics as well as in local Korean community affairs. Having been visible and active in fellow Koreans' affairs proved to be a significant source of financial support, if not votes. Most Koreans who donated money to fellow Koreans, did not live in areas or districts where the candidates ran. Camaraderie may have motivated them to see their own kind breaking into American politics hitherto perceived as a sacred preserve to Whites only.

Community activism may also have fueled the political motivation of candidates, driving them to fulfill their political ambitions beyond the confines of the Korean American community. The political skills they learned from Korean community politics may have proven just as useful when politicking to non-Koreans. Although, except for the one Korean American reelected in Hawaii, none of the other elected candidates would have made it without White majority support.

None of the eight who lost had any significant prior local political experience. This experience ties in with a generational factor. Of the seven successful candidates, five (71%) are first-generation Korean Americans, including a Chinese American, born and raised in Korea. Of the eight defeated candidates, three (37%) are first generation, while the rest (63%) are one-and-a-half, referring to those born in Korea but raised and educated in the United States, and second generation (three are one-and-a-half, and two are second generation).

First generation candidates were born, raised and educated in Korea. In America, they found themselves hamstrung by accent, and further disadvantaged by their limited experience with American traditions and lifestyles. Yet, this did not deter them from challenging politics—nor did it deter voters from voting for them. They were all elected. The majority of losers were from the one-and-a-half and second generation. They have had the advantage of an American education, earlier social training, and little or no accent. Yet, they lost. What may explain it?

First generation Korean American politicians are from the school of hard-knocks, hardened by the rough-and-tumble of Korean politics as well as self-made experience in business or elsewhere. They are also fueled by a desire to show the friends and relatives they left behind in Korea that they succeeded. And making it in White American dominated politics is the ultimate success. There must have developed in them a gall to challenge the seemingly unattainable. This why all first-generation candidates, no sooner than they were elected, made a pilgrimage to Korea, as if to report their success to their old homeland. One-and-a-half and second-generation candidates have had the advantage of American education, and adequate social training, yet a majority of them lost. Their lack of local political experience may account for some of it, but they may also have been disadvantaged by the absence of motivational factors.

While some in the first generation have a desire to fulfill their unfulfilled political ambitions back home, others—the majority—had left Korea with a great deal of distaste for politics as such. The latter group tended to persuade their offspring to go into so-called "safe" professions, like medicine, engineering, accounting, or law. We may speculate that some in this largely anti-political, American-raised generation have chosen to enter into politics out of a desire to blaze their own career paths. This kind of motivation, however, may not be a match for motivations honed over the years by the twists and turns of a typical first-generation life. The soft upbringing of the one-and-a-half and second generations may have well prepared them for idealism, but it has not given them the street-wise toughness needed to succeed.

If we associate Democrats with "liberal" ideals and Republicans with pro-business conservatism, a look at Korean American candidates' party affiliation will support the above explanation. The two Democrats, who are of the one-and-a-half and second generation, lost. The only Democrat who won is a third-generation state legislator in Hawaii. The three others who won partisan offices, are all of the first generation and are all Republicans. Republican party affiliation of first-generation Korean American politicians reflects a general pattern among most of the Korean electorate in California. One survey of party identification of Korean registered voters in fifteen Southern California cities found that 49.1 percent were Republicans, 29.4 percent Democrat, 19.8 percent Independent, and 1.7 percent, other (*The Korea Times,* Nov. 1, 1992, A8). This indicates that most Koreans are Republicans.

In conclusion, the following broad observations are offered. The year 1992 was a watershed for Koreans in America, a year in which a number of Korean Americans were elected to public office. How Korean American elected officials will do at governing remains to be seen. The Korean community may find its elected officials distancing themselves from it as they pay attention to the needs of their mostly non-Korean constituencies. At election times, though, these politicians may be seen turning back to their ethnic communities for funds. This may baffle most Korean Americans uninitiated in American politics as their hopes to gain immediate returns from their fellow Korean American politicians are dashed. The Korean community will soon learn to become an effective part of a coalition forged by each Korean American politician. This may be the only practical way of enabling Korean American politicians to help them.

Should the newly elected Korean American politicians of the first generation—given their close ties to the Korean American community and Korea—pursue too close a relation with their ethnic communities, some of them may not be reelected. Enclaves are comforting. But both the community and its politicians must learn when to break out of them and when to stay in them. Finding that balance may well be the most important ingredient in ensuring the success of both.

Political consciousness may have reached Korean Americans belatedly compared to other ethnic groups. Ironically, first generation Koreans, handicapped by a variety of odds, seem to be doing better than the less handicapped succeeding generations. This may prompt some rethinking on the part of the first generation about their parenting practices. They should raise their children in an open value system, allowing them to choose careers in fulfillment of their individual potentials rather than follow parentally guided norms.

A VISION FOR THE FUTURE

Angela Oh
President, Korean American Bar Association

Korean Americans are now confronting a real dilemma. The dilemma is this: shall we have more violence, shall we take the path of vengeance, or what other solutions can we find? What is the vision? Which direction are we to take?

We have already seen a tremendous amount of violence for the past year, and everyone is talking about more to come. My personal opinion is that we are not going to have an outburst similar to last year's riots. In fact, the more I look at that question and the possible outcome of the Rodney King civil rights case in federal court, I see that the main source of worries and, preposterously enough, some kind of urging for that to happen, is coming from rank-and-file police officers. This, indeed, is hard to believe. Of course, on the surface, the police right now are thinking in terms of prevention programs and public relations. But the average cop on the street is very frustrated about what happened last April. Many of them did want to act.

Our private investigations in connection with our civil rights are telling us that many of the cops on the street wanted to respond—only they could not. If they had, they would have been charged with insubordination, and under Darryl Gates that possibly meant days off and perhaps even the loss of one's job. There is a certain tension built up there, and it might break loose in some way. Presently the Los Angeles Police

Department has a lot of firearms—they are transferring them from all over the country. Should a confrontation happen, our high risk groups will be—across all racial lines—young boys, 14 to about 20 years old. They are the ones who are going to take to the streets, they are the ones who are going to do the property destruction—they are the ones who are going to get killed.

Vengeance is not the path that works. We lost Edward Lee. Why did that happen? People saw all this destruction done to their community. Some of them could not just stand by watching their property burn down, their livelihoods slowly turning into ashes. And, frankly, they should not have stood by. It was right, I think, to protect themselves in those circumstances. However, in the situation that developed, we lost Edward Lee. In that one death, we understood, as a community—and not only the Korean community—what happens when violence is met with vengeance. How many more lives shall we agree to sacrifice?

There are a lot of patrol groups starting to form in various segments of the community right now. Every Korean shop owner in Los Angeles has a gun. Let me correct myself: several guns. Many of them are not trained to use those guns. Many of them have employees who are not trained to use those guns. Many of them are calling my office as they are finding themselves on the other end of a criminal prosecution because they have used their guns improperly under the law. What does this mean for our community? It means, for instance, that between February 5 and March 20, 1993, 15 small business people in Los Angeles alone were killed or seriously injured by gun shots. Every other day, the Korean language media reports yet another shooting. There is a message that we need to take out beyond the Korean community and into the mainstream society right now: and that message is that the violence must stop. Everybody is focusing on the next riot—which may be six or seven weeks away, depending on how long it takes the defense to put on its case—and in the meantime, people are dying. People are being injured and people are killing each other. Nobody is paying attention today, right now.

Nobody is talking about the numerous gun stores that have been robbed in the last two months, and about the thousands of fire arms that are missing. That is not being widely reported in the press. We need to get these guns off the streets. And I am not saying to take them away from the Korean shop owners. Frankly, a volunteer surrender of guns would mean that probably those people who should have the guns would end up giving them away. We need to really push our law enforcement officers to go after those large caches of illegal weapons. I know that our intelligence in the LAPD must be able to identify where those things are. They may not want to move on them because of the risk of compromising some bigger investigation, but they know where those guns are.

So what are the needs now? What future direction should the Korean American community take? Out of a city of about 3.5 million, we number 72,900, according to the 1990 census. Out of a county population of almost 9 million, we number about a 150,000. We are not a "big" part of the community. One cannot start talking about political empowerment and "setting a political agenda" that will serve our interests: nobody is interested in less than one percent of the population. Less than one percent of the population is not going to move a political agenda by itself. Less than one percent of the population is not going to get itself elected into office—if that is your definition of empowerment. We have to begin to think in terms of strategic alliances.

Also, we have to begin to be smarter with our resources. The more I think about racial tensions in this town, the more I come to the conclusion that we are following the wrong path by having economic development programs in one arena, and racial harmony or human relations programs in another. The resources that now are being split in two directions, if brought together into one, could be tremendous.

The most strategic place for program and policy development is in the area of economic relationships, which

necessarily include racial issues as well. We hear a lot of talk
about the Black/Korean conflict, about cultural differences, and
we hear about Korean immigrants and their mentality compared
to the hundreds of years of oppression here of African
Americans. There is some truth in each perspective. But we
have to deal with the here and now. Here and now tells us that
the relationship that is most visible and most felt in South
Central Los Angeles is a particular economic relationship
between merchant and customer. We need to focus on how
those tensions develop, and then build programs around those
relationships that are not only about economic survival, but
human survival as well. Consider the tensions between Koreans
and Latinos in Koreatown. Koreatown has seen a tenfold
population increase since the 1970s, jumping from
approximately 1,900 residents to over 20,000 residents today. It
has been a phenomenal growth. However, Korean ethnic
residents amount only to about 23 percent of Koreatown's total
population. The rest is Latino. Again, the tensions are mostly
around economic, employer-employee type relationships; and
usually the Koreans are the employers and the Latinos are the
employees. We had better start paying attention to that
relationship and developing programs.

Where else are there opportunities that everyone can agree
on? The facts are indisputable. Take, for instance, housing.
Nobody is interested in talking about "Can we get along?" if
they don't know where they are going to sleep or what they are
going to eat that day. If you look at the Black and Latino
situation in south central Los Angeles, the biggest fights are
over who is going to get the next available housing unit—that
is, a two or three bedroom—for their family. Is it going to be
the new immigrant Latino family that has eight members, or is
it going to be the African American family that has been on the
waiting list for three years?

Perhaps the most important window of opportunity is youth.
We have already lost three generations in this society: first, the
generation that is sitting in prison, who has fathered the second
generation that is going down the tubes as we see the increase

of drug and gang activity, and a third generation composed of 12-year-old kids, who think it's funny to shoot an adult in his own place of business and then invite the rest of the community to come in and loot that store. Youth is the most crucial area where we have an opportunity for improvement, and I submit to you that we must focus in that area; otherwise, we will have a fourth generation lost. When I look at a 12-year-old kid who can commit that kind of crime, I say to myself: what happened to us out of the 1960s? Those are our kids. We grew up in a time when we were saying there has got to be social justice, there has got to be some questioning of how resources are distributed. We were about peace; we were about love; we were about stopping the war in Vietnam. These are our children who are out there carrying guns into high schools and shooting small business owners—and laughing about it. It's troublesome. We've done something wrong here.

When I talk about these problems, I am not talking just about Koreans. I am talking about this society, American society, of which we are a part. We are here. We are not going anywhere. You can tell me to go home. And do you know where I will go? I will get in my car and drive to Mount Washington, which is five miles outside of downtown LA—that's my home. I am not going anywhere else. I have no plans to leave. So, if we are to survive in Los Angeles, our problems must be solved here and solved now. That is the message I take to mainstream America.

The Korea Central Daily

April 30th, 1992 10 AM near the University of Southern California

VI

POLICY PROPOSALS

The Korea Central Daily

A boy participates in a rally in front of Los Angeles City Hall
on May 8th. His sign reads "I am a victim, too."

POLICY PROPOSALS:
RECOMMENDATIONS BY THE CONFERENCE ON NEW DIRECTIONS FOR THE KOREAN AMERICAN COMMUNITY

Multicultural Education:

- Create a multicultural urban education fund.
- Create and fund proactive outreach cultural centers.
- Create a curriculum that is less Euro-centric and more international in focus.
- Teach Korean Studies in public and private schools starting at an early age.
- Second generation Korean Americans' education in high school and college should include subjects on Korean culture.
- Develop high school/college mentor programs.
- Create prejudice-reduction programs.
- Develop leadership training among Korean American youth.
- Through education, enable American-born offspring to serve as a bridge between Korean and American cultures.
- Educate new immigrants in English, business, and citizenship.

Inter-Ethnic Policies:

- More minorities in journalism.
- Use care and integrity when reporting on Korean Americans and other minorities.
- Encourage Korean churches to serve as catalysts in resolving inter-ethnic conflicts, meeting spiritual demands, and assisting with overcoming cultural adjustments.
- Hold annual conferences on Korean American community issues.
- Establish an "anti-defamation league" to watch for signs of, and help prevent, scapegoating of Korean Americans.
- Establish and train workers for cross-cultural job opportunities.
- Create federal and state committies on multiculturalism (similar to those under the Canadian Ministry of Multiculturalism).
- Distribute scholarly documentation to refute the notion of any necessary conflict of interest between Korean American and African American economic development.
- Korean Americans should establish liaison with and ongoing dialogue with other like-minded groups to facilitate networking.
- Create a "trickle up" communications network, from grass-roots organizations upward, to media and elected officials.

Health Care Responses to Civil Unrest:

- Increase funding for community-level health care.
- Address all issues of post-traumatic depression disorder.
- Address all issues of mental health, and fund research on victims' treatment and improvement-of-health status.

Grass Roots Political Participation:

- Create greater Korean American political involvement: "We can all be activists."
- Encourage college students' participation in community political organizations.
- Establish a clearinghouse for volunteers for Korean American community activites.

Study the Feasibility of a Korean American PAC:

- Would it mean political empowerment?
- Establish a Blue Ribbon Commission to:
    (1) investigate the status of Korean Americans;
    (2) provide a blueprint for future public policies; and
    (3) involve public and private organizations in all policy implementation.
- Sustain regular contact with elected officials on key community issues.
- Set up a voter registration program for Korean Americans.
- Korean American leaders should "round table" on a regular basis to facilitate ending factionalism within the Korean American community.
- Those involved should include:
    (1) business, religious, and political leaders;
    (2) leaders of community organizations, (e.g., KABC, KAC, KAGRO, KYC, etc.); and
    (3) scholars from "think tanks" and academic institutions.

Law Enforcement and Crime Prevention:

- Encourage Korean Americans to join the Los Angeles Police Department, the Los Angeles County Sheriffs Department, or other law enforcement agencies.
- Qualified minority applicants should not be denied admission, excluded from promotion, or otherwise

suffer repression in any government or private-for-public institution.

- Centralize Koreatown under one police jurisdiction.
- Gun control—starting with gun-free schools and going on to tougher gun control laws throughout the state.
- Citizens deserve the assurance of effective police protection, not only in riot situations, but all the time.
- Adequate police protection would help reduce violent acts against Korean Americans, among others.

Anyone who buys a gun should assume full responsibility for such ownership, including learning to use it properly and to store it safely.

- Organize systems of community watch.

Community Economic Growth:

- Establish multiethnic committees to provide incentives for building community infrastructures and developing services, manufacturing, and retailing businesses.
- Encourage venture capital to be invested in communities that are predominantly Korean American.
- Smooth the introduction and/or operation of Korean-owned or operated businesses into non-Korean American neighborhoods.
- Join other groups in facilitating commercial loans for community business development.

Post Script: For a list of seven specific legal proposals, see the end of the chapter on the Korean American Bar Association above: pp. 131-132.

BIBLIOGRAPHY

Note: This bibliography does not include any items already cited in footnotes or listed in References following any of the chapters in this book. It is appended as a reference supplement for the readers.

Awonahara, Susumu. "All in the family: Self-employment among Korean Americans." *Far Eastern Economic Review* 11 (Mar 1991): 36.

———— and Shim Jae Hoon. "Melting pot boils over: Los Angeles riots dramatise plight of Korean Americans." *Far Eastern Economic Review* 19 (May 1992): 10.

Bilingual Education Office, California Department of Education. *Handbook for Teaching Korean-American Students.* Sacramento: California Department of Education, 1992.

[Block, Sherman]. "Los Angeles County Sheriff Sherman Block urges Justice Department to file charges against looters who singled out Korean businesses." *The New York Times,* May 5, 1992, A8.

Braus, Patricia. "Welcome to America, here's your phone: Immigrants' lack of knowledge of US telephone system." *American Demographics* (1993).

Brown, Ken. "Korean groceries failing in New York as recession drags on." *The New York Times,* Nov 29 1993: B12(N) B1(L).

Burr, Jeffrey A. and Jan E. Mutchler. "Nativity, acculturation, and economic status: explanations of Asian American living arrangements in later life." *Journals of Gerontology* 48 (Mar 1993): S55(9).

Burton, Jonathan. "Razed hopes: Korean Americans struggle to rebuild after riots." *Far Eastern Economic Review* 39 (Oct 1 1992): 26(2).

————. "A dream come true: Republican US Congress candidate Jay C. Kim." *Far Eastern Economic Review* 43 (Oct 29 1992): 55(2).

Bush, President George, "Remarks and exchange with leaders of the Korean community in Los Angeles." Transcript. *Weekly Compilation of Presidential Documents,* May 11 1992, p. 794.

Case, Tony. "Race issues and Asian journalists." *Editor & Publisher* 37 (Sept 12 1992): 13(2).

Cerrell, Joseph. "L.A. law (Joyce A. Karlin's campaign for judicial position in Los Angeles, California)." *Campaigns & Elections* 5 (Jan 1993): 57.

Chaffee, Steven H., Clifford I. Nass and Seung-Mock Yang. "The bridging role of television in immigrant political socialization." *Human Communication Research* 2 (Dec 1990): 266-323.

Chai, Alice Yun. "Freed from the elders but locked into labor: Korean immigrant women in Hawaii. *Women's Studies* 13 (Feb 1987): 223(12).

Chang, Won Ho. "Communication and Acculturation: A Case Study of Korean Ethnic Groups in Los Angeles." Ph.D. diss., University of Iowa, 1972.

Cho, Namju. "Check out, not in: Korean Wilshire/Hyatt take-over and the Los Angeles Korean community." *Amerasia Journal* 18 (Winter 1992): 131.

Choy, Bong Youn. *Koreans in America.* Chicago: Nelson-Hall, 1979.

Chung, Tong Soo. *Roots and Assimilation.* Elkins Park, PA: Philip Jaisohn Memorial Foundation, 1981.

Coleman, Wanda. "Blacks, Immigrants and America: Remembering Latasha." *Nation*, Feb 15 1993, 187.

Coplin, Gail Linda. "The Relationship of Degree of Acculturation and Causal Attributions in Korean and Samoan-American Students." Ed.D. diss., University of Southern California, 1981.

Evanoski, Patricia O. and Florence Wu Tse. "Career awareness program for Chinese and Korean American parents." *Journal of Counseling and Development* 8 (Apr. 1989): 472-5.

Fowler, Michael G. "An Analysis of the Problems of Korean Students in American Secondary Schools as Perceived by Korean Students and Parents and the Teachers in Public Schools." D.Ed. diss., University of Northern Colorado, 1978.

Fritsch, Jane. "Looters' booty a dream: Korean immigrants' Harlem store is plundered." *The New York Times*, July 18 1992, 25(L).

Gardner, Arthur L. *The Koreans in Hawaii: An Annotated Bibliography.* Honolulu: Social Science Research Institute, University of Hawaii, 1970.

Gibson, Margaret, and John Ogbu, eds. *Minority Status and Schooling: A Comparative Study of Immigrant and Involuntary Minorities.* New York: Garland, 1991.

Givens, Helen L. *The Korean Community in Los Angeles County.* San Francisco: R and E Research Associates, 1974. (Orig.: M.A. thesis, University of Southern California, 1939.)

"Group ends quest for racial peace: Organization on Black-Korean relations in Los Angeles decides to disband." *The New York Times*, Dec 26 1992.

Gurney, Kathleen S. "The Effects of Cooperative and Individualistic Achievement Conditions on Causal Attributions for Performance by

Korean and Samoan-American Students." Ph.D. diss. University of Southern California, 1981.

Han, Kyung-Chik. "Korean pastor wins prize." *The Christian Century*, Apr 8 1992, p. 360.

Han, Sang En. "A Study of Social and Religious Participation in Relationship to Occupational Mobility and Self-Esteem among Korean Immigrants in Chicago." Ph.D. diss., Northwestern University, 1973.

Herbert, Solomon J. "Why African-Americans vented anger at the Korean community during the LA riots." *The Crisis* 99 (Aug-Sept 1992): 5-7.

Hu, Arthur. "Us and them: An Asian take on L.A." *The New Republic*, June 1 1992, 12.

Hubler, William H. *Koreans in Emlyn: A Community in Transition*. Elkins Park, PA: Philip Jaisohn Memorial Foundation, 1978.

Human Rights in Minority Perspectives. Dong Soo Kim and Byong-suh Kim, eds. Montclair, NJ: Association of Korean Christian Scholars in North America, 1979.

Hyun, Peter. *Man sei!: The Making of a Korean American*. Honolulu: University of Hawaii Press, 1986.

Jackson, Harold. "We weren't listening: By not tapping into Rap's message of violence media failed to prepare public for rampage." *Nieman Reports* 46 (Summer 1992): 15-17.

James, George. "Police charge 2 in 16 robberies of Korean-owned business." *The New York Times*, Mar 5 1992, B2.

Jeong, Gyung Ja and Walter R. Schumm. "Family satisfaction in Korean/American marriages: An exploratory study of the perceptions of Korean wives." *Journal of Comparative Family Studies* 21 (Autumn 1990): 325-37.

Jo, Moon H. "Korean merchants in the black community: Prejudice among the victims of prejudice." *Ethnic and Racial Studies* 15 (July 1992): 395-412.

Kaff, Al. "Why Korean grocers select high-risk neighborhoods." *Human Ecology Forum* 21 (Spring 1993): 26-7.

Katayama, Frederick H. "Now come Korean landlords." *Fortune*, May 8 1989, 12.

Kelly, James. "In the land of free speech: Readers learn all about it in foreign-language papers coast to coast." *Time*, July 8 1985, 95).

Kim, Andrew H. N. "The Application of Needs Assessments to Educational Planning, Policy Development and Decision Making: Korean Immigrants in Hawaii's Public High Schools." Ed.D. diss., University of Southern California, 1983.

Kim, Bok-Lim C. "The future of Korean-American children and youth." In *The Education of Asian and Pacific Americans: Historical*

Perspectives and Prescriptions for the Future. Don T. Nakanishi and Marsha Hirano-Nakanishi, eds. Phoenix, AZ: Oryx Press, 1983.

Kim, Elaine H. "Home is where the *'han'* is: A Korean American perspective on the Los Angeles upheavals." *Social Justice* 20 (Spring-Summer 1993): 21.

———. "They armed in self-defense [Koreans in Los Angeles, California]." *Newsweek*, May 18, 1992, 10.

Kim-Goh, Mikyong. "Conceptualization of mental illness among Korean-American clergymen and implications for mental health service delivery." *Community Mental Health Journal* 29 (Oct 1993): 405-13.

Kim, Hak-Hoon. "Residential Patterns and Mobility of Koreans in Los Angeles County." M.A. Thesis, California State University, Los Angeles, 1986.

Kim, Hyung-chan and Wayne Patterson, eds. *The Koreans in America, 1882-1974: A Chronology and Fact Book.* Dobbs Ferry, NY: Oceana Publications, 1974.

Kim, Kerry Y. "The Role of Korean Protestant Immigrant Churches in the Acculturation of Korean Immigrants in Southern California." Ed.D. diss., University of Southern California, 1991.

Kim, Kwang Chung, Shin Kim and Won Moo Hurh. "Filial piety and intergenerational relationship in Korean immigrant families." *International Journal of Aging & Human Development* 33 (Oct 1991): 233-46.

Kim, Sangho J. *A Study of the Korean Church and Her People in Chicago, Illinois.* San Franicsco: Rand E Research Associates, 1975.

Kim, Sil Dong. "Interracially Married Korean Women Immigrants: A Study in Marginality." Ph.D. diss., University of Washington, 1979.

Kim, Woong-min. "History and Ministerial Roles of Korean Churches in the Los Angeles Area." D. Min. Thesis, School of Theology at Claremont, 1981.

Kincaid, D. Lawrence, and June Ock Yum. "A comparative study of Korean, Filipino and Samoan immigrants to Hawaii: socioeconomic consequences." *Human Organization* 46 (Spring 1987): 70-8.

Kirschten, Dick. "Minority report: Profiles of US House newcomers Eva M. Clayton, Luis V. Gutierrez and Jay C. Kim." *National Journal*, Jan 30, 1993, p. 254.

Korean-American Educational Commission. *Korean Studies Forum.* Pittsburgh: University of Pittsburgh. University Center for International Studies, 1976.

Korean American Literature (Miju munhak). Los Angeles: Miju Hanguk Munin Hyophoe, 1982.

"Korean grocer settles suit in girl's slaying." *The New York Times*, July 9 1992, A10.

Koreatown Weekly. Los Angeles, Oct 20, 1979-

Kwak, Tae-Hwan, and Seong Hyong Lee, eds. *The Korean-American Community: Present and Future.* Seoul: Kyungnam University Press, 1991.

Lee, Dong Ok. "Commodification of ethnicity: The sociospacial reproduction of immigrant entrepreneurs." *Urban Affairs Quarterly* 28 (Dec 1992): 258-76.

Lee, Felicia R. "Korean merchant holds on to dreams [Sang Han, a merchant whose business was looted during Aug 1991 riots in Crown Heights, Brooklyn, N. Y., reflects on the effect of disturbances]." *The New York Times,* July 21 1993, B11.

Lee, Mary Paik. *Quiet Odyssey: A Pioneer Korean Woman in America.* Ed., with introduction by Sucheng Chan. Seattle: University of Washington Press, 1990.

Liem, Channing. *Philip Jaisohn: The First Korean-American: A Forgotten Hero.* Korea: Kyujang Pub. Co., 1984.

Liem, Ramsay and Jinsoo Kim. "The Pico Korea workers' struggle: Korean Americans and the lessons of solidarity." *Amerasia Journal* 18 (Winter 1992): 49.

Light, Ivan H., Edna Bonocich and Charles Choy Wong. "Koreans in business." In *Awakening Minorities: Continuity and Change.* 2nd ed. John R. Howard, ed. New Brunswick, NJ: Transaction Books, 1983.

Lim, Shirley Geok-lin. "Assaying the gold: or contesting the ground of Asian American literature." *New Literary History* 24 (Winter 1993): 147.

Ludman, Elaine Kris, Keum Jee Kang and Lois L. Lynn. "Food beliefs and diets of pregnant Korean-American women." *Journal of the American Diebetic Association* 92 (Dec 1992): 1519.

MacFarquhar, Emily. "Fighting over the dream: The riots in L.A. left Koreans and blacks further apart than ever." *U.S. News & World Report,* May 18 1992, p. 34.

Mangiafico, Luciano. *Contemporary American Immigrants: Patterns of Filipino, Korean, and Chinese Settlement in the United States.* New York : Praeger, 1988.

Martin, Douglas. "Korean store owners join forces, seeking ties, opportunity and clout [Korean business owners in New York City push for more political clout]." *The New York Times,* Mar 22 1993, B11.

Melendy, H. Brett. *Asians in America : Filipinos, Koreans, and East Indians.* Boston: Twayne Publishers, 1977.

Miller, Jung Kim. "Health Beliefs and Health Utilization Patterns Among Korean Immigrants in Southern California." Ph.D. diss., University of Southern California, 1988.

Moon, Ailee, and Oliver Williams. "Perceptions of elder abuse and help-seeking patterns among African-American, Caucasian American, and Korean-American elderly women." *The Gerontologist* 33 (June 1993): 386-96.

Moon, Jeong-Hwa, and Joseph H. Pearl. "The alienation of elderly Korean American immigrants as related to place of residence, gender, age, years of education, time in the US, living with or without children, and living with or without a spouse." *International Journal of Aging & Human Development* 32 (Mar 1991): 115-25.

Mydans, Seth. "Koreans rethink life in Los Angeles." *The New York Times*, June 21 1992, p. 16.

———. "Korean shop owners fearful of outcome of beating trial [Civil rights trial of police officers accused of beating Rodney King]." *The New York Times*, April 10 1993, p. 1.

———. "Giving voice to the hurt and betrayal of Korean-Americans [Criminal lawyer Angela Oh speaks for her community in wake of Los Angeles riots]." *The New York Times*, May 2 1993, E9.

———. "Separateness grows in a scarred Los Angeles [Los Angeles shows few signs of progress and hope as the competition for scarce resources, jobs, aid, and political power strain ethnic relations]." *The New York Times*, Nov 15 1992, p. 1.

———. "Voting on judge's probation for killer [Joyce A. Karlin's decision in the case of a Korean grocer who shot a black youth in the back]." *The New York Times*, June 1 1992, A13.

———. "A target of rioters, Koreatown is bitter, armed and determined." *The New York Times*, May 3 1992, p. 1.

Norden, Edward. "South-Central Korea: Post-riot L.A. (The Korean community in Los Angeles, California)." *The American Spectator* 25 (Sept 1992): p. 33.

Oh, Yul Ja. "A Study of the Characteristics and Recreational Interests of Korean Immigrant Senior Citizens in Los Angeles." A.M. Thesis, University of Southern California, 1984.

Ong, Paul M. and Suzanne Heed, eds. *Losses in the Los Angeles Civil Unrest, April 29-May 1, 1992: Lists of the Damaged Properties and the L.A. Riot/Rebellion and Korean Merchants*. Los Angeles: Center for Pacific Rim Studies, University of California, Los Angeles, 1993.

Park, Chung-Hee C. "Ethnic identification, sociocultural adjustment, and school achievement of Korean-American youth in Los Angeles." Ph.D. diss., University of Southern California, 1981.

Park, Jang Kyun. "A Study on the Growth of the Korean Church in Southern California." D.Min. diss., School of Theology at Claremont (Calif.), 1979.

Peng, Ying, Leslie A. Zebrowitz and Hoon Koo Lee. "The impact of cultural background and cross-cultural experience on impressions of

American and Korean male speakers." *Journal of Cross-Cultural Psychology* 24 (June 1993): 203.

Pyong, Gap Min. "The structure and social functions of Korean immigrant churches in the United States." *International Migration Review* 26 (Winter 1992): 1370.

"Religious participation of Korean immigrants in the United States." *The Journal for the Scientific Study of Religion* 29 (Mar 1990): p. 19.

Rho, Jung Ja, and Walter R. Schumm. "Components of family life satisfaction in a sample of 58 Korean/American couples." *Psychological Reports* 65 (Dec 1989): 781(2).

Rohner, Ronald P., Byungchai C. Hahn, and Uwe Koehn. " Occupational mobility, length of residence, and perceived maternal warmth among Korean immigrant families." *Journal of Cross-Cultural Psychology* 23 (Sept 1992): 366.

Rosta, Paus. "Kim finds House seat costly [Rep. Congressman Jay C. Kim]." *ENR*, Feb 15 1993, p. 29.

Schine, Eric. "Koreans: Riot casualties the world doesn't see." *Business Week*, April 12, 1993, p. 24.

Shechter, Roberta Ann. "Voice of a hidden minority: identification and countertransference in the cross-cultural working alliance." *The American Journal of Psychoanalysis* 52 (Dec 1992): 339.

Shim, Jae Chul, and Charles T. Salmon. "Community orientations and newspaper use among Korean newcomers." *Journalism Quarterly* 67 (Winter 1990): 852-64.

Shim, Steve S. *Korean Immigrant Churches Today in Southern California*. San Francisco: R and E Research Associates, 1977.

Stein, M.L. "Coverage questioned again: Second Asian-American staffer at the Los Angeles Times says paper failed to present plight of Korean community during riots." *Editor & Publisher*, Aug 1 1992, p. 20.

———. "Coverage complaints: Asian and black journalists groups raise objections to media coverage of the Los Angeles riots." *Editor & Publisher*, May 23 1992, p. 3.

Sullivan, Ronald. "Five indicted in a robbery at a church; defendants linked to a Korean gang [Korean Flying Dragons accused of robbing 50 people at New. York Taberah World Mission, Queens, New York]." *The New York Times*, Dec 31 1992, B3.

Starczewska-Lambasa, Maris, ed. *The Ethnic Markets in New York City : A Study of Italian, Jewish, Polish, Chinese, and Korean Markets and Their Profit Potential for the Airlines, Banking, and the Dailies*. Hempstead, NY: Hofstra University, 1982.

Thompson, Rachel. "Korean women pin down U.S. boss [Pico Products' Bernard Hitchcock]." *The Progressive* 55:4 (Apr 1991): 15.

Ting-Toomey, S. and Felipe Korzenny, eds. *Cross-Cultural Interpersonal Communication*. Newbury Park, CA: SAGE Publications, 1991.

Waldrop, Judith and Thomas Exter. "Ethnic surge [Ethnic and racial diversity in the US based on 1990 census projections]." *American Demographics* 12 (Jan 1990): p. 25.

Whitson, Lesley H. "Taking a chance in a new country: Korean immigrants in US." *Nation's Business* 75 (Mar 1987): 59

Yoo, Jay Kun. *The Koreans in Seattle*. Elkins Park, PA: Philip Jaisohn Memorial Foundation, 1979.

Yoon, In-Jin. "The changing significance of ethnic and class resources in immigrant businesses: The case of Korean immigrant businesses in Chicago." *International Migration Review* 25 (Summer 1991): 303.

Young, Philip K. Y. and Ann H. L.Sontz. "Is hard work the key to success? A socioeconomic analysis of immigrant enterprise." *The Review of Black Political Economy* 16 (Spring 1988): 11(21).

Yu, Eui-Young. *Juvenile Delinquency in the Korean Community of Los Angeles*. Los Angeles, CA: *Korea Times*, 1987.

———— and Earl H. Phillips, eds. *Korean Women in Transition: At Home and Abroad*. Los Angeles: Center for Korean-American and Korean Studies, California State University, Los Angeles, 1987.

————, Earl H. Phillips and Eun Sik Yang, eds. *Koreans in Los Angeles: Prospects and Promises*. Los Angeles: Koryo Research Institute and Center for Korean-American and Korean Studies, California State University, 1982.

Yu, Elena S.H. "Functional abilities of Chinese and Korean elders in congregate housing." In *Ethnic Elderly and Long-Term Care*. Charles M. Barresi and Donald E. Stull, eds. New York : Springer, 1993.

————. "The health risks of Asian-Americans." *The American Journal of Public Health* 81 (Nov 1991): 1391.

INDEX

Note: This index references major terms and organizations whose names are frequently used. The page references cite basic discussions or definitions of the terms, categories, and organizations. The index also serves as a glossary for acronyms.